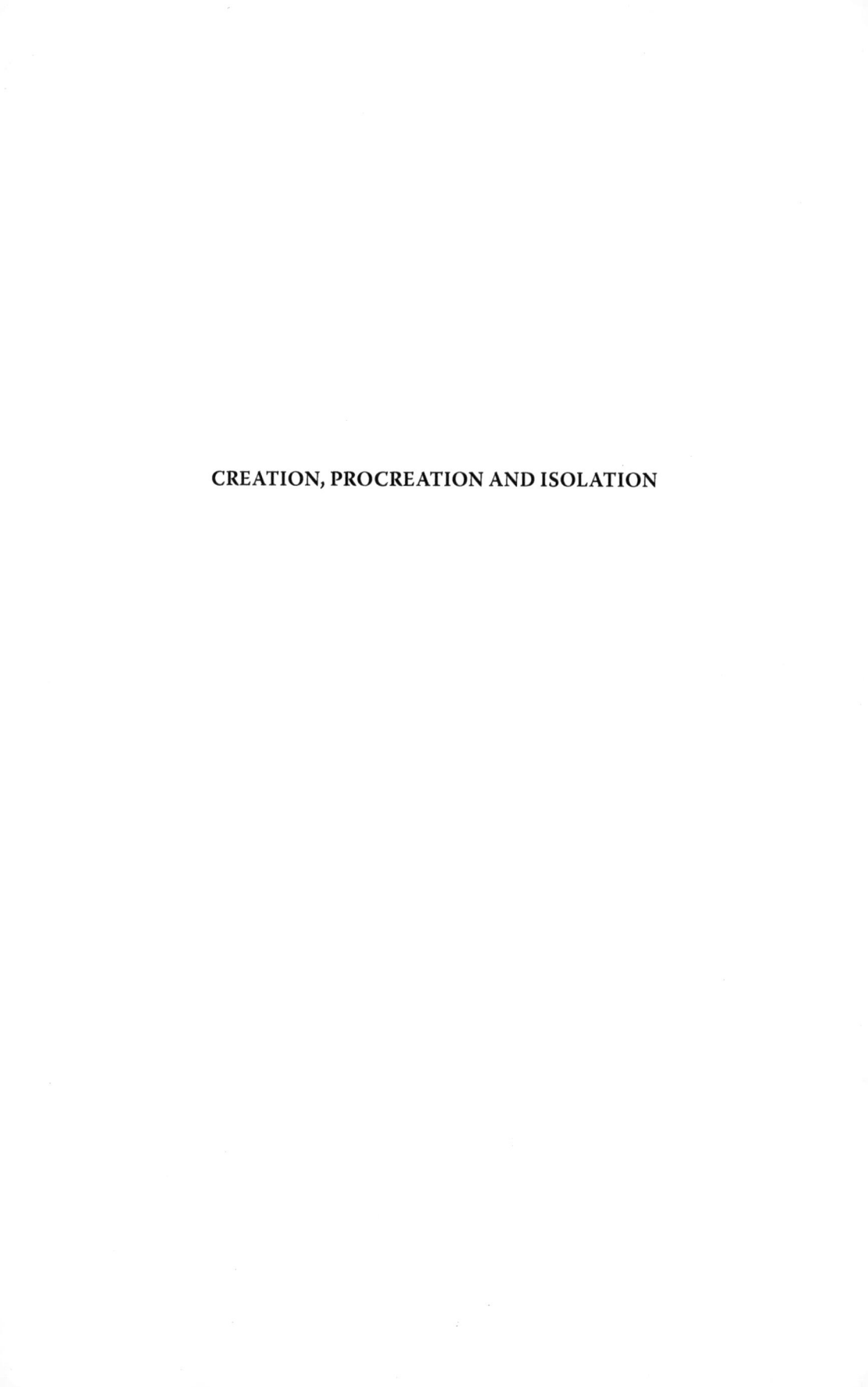

CREATION, PROCREATION AND ISOLATION

First published in 2024 by
Sean Kingston Publishing
www.seankingston.co.uk
Canon Pyon

© 2024 John Forrest.

All rights reserved.
No part of this publication may be reproduced in any form or by any means without the written permission of Sean Kingston Publishing.

British Library Cataloguing in Publication Data
A catalogue record for this book is available from the British Library.
The moral rights of the author have been asserted.

Cover image: *Adam and Eve* by Lucas Cranach the Elder, *c.*1510.
Currently in the National Museum, Warsaw.

ISBN 978-1-912385-54-6

Creation, procreation and isolation
An anthropological introduction to Genesis

JOHN FORREST

Sean Kingston Publishing
www.seankingston.co.uk
Canon Pyon

I dedicate this book to my beloved wife,
Deborah Blincoe, who died on 19 September 2007.
The world is poorer and dimmer for her passing.

Preface

This book grew out of my longstanding interest in the book of Genesis. I cannot read it without unearthing new riches. Both its grand popular tales and its smaller, lesser-known details fascinate me. I have lectured on Genesis in one context or another for over forty years. It was the first required book in a year-long Freshman Studies course that I helped design in 1981, and which I taught for many years at Purchase College, State University of New York. In addition, Genesis tales constantly popped up when I was lecturing in anthropology classes on practices of kinship, marriage, economics and ritual, as well as on various aspects of language and storytelling. The book was an endless store of cases, when I was searching for a familiar or concrete example to nail down an abstract generalization in anthropological theory. Aside from being a professional anthropologist (trained in both England and the United States), I am also an ordained Presbyterian minister, so, over the years, I have approached Genesis in the context of Christian preaching and teaching as well (my particular brand of Presbyterianism being characterized as 'modern' or 'liberal').

Before you close this book and put it back on the shelf because you think I am 'one of them' (whoever you think 'they' are), I would beg your indulgence. This book is merely one among many ways of approaching Genesis. It is not the only way that I view the text myself, by any means. Preaching from the pulpit is a world away from lecturing in the classroom. Furthermore, Genesis is a multifaceted work, and I am interested in all of its facets – and all ways of reading the text. I do not agree with all approaches to the text, but I want to understand the logic behind them. For example, I do not believe that Genesis 1 is an accurate description of the birth of the universe, but I want to know why some people think that it is. Maybe, therefore, you will also give me a chance to expose a facet of the text that may be new to you and explain my reasons for viewing Genesis from this angle. My interpretation here in no way disempowers a multitude of others.

I began my university career with a degree in theology at the University of Oxford that required me to be a competent reader of classical Greek and

Hebrew, as well as being conversant with various hypotheses concerning the origins and purposes of all the books of the Bible (which consumed almost all of my undergraduate training). During my time at Oxford I became aware, through friends, of the particular social anthropological tradition born there, and subsequently began informal studies myself – complementing (uneasily, at first) my theological studies of ritual, kinship and marriage. I was, however, less than pleased with my options in England for further study in social anthropology, and so moved to the USA, where I took an MA in folklore, and then a Ph.D. in cultural anthropology at the University of North Carolina. From there, I was hired to teach anthropology at Purchase College at the State University of New York, specializing in the analysis of religion among other things. Ten years later I was accepted for ordination via examination by the Presbyterian Church (USA) and became a parish minister in upstate New York in addition to being a professor of anthropology. Currently I live in Phnom Penh in Cambodia and teach early church doctrine and Reformation history at the International Theological College and Seminary.

Because of my mixed academic training, I am aware of, and comfortable with, at least three quite different ways of approaching Genesis (though there are of course more than three): 1) as a sacred document for use in a ritual/religious context; 2) as an orally transmitted group of texts that were eventually written down and edited, and which can be interpreted using the tools of textual analysis including form and source criticism; 3) as a series of narratives revealing cultural norms in a particular time and place. Each of these approaches can be broken down into subcategories and sub-subcategories. For example, in considering Genesis as a sacred document, are you a Jew, Christian or Muslim? If you are a Jew, are you orthodox, conservative or reformed? ...and so on. The point you start from, will determine how you examine the text and what you see in it. Because of my training, I am familiar with all three approaches in general, but in this work I am going to be using approach 3) exclusively.

The more I examined Genesis from different angles as a scholar, the more I realized that the work was a remarkable, perhaps unique, book for anthropological investigation. What dawned on me slowly, as I probed the familiar, and less familiar, stories of Genesis, was that while the book in its final form had been constructed to serve many varied purposes, the one function that scholars seem to have missed was that it was crafted as a cultural survival manual – although not always deliberately and consciously so, and most certainly not as its only, or even primary, function. In this book I am going to explore my hypothesis, piece by piece, that key ideas at the heart of Genesis, when adhered to strictly, saved a group of Judeans/Jews from cultural extinction during the period called the Exile or the Babylonian Captivity (c.597–539 BCE). Subsequently, Genesis played an active role in developing religious and social practices that endured for centuries, with a similar effect of warding off forces that could weaken their cultural integrity. The Exile is my main focus, but I will touch briefly on the enduring legacy at the end.

Cultural anthropologists and biblical exegetes have much to learn from one another, but an unfortunate gap between the expertise and interests of the two groups has often hampered fruitful interchange in the past. In part, the gap exists because the two areas require mastery of different skills, and the two sets of scholars have markedly different agendas and expectations. They are asking different kinds of questions and are on different research trajectories established by their respective disciplines. We are not really talking about just two camps anyway, but multiple camps on either side of the gap. An evangelical Christian commentator is going to approach Genesis very differently from a reformed Jewish one, and both are going to be at odds with Hasidic rabbis. By the same token, a structuralist anthropologist and a cultural materialist are going to view the Bible in markedly dissimilar ways. The two kinds of anthropologist might be able to sit in the same room and argue – even though they may never come to agreement – because, at minimum, their goals and methods are similar enough for some measure of discourse. But put a cultural materialist and an evangelical Christian in the same room, and there is almost zero chance of communication between them on any level, even though the text in front of both of them is the same: their starting points and frames of reference are fundamentally incompatible. Put a basketball team up against a volleyball team in the same gym and you are not going to get any meaningful play between the two teams because their rules and expectations of what qualifies as a 'match' are incompatible. Watch any debate you like between an evangelical Christian and an evolutionary biologist concerning the origins of *Homo sapiens* (there are plenty on YouTube) and my point will be immediately patent. The one treats Genesis 1 as the inspired and inerrant word of God that counts as sufficient evidence for understanding human origins, whereas the other draws on fossils and other physical remains from the geological record and uses them to draw conclusions. They might as well be speaking different languages. Their basic methods and theory do not mesh at all.

For some time now, scholars of the Christian sections of the Bible (called the New Testament by some Christians) who are interested in the life and times of Jesus of Nazareth have been willing to learn from social scientists in their efforts to build a broad picture of the cultural context of his ministry, the people who surrounded him, and the new church that developed after his death. John Dominic Crossan, for example, who started his academic career as a Jesuit priest, has employed contemporary anthropological theory to interpret the Jesus of the gospels as a flesh-and-blood historical man (e.g. Crossan 1991,

1994). Approaching the text from another angle, social scientists such as Bruce Malina have been able to contribute an anthropological perspective to the Greek texts (e.g. Malina 1981).

Scholars of the Hebrew Bible (called the Old Testament by some Christians) have tended to lag behind in this approach. For example, a technical commentary on Leviticus by a well-respected Hebrew Bible scholar, published in 2003 in a widely available series of commentaries, contains only one reference to anthropology: Sir James George Frazer's *Golden Bough*, published in 1890, and now entirely discredited by modern anthropologists (Levine 2003). In other words, Levine sees no point in incorporating serious contemporary anthropology into his commentary, and has no interest in finding out what anthropology has to offer him, any more than he thinks that quantum mechanics or phenomenology will further his insights.

The archeology of the region occupied by the ancient kingdoms of Judah and Israel has, for many decades, been concerned with a number of historical claims made in the Hebrew Bible – 'Did the Exodus actually happen?', 'Was David king of a united monarchy of Israel and Judah?', 'Did Solomon build the first temple?', 'Did David and Solomon even exist?' etc. – and in analysing archeological evidence in relation to these questions, theoretical insights from cultural anthropology inevitably seep in. But there is a fundamental difference between investigating historical claims about people (and events), and exploring the evolution of ideas. This book is about the latter – the domain of cultural anthropology.

There are many reasons why conventional biblical textual criticism and cultural anthropology are typically miles apart. The two are venerable disciplines with long histories of their own. They have their own vexing questions and their own methods of answering them. Frequently, the concerns of one side are irrelevant to the other. Because of this longstanding division, it is an enormous challenge to gain expertise in both fields, with little encouragement from either side. Both sides have turf to protect, and can look with suspicion on anyone appearing to trespass. For example, in the past there have been some notable efforts by well-known anthropologists, such as Mary Douglas, Marvin Harris and Edmund Leach, to make sense of Judaic law (most notably concerning food laws), but their efforts have either been ignored or savagely criticized by biblical scholars – and for good reason. I agree with many of the critiques, because these anthropologists had a limited understanding of the Hebrew Bible and its geographic and historic contexts. They are pushing their own cherished anthropological theories using biblical references as a small component of their overall data to buttress their claims, without taking into account any of the scholarly exegesis of these references. In this book I want to assist in the process of bringing Hebrew Bible scholarship and cultural anthropology together in areas where they may profit one another. Because I am formally trained in both cultural anthropology and biblical analysis, I can bridge the divide between the two fields better than most – I hope.

Although this is a work of serious scholarship, I want to keep the level of discourse relatively simple and straightforward, so that the ideas are accessible to as wide an audience as possible. The book can act as a supplement to standard texts in introductory anthropology because it deals with the basics of marriage, family, kinship, ritual, exchange and so forth, and can also be used in adjunct fields such as religious studies. It is also suitable reading for rabbis and Christian pastors, as well as for the interested laity. To that end, the text is not overburdened with footnotes and inline citations – just enough to point in the right direction. I include at the end of each chapter a list of suggested readings in case certain topics inspire a desire for deeper knowledge of them.

You will also see that on occasion (not often) I use various other parts of the Hebrew Bible to contextualize Genesis. This practice stems from my considered position on the texts and ideas that were available to the redactors of Genesis when they were assembling the book. As a simple example, I sometimes use quotes from the prophets Ezekiel and Deutero-Isaiah to flesh out my ideas, because they were living in exile in Babylon when they were actively writing. They lived the Babylonian experience, and I can draw on that experience as eyewitness testimony to conditions at the time. Also, Genesis is a book of tales not of law, so there are times when I need to shift to actual law codes (that the exiles would have been aware of or were in the process of compiling) to explain the legal implications of the tales.

Acknowledgements

I owe an enormous debt of gratitude (and respect) to Barbara Miller who worked tirelessly on earlier drafts of each chapter of this book and then gave the final draft of the whole work a polished and invaluable critique. Also, thanks to Katie Nelson for inspired comments, especially on the role of women in Genesis. Thanks also to the many anonymous reviewers of drafts, who provided valuable insights.

Contents

Chapter 1	Everyone has an agenda	1
Chapter 2	Judah in exile	23
Chapter 3	What's in a word?	41
Chapter 4	The creation formula	55
Chapter 5	Don't let your daughter marry an angel	70
Chapter 6	What's in a word?	82
Chapter 7	Be fruitful and multiply	100
Chapter 8	What's my line?	114
Chapter 9	The last shall be first	130
Chapter 10	Matriarchs, Mother Eve and gender	146
Chapter 11	Towering arrogance	162
Chapter 12	The farmer and the cowman can't be friends	173
Chapter 13	It isn't over even when it's over	191
References		206
Index		221

1

Everyone has an agenda

An anthropological perspective
Genesis is unlike any other book in the Bible. Indeed, it is unlike any other book you are likely to come across. Almost everyone brought up in some part of the world where Judeo-Christian culture has left its mark will be aware of many of its themes, such as, Adam and Eve, Noah's Ark or the Garden of Eden, even without ever having read the actual tales. These images are indelibly marked on the collective consciousness of generation upon generation of people. They appear in countless works of poetry, art, song, literature, advertising and film, and are expected to be instantly recognizable. There are also passages, such as the extremely short description of primeval sexual relations between heavenly beings and women (Genesis 6:4), that are much less well known.

Genesis is a dense, rich, complex and multifaceted work. Yet, it is not an especially long book. In one edition of the original Hebrew it contains 32,046 words (a little more in English translation). By simple word count it is, in fact, the second longest book in the Bible, but, even so, you ought to be able to read a work of that length (about 90 double-spaced, typed pages) in a short period. Admittedly, some English translations are hard to fathom, but there are contemporary language versions that smooth out the text so that the reader does not have to keep reaching for the dictionary. Nonetheless, Genesis does not read like a simple narrative nor even a standard history text. It can be tough going to read it straight through.

Some of the tales in Genesis are short and simple, some are long and complex. If you start at the beginning and work your way through to the end, you soon realize that the book can be broken down into chunks that are understandable on their own, and you may wonder, when you have finished, whether it is a single narrative at all, or a series of disconnected units joined together by basic chronology alone. In chapter 1, for example, God is supremely transcendent, brooding in spirit over an infinite dark watery chaos that represents the entire universe, and then calling light into existence out of nothing by a simple command; whereas, in chapters 2 and 3 he plants a garden and walks in it in the cool of the evening, much like a human gardener would do. They seem like two different gods entirely. There are some well-known works of European literature, such as, Chaucer's *Canterbury Tales* and Boccaccio's *Decameron*, that bear some similarity to Genesis in that they are built out of discrete components, but few such works, if any, are held together in a manner at all like Genesis. Nor have many been approached and dissected in quite so many diverse ways.

Initial exposure to the text of Genesis can come in many forms. Many people encounter elements of it as children, through regular attendance at temple or church, in which case an adult likely acts as a mentor, picking out salient stories and giving them an interpretation in ways that children can understand. Likewise, many adults are guided through passages by rabbis, priests, pastors or teachers of one sort or another. Even with a user-friendly translation, simply picking up a Bible for the first time and making a stab at reading Genesis presents numerous challenges. Having someone to provide a context for reading, or an interpretation, can be of great assistance. But more than with most other texts, even within the Bible, Genesis is a multilayered, complex book that can be read in many different ways.

The density of Genesis is immediately obvious. Rabbis, priests, Sunday School teachers, scholars and cantors can take small segments of the book, maybe even one or two verses, and write, preach or teach lengthy expositions on them. What should also be obvious when you experience such expositions, is that every interpreter of Genesis has an agenda. There are numerous verse-by-verse commentaries on Genesis (e.g. Prager 2020; Sarna 2001; von Rad 1961; www.biblegateway.com/resources/matthew-henry/Genesis), as well as thousands of books that focus on special aspects of Genesis (e.g. Dundes 1999; Leach 1969; Niditch 1993; Sailhamer 2008; Steinberg 1993). Each one of these books approaches the text from a particular point of view, whether explicitly stated, or implicitly understood. Nahum Sarna is a Torah scholar, for example, and his commentary uses a standard Hebrew text. Gerhard von Rad, by contrast, was a German Lutheran biblical scholar and theologian. You would be correct in assuming, without even opening them, that these commentaries are radically different. If you were raised in a Jewish household you might pick Sarna over von Rad as a suitable interpretation for your needs, and if raised as a Christian, the reverse. But some Jews will object to Sarna's exegesis, while some Christians will dislike von Rad's. Many readers will find both commentaries far too scholarly for their purposes, and may prefer a sermon, an internet video or a simple storybook in plain language. There is a superabundance of all kinds of exegeses for all tastes.

In this welter of interpretations, every interpreter is making a particular point, and I make no bones about the fact that in this work I am doing the same. I want to be up front about my agenda. I am not saying that my analysis in this book is in any sense the best or the only interpretation of Genesis; far from it. My interpretation emerges from my own intellectual background. By training I am a cultural anthropologist and, as such, I treat all texts in a particular kind of way. I am also an ordained Presbyterian minister, though I have been at pains to mute that voice in this work. My academic training in theology has been of use in preparing this book only inasmuch as I had to learn biblical Hebrew in order to interpret the texts, and I had to compare multiple commentaries on Genesis for scholastic purposes.

Cultural anthropologists spend a great deal of time and energy debating how to interpret cultures and their cultural texts. I was educated in a school of thought that sees every culture in the contemporary world, and in the past, as a distinctive pattern of ideas and behaviours. We attempt to decipher these patterns and to translate them into terms that make sense to people in other cultures. The concept of culture is arguably anthropology's greatest contribution to modern social scientific investigation, although these days it is a deeply contested concept. Nonetheless, as a rule of thumb, many anthropologists still define culture as the system of rules, values, ideas and norms that holds societies together and gives them their distinctive character. This system of rules and values guides the behaviour of the individuals who live within it and forms their world-view, through which they make sense out of the world in which they live. Thus, members of one culture hear thunder and go indoors because they interpret the sound as a sign that rain is imminent, whereas members of another culture hear thunder and go to a religious specialist because they interpret the sound as the voice of the gods. For the anthropologist the question of whether thunder is 'really' a sign of rain or the voice of the gods (or both or neither) is not terribly important. What matters to the cultural anthropologist is the place that thunder holds within that culture.

One guiding principle of my brand of cultural anthropology is that the shared behaviours and beliefs in a given culture, no matter how odd or irrational they may appear to an outside observer, make sense once one takes the time to understand the whole pattern of the culture from the inside. Therefore, one of the main contributions of this kind of anthropology is cultural analysis on a holistic level. One of the ways anthropologists understand the parts of culture is by understanding the workings of the whole. This is a little like understanding the parts of a complex machine, such as a car engine, by understanding the design of the whole. A spark plug viewed in isolation may seem like an incomprehensible object, but when fitted properly into an operating engine its form and function make perfect sense. To be fair, this approach has its critics within the discipline, but it is well established. The most obvious critique of this stance is that culture is not like a machine, not even a very complex one. Cultures are self-conscious, evolving phenomena, with some components working well and others badly, and with nothing fitting very well together. Cultures deal with the messy realities as best they can, trying to make some kind of logical sense out of complex experiences.

The style of cultural anthropology I employ here argues that all behaviour, thoughts, and objects exist within a cultural context and derive their values from that context. This way of thinking is sometimes called a 'text-in-context' approach, where 'text' can be any behaviour – language, gesture, ritual – and the 'context' is the whole system that makes up the culture. My anthropological take on Genesis is a text-in-context approach, such that understanding the text of Genesis requires an understanding of the context of the culture that produced it. Let me be clear from the outset, however. This approach is only one of many, and it is not universally agreed upon by any means. There is not much agreement among anthropologists concerning the interpretation of cultures. (Useful readings on anthropological approaches to culture, and the various debates, can be found at the end of the chapter.)

For contemporary cultures, the most frequently employed method of understanding cultural context by anthropologists is participant-observer fieldwork. Using this method, the anthropologist lives with a community for a year or more and engages in all the activities common to the people (e.g. Robben and Sluka 2012). For historic cultures, such as those of the Bible, participant observation is not possible. Instead, three approaches can be combined to lay bare the culture in question. First is archaeology, whose methodologies have reached a level of considerable sophistication. The archaeology of the land of the Bible has a rich history and has produced an enormous wealth of information about the development of culture in the region (e.g. Dever 2017; Finkelstein 2013; Mazar 1973). Such archaeological findings can be supplemented by biblical and extra-biblical texts, and can also complement them, if these texts are used critically and with care. The second approach is cross-cultural comparison (e.g. Fedorak 2013, 2017). Information generated by participant-observer fieldwork in many cultures with similar environments and subsistence bases helps us to build up common patterns that can then be used to analyse historic cultures. This approach has its dangers and weaknesses, however. What counts as 'common patterns' can be, and has been, vigorously contested.

Third, I occasionally refer to other books of the Bible to help contextualize the ideas of the 'redactors' of Genesis (which was pieced together from several different kinds of source material in a process known as 'redaction'; the people involved are the 'redactors').[1] For example, Ezekiel and Deutero-Isaiah were Judean exiles. They were coping with the rigours of living in exile in a foreign land, and are the best we have in the way of eyewitnesses (that is, surrogates for interviews or participant observation). Slightly farther afield, I occasionally refer to legal codes in Leviticus and the Deuteronomic corpus, especially in relation to kinship and marriage, because these codes were current for the exiles. Genesis presupposes the existence and the validity of these codes (in some form, not necessarily as finished books).

Some of what I have to say about Genesis as a cultural anthropologist has been noted before, but I am going to approach the text in a way that I believe is original because my opinion concerning the culture that formed the context out of which Genesis as a (mostly) finished book arose, goes against the common scholarly consensus (although my viewpoint is gaining ground), and for me the cultural context of the original text matters greatly for my interpretation. Some commentators, particularly evangelical Christians, will tell you that the book contains timeless truths that need no cultural context to explain them (e.g. Ham 2006). Others will tell you that any reading of any text is irredeemably coloured by the cognitive and intellectual background of the reader regardless of the cultural values of the writer (e.g. Derrida 1990). Both approaches have their followers, but I am not going to be one of them. For me, the cultural context out of which the book grew is fundamental to my interpretation of one of its original purposes, namely, as a culture-survival manual.

Delving into the cultural context of Genesis raises two major challenges. First, the book was written and compiled over a period of hundreds of years in different places. So, there is no such thing as 'the' cultural context of Genesis. There are many cultural contexts over that long period of time. Before I can begin my interpretation, I have to determine what contexts I want to deal with. This challenge leads to the second one. Experts do not agree about when and where most of Genesis was written (e.g. Davies 1998; Hendel 2012; Ska 2006; van Seters 1992).

Arguably, Genesis is the most contested battleground of the entire Bible. Whatever you say about Genesis, someone will disagree with you – often

---

[1] Theories of the redaction process of Genesis have evolved and changed markedly over the past hundred years or so. For much of the twentieth century, the documentary hypothesis (see below) of Julius Wellhausen (1878, 1883, 1894) held sway, but it has been seriously revised from the 1970s onward (e.g. Baden 2012, Nicolson 2003, Saeboe, Ska and Machinist 2014).

vehemently. The crux of the matter that makes or breaks everything I am going to say in this book concerns my personal determination of when, where, by whom and, most especially, why Genesis was redacted into a finished book. Genesis is not like a modern, single-authored book. An individual did not sit down one morning and decide to write it from scratch beginning at verse one and going all the way through to the end (although there are rafts of people who will argue with me about that point). Unlike a contemporary novel, Genesis is not overtly driven by a single narrative with a beginning, middle and conclusion, although it has elements of such a structure. Genesis is more like a patchwork of stories (with their own beginnings, middles and ends): you can isolate small details in the stories, or you can take in the totality.

The first eleven chapters of Genesis consist of short stories that are only loosely tied together (primarily by chronology). Each of them can be read as an individual module without reference to the others. Later chapters focus on a series of related men, namely Abraham, Isaac, Jacob and Joseph, known collectively as the patriarchs.[2] The stories in these chapters can also be read as self-contained units, but there are threads that tie the pieces together into longer sagas. These threads are primarily genealogical, as well as chronological.

For hundreds of years, biblical scholars have put forward various arguments concerning the origins of the individual narratives that make up Genesis. The best known is generally called the documentary hypothesis (Friedman 1987). This hypothesis has taken many forms over the past hundred years, but its basic tenet is that Genesis was crafted out of traditional tales originating in diverse ethnic enclaves throughout the Near East. Although the documentary hypothesis in all its guises is fascinating, I am going to ignore it because it is not relevant to my interpretation (and because these days its importance is drastically waning within biblical scholarship – see, for example Carr 2014). The only aspect of the hypothesis that we need to accept in order to proceed is that the various components of Genesis came from many different writers, times and places, but were ultimately shaped into a single book. Here I care only about how the book was compiled into a finished whole, not about the provenance of its sources.

I can use the patchwork quilt as an analogy for my approach to Genesis. One type of quilt is known as a scrap quilt because it is pieced out of scraps cut from various sources – old shirts, dresses, curtains and so forth. The original maker of the quilt can identify the sources of each of the patches, but when

---

[2] I am aware that 'patriarch' is a gendered term, but in this case the gender is apt: they are all men – Abraham, Isaac, Jacob and Joseph. One might object to the suffix /-arch/ with the connotation of 'ruler', but they are all heads of significant lineages, and, as such, the suffix is apt also.

she has sewn them all together, a finished pattern emerges that overtakes the interest in the origins of the individual pieces. Thus, while I readily admit that Genesis is pieced together from radically diverse sources, the finished product has a definable pattern that shapes the whole. The Flood narrative is an excellent example. The whole narrative begins with tales of giant warriors and with sexual encounters between heavenly beings and human women, moves on to the Ark, and then concludes with Noah's drunkenness. These components obviously come from different sources with different original purposes, yet they have been stitched together to form a whole that is clearly greater than the sum of its parts and in which their original purposes have changed to serve a larger pattern.

In general, the pieces that make up Genesis do not always fit together terribly well for the modern reader. To us, certain segments appear to flatly contradict others. I deal with this problem more fully later on. For now, it is best to avoid being ethnocentric, that is, to avoid using our own cultural biases to judge aspects of another culture. Do not assume that the apparent contradictions and paradoxes in the book mean that the people who put Genesis together were incompetent. What may look odd to us was likely created in that way for good reasons, and we need to find out what those reasons were.

Who's who and where's where

The focus of this book is the ancient kingdom of Judah and its historical tribulations, but in order to understand that cultural context it is necessary to consider the kingdom's wider geographic circumstances, including the ever-changing ethnic composition of its neighbours and imperial masters. What to call the various regions within the land of the Bible and the numerous ethnic groups who have occupied it at different times is a problem that has vexed scholars for centuries (Arnold 2014). Even the Bible itself is inconsistent. What you call the people and their homelands has profound social and political implications down to the present day. Accepting that these are hotly contested and divisive issues, and that it is impossible to make such decisions without offending someone, I am going to follow practices that are accepted widely by archaeologists and biblical scholars. The overall geographic region of the land of the Bible I am going to refer to as the Levant most of the time. Sometimes I refer to it as Canaan because I want to emphasize the historic period when it was occupied by Canaanite peoples. During a significant portion of ancient history, the territory was divided into two kingdoms: Israel, made up of ten tribes (more or less) in the north, and Judah, made up of two tribes (more or less) in the south.[3] Generally, when I use these terms I am referring to the regions occupied by these two kingdoms, or to the nations themselves, mindful that the geographic boundaries were fluid. Sometimes, however, the Bible refers to the two kingdoms collectively as Israel. This is because the twelve tribes that comprise the kingdoms of Israel and Judah together were considered to be historically related in some way or other, and were treated as a whole for certain political or theological purposes – although exactly how they were related is endlessly debated by scholars (e.g. Dever 2001; Finkelstein and Mazar 2007).

Technically (that is, biblically), the term 'Israelites' refers to the members of all the twelve tribes of Israel: the peoples of Israel and Judah taken as a whole, because the twelve tribes are all supposedly descended from the twelve sons of Jacob/Israel. I occasionally use the term in this overarching sense. When I use the term Judeans, I am referring specifically to the people of the nation of Judah (the Yehudim in Hebrew). They are the people who are the prime subjects of this book and, nominally, the ancestors of the people now commonly called Jews.

How the nations of Israel and Judah actually arose historically, as opposed to how they arose according to the Bible, is the subject of extensive debate among archaeologists nowadays (e.g. Dever 2017). On the most general level, there is an emerging consensus that while Israel and Judah may have coalesced into states some time around the tenth century BCE (heavy emphasis on 'may'), they were a far cry from the glorious kingdoms described in the Bible. Israel was certainly the oldest, richest and most powerful, with Judah emerging some time afterwards as a much poorer and more isolated vassal state. Judah is named for Jacob's fourth son, Yehudah. In Hebrew, a person from Judah was a *Yehudi*, which was translated in the Septuagint (a Greek version of Hebrew sacred texts produced from roughly the third century BCE onwards) using the Koine Greek term *Ioudaios* (Greek: Ἰουδαίος; pl. Ἰουδαῖοι, *Ioudaioi*) – dropping the /h/ sound from the Hebrew. The Latin term, transliterated from the Greek version, is *Iudaeus*, and from these sources the term passed to other European languages. The Old French *giu*, earlier *juieu*, had dropped the /d/ sound from the Latin *Iudaeus*. The Middle English word Jew derives from Old English, where the word is attested as early as 1000 CE in various forms, such as Iudeas, Gyu, Giu, Iuu, Iuw, Iew. The Old English name is derived from Old French (see OED entry 'Jew').

---

3 Historically, the kingdom of Judah's territory appears to have included the lands of the tribes of Judah, Benjamin and Simeon (plus some Levite cities). But the tribes of Simeon and parts of Levi are counted among the so-called ten 'Lost Tribes of Israel' which were deported following the Assyrian conquest of Israel in 722 BCE.

The history of the kingdoms of Israel and Judah was once believed to be accurately, or reasonably accurately, recorded in the books of Samuel and Kings. But by the late 1980s into the 1990s, archaeology had called into question much of the reliability of the biblical record (e.g. Grabbe 2007). This larger story is a tale for another time. Nonetheless, two major events in the region recorded in the Bible, and relevant to this book, are abundantly confirmed by sources outside the Bible and by modern archaeology. The first is the final destruction of the northern kingdom of Israel in around 722 BCE by neo-Assyrian forces under Sargon II. The Assyrians amassed wealth by having tribute paid to them by modestly rich vassal states such as Israel, so when Israel rebelled in the eighth century there was likely to be a retribution, if only for financial reasons. But there was more than wealth at stake. Israel was strategically located on natural land routes between Africa, Asia and Europe. Thus, if an Assyrian emperor wanted to wage war with Egypt, for example, he had to take his army through Israel. Likewise, if an Egyptian army was intent on conquest in Mesopotamia. Taking a large army to the west of Israel by sea was not feasible, and to the east was arid desert. The land bridge through Israel was the obvious and preferred route.

When Israel refused to pay tribute to Tiglath-Pileser, it felt the full might of the neo-Assyrian empire, not simply because the rebellion was intolerable on its own merits, but also because of the strategic importance of the land routes. The campaign may have taken as many as twenty years to complete, but it was relentless under four successive emperors because they were determined to have open access to the land routes. When these emperors concluded their various campaigns in Israel, they forcibly deported the residents of the territory to different parts of the empire, and their fate has largely been lost to history. These Israelites have become known as the Lost Tribes of Israel, and they have been the subject of countless idle speculations (e.g. Gonen 2002). On the other hand, it is contended by many scholars that a handful of scribes and priests from Israel managed to escape south to Judah, bringing a number of oral and literary traditions with them. According to some older forms of the documentary hypothesis, for example, it is argued that the E, or Elohist, source material of Genesis is derived from traditions acquired from refugees from Israel (e.g. Baden 2009).[4]

Let us be clear on one vital point, though. At the time of the conquest of Israel by Assyria, according to the academic consensus I ascribe to, virtually none of the books of the Hebrew Bible existed as finished books, and what did

---

[4] The Documentary Hypothesis argues that Genesis has three primary sources, J (the Yahwist) from Judah, E (the Elohist) from Israel, and P (Priestly Source) made up of temple priests from Jerusalem.

exist was either Judean or reflected the Judean perspective that the deity יהוה (which I will transcribe in this work as 'Yahweh')[5] dwelt in the temple in Jerusalem and was supreme over all other gods. There were plenty of oral and written sources, as well as religious and ritual traditions, in existence of course, many of which are now either lost or folded into other books at a later date. But only the prophetic books of Amos and Hosea were available in anything like the finished form we have them in now. Amos and Hosea rail against the excesses of the fabulously rich nobility of Israel, predicting utter doom and destruction should it continue. The survival of these books is undoubtedly due to the fact that the destruction of Israel prophesied in them, occurred. Henceforth, with Israel out of the way, Judah grew and flourished. Unlike Israel, Judah decided that paying tribute to Assyria was more sensible than resisting militarily, and thus was able to ride out the storm while Assyria asserted dominance in the region.

During the relative calm of the period following the destruction of Israel, scholars in Judah put their minds to determining why, powerful though it was, it had been utterly crushed by Assyria, yet they, a small and weak neighbour, had survived and subsequently prospered. The contemporary academic community is divided at present concerning the formal literary output of this period in Judah's history. I tend to support the opinion that so-called Deuteronomic history (named for its first book) – Deuteronomy, Joshua, Judges, Samuel and Kings – was substantially written in the seventh century by scholars now called the Deuteronomists (Schearing and McKenzie 1995). One of the lynch pins of Deuteronomic history is that unwavering faith in Yahweh (the national God of Judah), as archetypically demonstrated by David and Solomon, leads to glory; and apostasy, as exhibited by many subsequent monarchs of Israel and of Judah, was the recipe for disaster (with the complete annihilation of Israel as proof). The only hope for the long-term survival and prosperity of Judah was strict adherence to the religious code of Yahweh.

In this same period, in the mid- to late seventh century BCE, it is now increasingly argued that the eighth-century poetic prophesies of Isaiah ben Amoz were reworked to incorporate prose sermons that reflected a Deuteronomic perspective to produce a finished book now represented by Isaiah chapters 1 – 39, sometimes called Proto-Isaiah (e.g. Stromberg 2011). Proto-Isaiah prophesied that a Messiah (an anointed one, or king) would arise in the Davidic line and lead Judah on to victory, restoring the former glories of the original Davidic kingdom. Both the lessons taught by this brand of history

---

5 The four letters which make up the deity's name – יהוה – are the source of an immense amount of discussion. For the sake of simplicity, I am going to sidestep this discourse.

and this style of prophecy were sadly misguided and led to a major catastrophe in Judean history that I describe in greater detail in Chapter 2.

The brief version, for now, is that in the early sixth century BCE, Judah, centred on Jerusalem, rebelled against its imperial Babylonian overlord (successor to the Assyrian empire) and in consequence was crushed into complete submission. The Babylonians left the city of Jerusalem a smoking pile of rubble; they tortured, raped and slaughtered untold numbers of its population. Those who survived, if they were poor, were left behind to eke out a living in the remains. The conquering generals forcibly relocated almost the entire upper echelon of royalty, professionals, priests, artisans and intellectuals to Babylon. As far as they knew, they would never see Jerusalem again; and most of them did not. They had to find some way to survive in a strange land. My argument is that the creation of the book of Genesis in exile in Babylon was a major part of that survival strategy.

Geographic dislocation is a potent weapon for dealing with a troublesome ethnic minority. Rulers of large multicultural states have used it with great effect for millennia. The Assyrians had done exactly that with the population of Israel, and utterly neutered their power. When Native American tribes proved too rebellious for the Euro-American populations of New York, Idaho or North Carolina to cope with in the nineteenth century they were shipped off to reservations in Indiana and Oklahoma. Stalin repopulated vast regions of the Soviet Union in an attempt to break down local ethnic resistance to Slavic dominance. The result of such forced migration is often the extinction of the inconvenient minority, thus constituting either genocide, the mass slaughter of a people, or ethnocide, the destruction of a cultural way of life, even if some of the people survive.

A critical factor affecting survival of a culture in a situation of forced displacement is that cultures and ethnic identities are often distinctively tied to geographic features of their place of origin. Mountains, groves or rivers can have overwhelming significance in the life of a people, such that if you take that people away from those places, there is a good chance that significant aspects of their culture will be lost, because they have been separated from the locations that give it meaning and, thereby, power. The Judeans in exile faced that threat. Mount Zion and the temple in Jerusalem were the axis of all Judean culture. With the inability to sacrifice and worship at Solomon's temple in Jerusalem, it was quite possible that Judean culture would disappear.

A second threat arises for people who are relocated into the midst of a big, powerful, alien culture: assimilation. In that situation, in the midst of a dominant and potentially attractive culture, there are two clear paths you can take. One is to isolate and insulate yourself as much as possible from the dominant culture. You maintain your language and customs in every way you can within the foreign land, and, thus, create continuity with the past and feel comfortable in your little enclave. The price you pay is that you remain a small, weak, oppressed minority surrounded by people who may look down on you and even despise you. The second path is to abandon your traditional roots and to adopt the language and culture of the dominant group. You may never fully assimilate into the new culture, but you can at least begin to share in its wealth and power. The result is a diminution in your oppression, but that benefit carries with it the cost of losing your culture.

Options of the oppressed

In *The Colonizer and the Colonized* (1965) political theorist Albert Memmi investigates the relationship between powerful imperial cultures and their subordinate peoples. He charts the options for oppressed groups, and examines the consequences of their choices. Memmi was a Jew born in Tunisia in 1921. At this time, Tunisia was under French colonial control. Arabic was his first language and Tunisia was his home culture. However, he attended schools in France, Tunisia and Algeria, and thus saw colonial imperialism from the standpoint of both the oppressor and the oppressed.

Memmi's understanding of the colonial imperial situation of oppressed groups and their masters is a clear and cogent analysis. He argues that the colonial masters and the colonized peoples each have two choices: they can accept the colonial situation and try to make the best of it, or they can reject it and seek alternatives. For our purposes, his analysis of the options of the colonized is valuable for understanding the situation of the Judeans in exile in Babylon.

Memmi's analysis was originally meant to model the situation of populations who had been conquered and then colonized by outside forces. These populations were not displaced, but their power had been taken from them. The Judean exiles were not in this situation. They had been conquered, but then they had been moved to a new geographic location. Nonetheless, we may speak of them as 'the colonized' and use Memmi's insights to understand their dilemmas. Memmi suggests that oppressed groups have a fundamental choice to make. They can either accept their position and make the best of it, or they can reject their position and fight against it.

The colonized who accept the colonial situation

A common response of people who are oppressed is to emulate the power of the culture that controls them and try to assimilate to it. According to Memmi, assimilation inevitably involves rejection of one's native culture, perhaps even one's own family, and, by extension, involves rejecting oneself. Assimilation bears with it the burden of self-hatred. For the sake of advancement in an imperial or colonial situation, self-loathing and identity rejection may seem like an acceptable price to pay for a measure of status and perhaps power. All ambitious people must accept the personal and psychological consequences of their ambition. The fatal problem is that oppressed people attempting to assimilate to the dominant culture can appear ridiculous to the people they are trying to emulate, and so are ultimately rejected by them to one degree or another, while also being despised by other members of their own culture who refuse to assimilate.

Memmi's analysis has been given a more nuanced guise in recent years because his original formulation was too one-dimensional in light of current ethnography. Some colonized people may, indeed, succumb to his prescribed fate, but others may find subtler ways to accommodate to the colonial situation. It is possible, for example, to become bicultural (similar to being bilingual). That is, you learn to operate effectively in two radically different cultures by switching between the two as necessary (in the same way that you can switch languages). This approach softens the sense of self-rejection because you maintain both cultures internally. Nonetheless, the asymmetry of power and wealth between the two cultures remains.

The colonized who reject the colonial situation

This is the group to which many of the Babylonian exiles belonged. Memmi sees the colonized who reject their situation as tending primarily to a nativistic outlook. Nativists are members of oppressed minority cultures who seek to remove from their traditional culture, including their dress and personal behaviour, as many traces as possible of the culture of the imperial power group who control them. Language is an important starting point. Nativists speak and write in their local language and refuse to use the language of the hegemonic elite. These actions can be deeply threatening to that elite, whose members do not understand the minority language and, therefore, cannot be sure what is being said about them.

In the nineteenth century, when the British government wished to control the subject Irish in Ireland, it banned the use of all dialects of the Irish language (Gaeilge) in schools, and their use in the law courts was periodically banned over centuries (Crowley 2000). In the early twenty-first century Turkey has made efforts to ban the Kurdish language, including its teaching in schools, in Kurdish regions (Nelles 2003). Once in a while, the United States government and various state and local agencies attempt to make English the official language of the country. If they succeed, they will erode the power of minority cultures who speak languages other than English, as is their intention. (Crawford 2000).

Much of a culture's identity is wrapped up in the language it uses. If the language of a minority culture dies, the act of assimilation into the mainstream is effectively accomplished. Cornish, the Celtic language of Cornwall in southwest England, became extinct in the eighteenth century, and for all intents and purposes Cornwall, though still regionally distinct, is now essentially English. Folklore has it that the dying words, in 1777, of the last fluent native speaker of Cornish, Dolly Pentreath, were, 'Me ne vidn cewsel Sawznek!' ('I don't want to speak English!') Attempts to revive the Cornish language over the course of the twentieth century and into recent times have been modestly successful, with about 300 fluent speakers at the beginning of the twenty-first century. However, it is not possible through language revival to restore the culture on which Cornish was based. Once the language dies, the culture it supports dies or radically changes to the extent that it is no longer recognizable as distinct (Siarl 2013).

A distinctive religion, like a distinctive language, is often the key to the success of nativist separatism. It establishes a sacred space where local communities meet and reaffirm their identity, and it provides visual symbols of power. Religion also supplies potent annual rituals, what anthropologists call 'rites of intensification', such as the pilgrimage to Mecca or Yom Kippur services, when the nativist community can unite and parade (metaphorically and actually) its distinctive symbols. Religion provides the community with significant rites of passage, such as marriage ceremonies, funerary practices and puberty rituals, which reinforce its values. Religious activities can bring together all manner of aesthetic forms that vitalize the community: food, dance, music, poetry, clothing and the like. Religion can be a powerful glue that holds the nativist movement together, empowers its members, and reminds them of their specialness.

Many examples of such separatist behaviour are found historically, and in the modern world: the Chechens, Basques, Ainu, Scots, Welsh, Mari, Native American cultures throughout North and South America, and Australian Aborigines all employ similar nativistic tactics to distinguish themselves from the dominant culture. But such behaviour has negative consequences. As Memmi notes, rebellion against the dominant culture tends to reinforce the power structure. Jean-Paul Sartre confirms this sentiment in his introduction to *The Colonizer and the Colonized* when he states, 'A relentless reciprocity binds the colonizer to the colonized.' (Memmi 1957:24). Every adolescent knows that when you rebel against your parents you merely confirm their power over you. You do not rebel against the powerless or insignificant. All the energy that goes into nativist separatism powers a system of oppression, and constantly ties the dominant and subordinate cultures together. Even when the subordinate culture singles out something in the dominant culture to hate and reject, the dominant culture is still calling the shots. Nativist dress, music, foodways and other practices are what they are, in part, precisely because they are not what the dominant do. They are responses to the dominant culture and not independent of it.

While Memmi's analysis is applicable in a wide variety of circumstances, I believe it is incomplete. There is a third alternative, what I call the 'Genesis option', which is distinct from Memmi's two paths. The Genesis option requires utter disengagement from the dominant culture. If a minority culture builds a wall around itself and refuses to recognize other cultures as legitimate, or to interact with them on any level, the cultural power of the dominant group becomes irrelevant. While Memmi does not consider this possibility, it is a potent, though rarely used, option: in large part because it has consequences that few are prepared to accept, and it is difficult to maintain.

I call this third path the Genesis option because I believe its basic tenets are laid out in the book of Genesis in the form of a series of interconnected moral tales. My belief is that the first edition of Genesis was put together by some of the priestly leaders of the Judeans in exile in Babylon as a manual for survival in a hostile and oppressive environment. This dating of the initial redaction of Genesis runs counter to the prevailing academic opinion which places it later, that is, after the Exile (e.g. Carr 2011; Ska 2006).[6] Dating during the Exile makes more sense to me because of the themes I point out in this work. I will note, however, that the first edition of Genesis was by no means the final edition. Editors kept playing around with the text for centuries. I cannot get too deeply into the editorial history of Genesis without getting enmeshed in the complexities of source criticism. Instead, I will simply demonstrate that the core book (with or without later edits and additions) can, and did, work as a survival manual for an oppressed people.

Genesis answers two fundamental questions: 1) who are we as a people? and 2) how do we maintain that unique, individual identity? The stories contained in Genesis all repeat a limited set of themes concerning the dangers of assimilation to a dominant culture and the necessity of being entirely cut off from it. Whether or not Genesis was consciously redacted with this end in mind, or whether survival in a hostile culture was the primary purpose for creating the work are not important questions. I am concerned only with the effective outcomes, regardless of intentions.

---

6 The later dating is based on the belief that canonical Judaism is a post-exilic phenomenon, the necessary texts and associated practices crystallizing in the new-found freedom of a reconstructed Jerusalem. I tend to favour an exilic setting, because during those times, in the absence of a temple and sacrificial worship, sacred texts would have been fundamental to religious praxis.

Genesis worked as a survival manual for the exiles because it laid out the necessary social principles to be followed in simple stories that every reader could understand and interpret, rather than codifying them into formal laws or commandments. Genesis contains very little in the way of direct moralizing or explicit instructions on how to behave. The exiles did have books of laws as well as the stories of Genesis. Books like Leviticus and Exodus, which were probably also redacted, in some form, during the Exile, are filled with law explicated in exquisite detail. You can find out, for example, what penalty to exact of a man who, in fighting with another man, accidentally injures a pregnant woman, who, in consequence, gives birth prematurely though the baby is fine (Exodus 21:22). But law books are for lawyers. Genesis is for everyday people. What is more, the laws codified in the law books all rest on the principles exemplified in the narratives of Genesis. Genesis is the cornerstone of the whole enterprise. When you understand the lessons embodied in the truly human tales of Genesis you can understand the reasoning behind the specifics of the dry and seemingly impersonal law in Leviticus and Exodus.

Genesis repeatedly tells the Judeans in exile, through rich stories, that they are to stay as far away from imperial powers as possible and maintain their own distinct lifestyle. They are neither to respond to nor engage with their oppressor's culture and its values. The main components of the Genesis option enshrined in these tales are:

- Radical isolation from other cultures, both physical and symbolic. This stance includes cultural behaviours such as language, religion and foodways that are rooted in history and serve to separate the Judean community from the mainstream. Avoidance of multicultural urban centres is also vital to the task.
- Kinship rules that enforce patterns of marriage and inheritance within the community of Judean exiles. Those who marry outside the community are severely condemned and may be forced out.
- A procreative ethic that strongly values reproductive sexual behaviours and condemns non-procreative sexuality. Women with many offspring have high social status.
- Condemnation of assimilationist words and actions. Any imitation of, or attempt to assimilate with, other cultures is expressly forbidden.

The substantive chapters here explore these survival strategies in detail by examining the tales that underpin them. When viewed as a culture-survival manual, Genesis appears in a wholly new and surprising light. Genesis gave the exiles the tools not just to survive, but to prosper in an inhospitable environment. As such its message can transcend the specifics of the Babylonian captivity and speak to oppressed groups in all places and times.

Genesis: neither historical narrative nor myth

The narratives in Genesis are not equivalent to modern historical studies. Most of its stories are not, and cannot be, confirmed by archaeology nor any other extra-biblical sources or empirical inquiries. Many modern anthropologists and theologians call the Genesis narratives 'myth', but I shy away from this term because it is ethnocentric. Some cultural anthropologists and biblical commentators apply the label 'myth' to the sacred narratives of non-Western cultures or of cultures of the past. These scholars view such narratives as fictional when investigated from a scientific historical perspective, but the original authors probably perceived them as true in some sense. Many modern Western scholars, including anthropologists, are thus in the habit of downgrading the narratives of non-Western cultures as bad history because they do not meet Western scientific standards. Such a stance is inherently ethnocentric.

In the modern world it is common for people to accept many tales as true because they affirm something that they want to believe (for whatever reason), even though they are quite demonstrably false. A story of this sort, frequently circulated on the internet, involves the fathers of Winston Churchill and Alexander Fleming. The story has it that the senior Fleming, a struggling Scots farmer, saved the senior Churchill from drowning. In gratitude Churchill paid for Fleming's son's education. The younger Fleming went on to be a doctor and was the discoverer of penicillin. When Winston Churchill was struck down with a virulent form of bacterial pneumonia, Alexander Fleming saved his life with penicillin.

While this story contains no truth whatsoever, it won't die. Western readers want it to be true because it is a good story and because it says something important about charity and kindness. One could go further and say that all of fictional literature has this character: it speaks to what we consider fundamental truths. The narratives of Genesis can be construed in this way also, although there are many sects of Christians and Jews who argue that they are inerrant historical tales. Whatever the historical status of Genesis, these narratives appear to outline vital cultural truths for ancient Judeans. Whether they took them as literally true or not is not especially relevant. The tales helped ground the abstractions of their world-view in something concrete.

Did Jacob, the father of the twelve tribes of Israel, exist historically? Did he really have twelve sons by four women? Did the family end up in Egypt, where the descendants were oppressed by pharaohs? Did they escape and wander for forty years in the desert? Did they ultimately enter Canaan and conquer it, settling in twelve distinct tribal zones? From a modern scientific/historical perspective, there is serious doubt about such claims. Archaeological evidence supports none of these narratives. I am much more in favour of the argument, supported by archaeology, that twelve linguistically and culturally related Semitic groups emerged over a long period of time in Canaan, and established themselves in local pockets where they grew and flourished. Sometimes they lived in harmony with the Canaanites, sometimes not. Eventually these Semitic groups banded together in loose confederations which ultimately evolved into two states, Israel and Judah, with some shared values (e.g. Dever 2017).

This discussion brings me to a critical point about biblical stories. They, like other historical narratives, sacred or otherwise, are not told to explain the past: they are told to explain the present and to provide guidance to people living in the present. If present circumstances undergo radical change, the past may have to be reworked or rethought to accommodate the change. This sounds a bit like *Nineteen Eighty-Four*, I know, but modern dictators did not invent the idea that the past serves the present. In the case of Genesis, the 'present' to be explained (for the original context), was the present of the priests and scholars who put the book together in some kind of finished form during the Babylonian exile.

Why human cultures want to root their present world-views in the past, and why the past has such power, is a question that is well beyond the scope of this book. Nonetheless, it is clear that Genesis is laying out a vast and unchanging pattern for the entire world. It explains the present of a very small, oppressed minority people, and sets their history on the world stage, showing how all of world history and culture intersects with them. The ancient Judeans staged themselves literally as the centre of the universe and Genesis provided them with a manual of culture survival so that they could retain their central position ideologically, even if not physically.

I call this concept of history the origin-as-essence world-view (Forrest 1999). This world-view is based on the basic principle that events from the earliest history of the world established a pattern that shapes everything that is to come. Everything in the present can be explained in terms of that pattern which was laid down by God at the beginning of time, and which governs everyone's lives into the present. Even though the world may appear to change over time, the underlying pattern is unchanging and directs everything that people experience.

In the modern Western world, the scientific thinking generated by the Enlightenment and its aftermath, including the Industrial Revolution, has led to the dominance of a world-view that contrasts sharply with the origin-as-essence model. Theories such as natural selection and the biological evolution of species suggest that the world is not archetype oriented, with a stable and unchanging underlying essence; rather it is fluid and constantly in the process of developing and changing (although the governing scientific principles are unchanging). Because of this world-view, contemporary people in the developed world can easily imagine a future that is very different from the present: an idea that is not distressing but instead provides a sense of agency and optimism. They can therefore conceive of themselves as the controllers of their own destinies, and not beholden to the natures of their parents and forebears. The ancient Judeans, by contrast, were much more archetype oriented. Jacob was imaginatively resourceful, therefore all of his descendants into the indefinite future will be imaginatively resourceful. Once the archetype is created it persists. The narratives of Genesis explain how this eternal pattern was created in the first place.

Whether cultural analysis should be dominated by a pattern- or a process-orientation is a question that has dogged cultural anthropology for a century. Alfred Kroeber famously asked whether the study of culture was one of the sciences or one of the humanities, and ended up hedging his bets – calling it the most scientific of humanities and the most humanistic of sciences (Kroeber 1935). The contrast he espoused was between what he called 'history' and what he called 'science', which are not necessarily the way these terms are used popularly. By 'history' he meant the study of people without respect to the passage of time. What patterns of behaviour do they display – always? This is what anthropologists call synchronic (syn = without, chronic = time) analysis. Contrast this view with 'science' that deals in cause and effect. Science wants to confirm that if I perform action A under controlled conditions, event B will always occur. It is interested in process. What anthropologists call diachronic (dia = through, chronic = time) analysis. Viewed globally, we can see that pattern and process are deeply related. Linnaeus devised a pattern to organize the taxonomy of plants and animals (with no interest in time), and Darwin hypothesized a process that happened through time and explained the pattern. For a more extended analysis of pattern versus process in anthropological theory, consult the first chapter of my *History of Morris Dancing* (Forrest 1999).

Unfortunately for a culture that is dominated by a pattern orientation, such as that of the Judean exiles, there are times when their cultural circumstances change so radically that the underlying pattern to world history, which they have put forward to explain everything, seems to no longer apply, and something new has to be done to explain the changes they are experiencing. One course of action is to switch world-views entirely and to become more process oriented. This line of action is problematic on all kinds of levels. Most importantly, when a culture shifts its world-view, it can alter beyond all recognition. This was the last thing that the Judean exiles wanted or needed.

The solution to this problem, achieved by the redactors of Genesis, was to widen the historical narrative of the origins of the Judean people from a relatively local, and contemporary historical viewpoint, as held by the Deuteronomists and Isaiah before them (see Chapter 3), to a global and eternal one. Thus, instead of seeing Yahweh as their national god with the specific everyday problems of Judah as his concern, as they had previously, the Judean editors of Genesis, living in exile in Babylon, opened up the history to situate Yahweh as the creator of the entire universe, with all peoples, places and things created by him and under his control. In this way they could remain pattern oriented, the difference being that now the pattern was all encompassing, and what was once seen as a major local catastrophe – namely, the destruction of Jerusalem and the temple – could now be viewed as a small component of a giant cosmic (and cyclic) pattern with Judah as the centrepiece. Sin and disobedience could cause hardship, and drive the Judeans away from the physical centre for a time. But with a grand overview of all history from the beginning of time within which to situate all events, the fate of Judah could be seen as a series of cycles of decline and restoration, and the Exile could be fitted into one of those cycles. All would be well when the Exile cycle ended, but, to achieve a happy end to the cycle, the Judeans had work to do. They had to keep themselves holy (the Hebrew word for 'holy', קדוש, also has the semantic connotation of 'set apart').

Overview

My anthropological analysis of Genesis begins with an examination of the Exile, the calamitous event that led to a radical rethinking by Judeans of their relationship to God (Chapter 2). This chapter also deals with the events that led up to the Exile, including a sense of what their world-view had been beforehand. They had not only lost their temple, the principal locus of their worship, they were also dislocated from Jerusalem, the centre of their ethnic identity. They needed something else that was tangible to become their symbolic focus, and they needed assurance that God had not deserted them. Books like Genesis became the new temple for them (Chapter 3). By examining some issues concerned with the Hebrew language and the power of Hebrew written texts it is possible to understand how Genesis became a surrogate for the temple: God was no longer seen as residing in a physical building or place, but, instead, was alive in words. These two chapters provide the basic cultural background necessary to understand the body of the analysis of Genesis which follows.

The next several chapters provide my cultural interpretation of a selection of key texts in Genesis to show how these themes worked together to help the Judean people maintain their cultural isolation and, hence, their cultural identity, especially when it came to sex, marriage and kinship. First comes the story of creation to see how the various acts described in the narrative reinforce an ethos of separation and isolation (Chapter 4). Next is a section on just how furious God is when his chosen people select the wrong mates for procreation (Chapter 5). The selection of the right partner for marriage and reproduction occupies huge portions of Genesis. I examine the complexities of incest laws (Chapter 6) and procreation (Chapter 7), leading on to a discussion of patterns of descent (Chapter 8) and inheritance (Chapter 9), and concluding with an analysis of the roles of women in the narratives (Chapter 10). Finally, there is a consideration of why cities are the epitome of evil (Chapter 11) and why the free life of the cattle herder and the shepherd are the right models for the people of Exile to emulate, rather than the settled life of the village farmer (Chapter 12). The touchingly, and sometimes excruciatingly, human tales that Genesis employs to teach the exiles these lessons emphasize repeatedly the main tenets of the Genesis option: grow strong and numerous in complete isolation from the taints and temptations of other cultures. To conclude, I (very) briefly examine the validity of the Genesis option in the time since the Exile, and, especially, as a continuing set of guiding principles for Jews in the modern world (Chapter 13).

Along with the many passages from Genesis, I introduce concepts and topics in cultural anthropology related to gender roles and sexuality, state powers, the transition from foraging to herding and agriculture, kinship and marriage systems, and religion in society. Through a combined attention to text and context, I hope to show that Genesis has at least one more dimension than was evident before. A text-in-context analysis adds a vital dimension to the power of Genesis by revealing its role in the survival of a people living in a dangerous world. I hope to show that Genesis helped save Jewish culture from extinction during the Exile, and in the centuries that followed.

Further reading

I supply Bible quotations in this text to complement the discussion. You may, however, want to consult the Bible itself for a fuller reading of the brief selections provided. I use the New Revised Standard Version (NRSV) because it is a reasonably accurate and readable translation. Many people are familiar with the Bible via the Authorized Version (AV), commonly called the King James Bible. While that version will suffice, its language is old fashioned and does not convey the freshness and vitality of the original texts as well as the NRSV does. It also contains numerous errors. Your best option for analysis is to study the original Hebrew.

The documentary hypothesis concerning the construction of Genesis and the other books of the Old Testament out of older source material has a long history. Richard Elliot Friedman's Who Wrote the Bible? (1987) is a user-friendly introduction to the hypothesis, although it is now dated. Joel

S. Baden's The Composition of the Pentateuch: Renewing the Documentary Hypothesis (2012) is more up to date, and more critical.

The culture concept has been the backbone of anthropology since the late nineteenth century. E.B. Tylor's *Primitive Culture* and his definition of culture as 'that complex whole which includes knowledge, belief, art, morals, law, custom and any other capabilities and habits acquired by man as a member of society' (1871:1) gets paraphrased repeatedly in introductory texts, with some major and minor changes. At one time, anthropologists thought that culture was as axiomatically real as species in biology, and treated the concept in analogous fashion. The tacit assumption of ethnographers was that the Nuer, Tikopia, Maring etc. lived in well-defined bounded cultures that could be observed and described as independent, self-contained units. As fieldwork shifted from small, relatively isolated communities to larger populations with constant interrelations with other communities, the culture concept took a beating. Some even questioned whether it would survive – e.g. Norma González in 'What will we do when culture does not exist anymore?' (1999). Nonetheless, culture still stands as a workable category of discussion. One enduring classic that unpacks many of the key issues is Clifford Geertz, *The Interpretation of Cultures* (1973).

Albert Memmi's *The Colonizer and the Colonized* (1965) was banned in many countries and often confiscated by colonial police. When an academic has that kind of impact you know he is saying something important. Some of Memmi's other writings add depth to that book and to the general arguments in this chapter. These include *Portrait of a Jew*, (1962) and *Decolonization and the Decolonized* (2006). Other works on colonization include Frantz Fanon's *The Wretched of the Earth* (2004) and *Black Skin, White Masks* (1967).

On the role that indigenous languages play in the resistance to colonization, and how colonizing powers seek to control language usage, I recommend the following works: Jon Reyhner (ed.), *Revitalizing Indigenous Languages* (1999), David Crystal, *Language Death* (2000), and Joshua Fishman (ed.), *Can Threatened Languages Be Saved* (2000).

For a sample of anthropological studies of ethnocide and genocide, see the chapters in Alexander Laban Hinton (ed.), *Annihilating Difference* (2002).

The analysis of Genesis as a series of myths and folktales has a long history, beginning at least one hundred years ago. For a modern encapsulation of these theories see Alan Dundes, *Holy Writ as Oral Lit* (1999). See also two books by Susan Niditch, *Folklore and the Hebrew Bible* (1993) and *Oral World and Written Word* (1996), as well as Patricia Kirkpatrick, *The Old Testament and Folklore Study* (1988) and Edmund Leach, *Genesis as Myth and Other Essays* (1969). For a more complete exposition of the origin-as-essence model, see chapter 1 in my *The History of Morris Dancing* (1999).

2

Judah in exile

According to biblical accounts, the early tenth century BCE was a time of glory for the twelve tribes of Israel living in Palestine. The nation-states of Judah and Israel combined to form a powerful united monarchy under the legendary kings David and Solomon. David was a strong military king crushing all his enemies before him, and Solomon set out on an ambitious plan of imperial consolidation that included a massive building program throughout the land. The temple and palace complex he constructed in Jerusalem were the envy of the ancient Near East. But the unity created by the charismatic power of these two kings could not last. Under Solomon's son, Rehoboam, the union collapsed and Israel, under the rebel king Jeroboam, split off from Judah some time between 931 and 922 BCE. They remained as separate kingdoms for two centuries, until Israel was destroyed around 722 BCE.

Life in a contested land
The biblical accounts of the history of the kingdoms of Israel and Judah must, however, be taken with more than a small grain of salt. They are not strictly history in the modern sense of the word, and, as more and more sophisticated archaeological methods have come to bear on them, the factual basis of these narratives has been called into question. This divide is especially obvious if we compare the archaeological record and the biblical texts concerning the early days of David and Solomon (Finkelstein and Silberman 2006); less so in the latter days of the Judean monarchy, because these passages deal with current events or recent history for the writers. This fact need not worry us unduly, however, because the key point to take from all the histories is that the region of the Levant in general has always been a contested land (and still is).

Archaeology confirms that there were long periods when Israel and Judah's neighbours to the north in Mesopotamia and to the south in Egypt were strong empires, often vying with one another for regional dominance

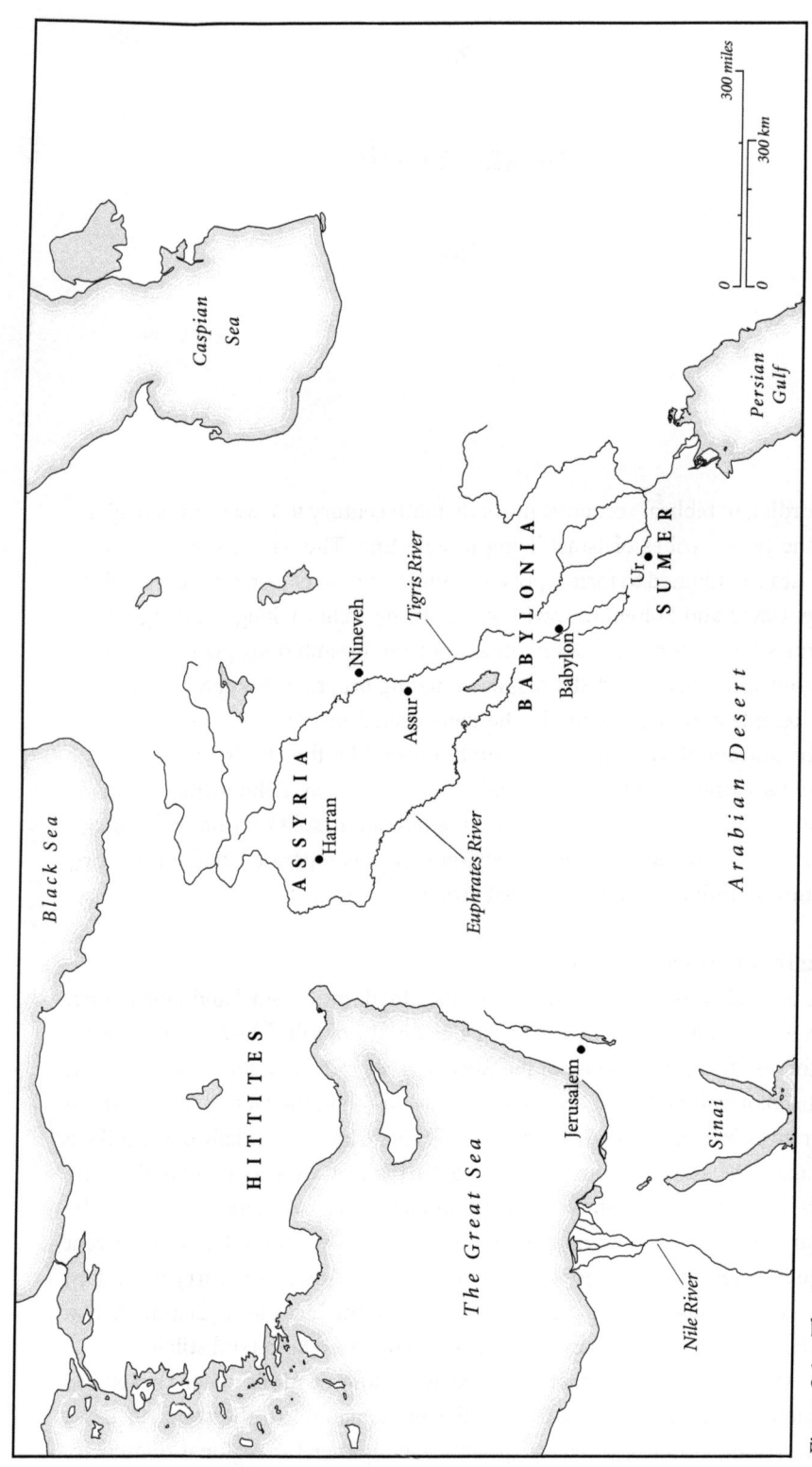

Figure 2.1 The Ancient Near East in the time of Samuel and Kings.

(see, for example, Stern 2001). But occasionally there were tranquil periods when the power of these empires waned. When their neighbours were weak, Israel and Judah could flourish, but when these neighbours were strong, Israel and Judah suffered. Though small, Israel and Judah had wealth generated by rich farmlands and pasture. More importantly, these kingdoms controlled critical land routes connecting Europe, Asia, and Africa. If you wanted to move an army or commerce swiftly from Egypt to Asia Minor or Mesopotamia (or vice versa), command of the territory of Israel and, to a lesser extent, Judah was pivotal. The region of the Levant is a natural north-south land bridge, and powerful empires had to have control of the region if they were to have easy access north or south. There were no other choices. To the east was impenetrable desert and to the west was the sea, both of which were unsuitable for the movement of large armies. Through the Levant, however, there were several natural land corridors.

Israel and Judah, consequently, were subjected to a series of imperial masters, including Egypt, Assyria and Babylon, under whom they laboured or against whom they sought to rebel. Much of the Hebrew Bible was the product of a people who found themselves on the main crossroads between endlessly warring titans. As these tiny nations were conquered and reconquered for the umpteenth time, priests, scholars, prophets, kings and peasants would no doubt have asked, 'Why us?', and have wanted a better answer than, 'You're in the way'. This part of the world is still geopolitically critical, and the people who live there continue to suffer accordingly.

The northern kingdom of Israel was by far the richer and larger of the two kingdoms. It accounted for ten of the twelve tribes of Israel and occupied fertile arable plains. The southern kingdom of Judah was occupied mainly by hill farmers and shepherds scraping a living out of difficult territory. But Judah had Jerusalem as its capital, and the city was an important centre of ritual and intellectual culture, with ample resources for a small state. Israel was the greater prize when colonizing tyrants came looking for people to tax or for a convenient trade route. Even so, Judah also had its temptations, such as the riches of the temple and palaces in Jerusalem. While the overlords exacted tribute money from both kingdoms, they also wanted settled peace. They wanted to be able to move around the region freely without having to tie up too many troops maintaining order.

In the later eighth century BCE (when archaeology and the Bible become much more mutually consistent), Assyria was the emerging superpower to be reckoned with in the Near East. Hoshea, the king of Israel became a client of Assyria for a time, but then unwisely tried to shift allegiance to the Egyptian pharaoh. Assyria got wind of the rebellion and besieged the central region of

Samaria for three years. It finally fell around 722 BCE. According to the book of Kings (2 Kings 17:3–6), the inhabitants were deported to various parts of the Assyrian empire. They eventually became known as the Lost Tribes of Israel, because for all intents and purposes they disappeared from history. You can read many fanciful accounts of where they ended up and who they are today: ancient Britons, Mormons, the Japanese, native Americans, west Africans (see, for example, Parfitt 2002).

The lessons of the disastrous fate of their neighbouring state and ethnic kin were not lost on the Judeans. They hunkered down and survived, eventually to see the waning of Assyrian power. From the mid to late seventh century BCE, the relative weakness of the surrounding empires allowed Judah to flourish in a bright renaissance of intellectual and religious splendour. Under King Josiah (640–609 BCE) a group of visionary scholars began collating a somewhat fragmentary body of historical works (many of which had existed for centuries prior as folk stories in the oral tradition) into a continuous narrative concerning the fortunes of the twelve tribes of Israel from the days of the exodus from Egypt to the time of Josiah's reforms. This narrative is contained in the books of Deuteronomy, Joshua, Judges, Samuel and Kings. The dating of the redaction of this history (generally called Deuteronomic or Deuteronomistic history) during Josiah's reign has been contested over much of the late twentieth century down to the present, and I give some suggested readings at the end of the chapter for further study if you are interested. For present purposes, I am siding with the moderate consensus that sees the production of Deuteronomy and Deuteronomic history as a product of the revitalization movement during Josiah's reign, and I am not going to deal with edits that the books underwent, before, during and after the exile (see Albertz 2000; Ausloos 2015).

What makes the Deuteronomic historical narrative so extraordinary is that it is quite unlike the chronicles and archives of the kings of the ancient world. Most ancient historical writings are puffed up accounts of the battles and conquests of the mighty, written for their own vanity and to stamp their names on history. The Deuteronomic historians, by contrast, asked a beguiling question that made their style of history unique for their era: 'Is there a single discernible pattern in all of our history that explains why some times are good and other times are bad?' This 'why?' question is genuine history in the modern sense, although the use of 'God's will' to answer the question would not be approved by modern historians (and their use of sources is of course also unacceptable in modern terms).

The Deuteronomists were not particularly interested in world history or grand visions of the social forces that drive history in general. That vision comes later in Genesis. They were concerned only with their own little corner of the earth. Why had Judah survived when Israel had been destroyed? What made the united monarchies powerful under David and Solomon but weaker under other kings? What makes a good king? The Deuteronomists believed they had found a simple and elegant solution to all these questions: the answer lay in their sense of ethnic purity and tradition. Put simply, Deuteronomic history casts the Israelites and Judeans as people with an ethnic destiny. That destiny was rooted in the temple in Jerusalem.

The Deuteronomists began what anthropologists call a revitalization movement (e.g. Wallace 1956) or a nativistic movement (e.g. Linton 1943; Donigue and Metzner 2017), that is, a socio-political movement, often with a single person, or 'messiah', as the saving leader, that seeks to restore the vitality of a culture by purifying it, and which uses a key set of traditional values and symbols to focus the movement. The Deuteronomists' notion was that the tribes of Israel had once had a pure culture that over the years had been diluted by foreign influences. I am not going to debate the legitimacy of this notion, but simply lay out its tenets. There were dozens of Canaanite holy sites and pagan (non-Judaic) shrines scattered across the countryside, many of them pre-dating the traditional time of arrival of the Israelite peoples. The Canaanites were also famous for their worship of Ba'al and allied deities. Such cults were popular with the Israelites over the years, taking over for many people from the traditional cult of sacrifice in the temple. Statues and symbols of the Ba'al cult appeared in the temple under some Judean kings. When the land was dominated by foreign powers, all sorts of exotic paraphernalia showed up in the temple, from astrological symbols to statues of Egyptian gods.

The Deuteronomists had a simple and clear-cut message. The kings of Israel and Judah who tore down the pagan shrines and chose to worship the high god of Israel in traditional manner, in Jerusalem, prospered. The archetype was David, a warrior king. His line was the one from which the true saviours of the nation would come once again. Those kings who rejected traditional worship and who, instead, courted foreign powers and imported foreign culture and traditions were the ones who ultimately met with doom. The northern kingdom was destroyed by Assyria because its kings lost their cultural and ethnic identity. Assimilation was their death knell.

The Deuteronomists thought they had found the formula that would provide their own salvation. They had created a classic messianic revitalization movement with Josiah, descendant of David, at its centre. What he had to do was purge the kingdom of all foreign influences and re-establish the old traditional, ethnically pure culture of Judah. When the culture had been fully purified, the king and his people would rise to new heights to rival the legendary kingdoms of old.

To some extent the Deuteronomists' analysis of history was a matter of making the facts fit the theory. Some apostate kings, that is, kings who had rejected traditional religion and values in favour of foreign influences, had done quite well for themselves. Conversely, Solomon, the archetype of the 'good' Davidic king, was not averse to bringing outside influences to court. He had a large number of foreign wives, for example, and many of them brought alien cultural practices with them. The Deuteronomists made note of Solomon's weaknesses and their consequences, but they were not fatal to his lasting reputation. What counted most for the Deuteronomists was the overall vision, rooted in an idealized past, of a heroic leader who succeeded because he was loyal to a specific cultural and ethnic ideal.

Josiah, inspired by the Deuteronomists' theories, set out on a path of sweeping cultural reform to purify Judean ethnic identity. Of course, it is possible to characterize Josiah as a willing puppet of the Deuteronomists; we know almost nothing about him outside of the biblical record, which is troubling when it comes to making an historically accurate analysis of his actions. We rely greatly on the Deuteronomic account which begins:

> 22:1. Josiah was eight years old when he began to reign; he reigned thirty-one years in Jerusalem. His mother's name was Jedidah daughter of Adaiah of Bozkath. 2 He did what was right in the sight of the Lord, and walked in all the ways of his father David; he did not turn aside to the right or to the left. 3 In the eighteenth year of King Josiah, the king sent Shaphan son of Azaliah, son of Meshullam, the secretary, to the house of the Lord, saying, 4 'Go up to the high priest Hilkiah, and have him count the entire sum of the money that has been brought into the house of the Lord, which the keepers of the threshold have collected from the people; 5 let it be given into the hand of the workers who have the oversight of the house of the Lord; let them give it to the workers who are at the house of the Lord, repairing the house, 6 that is, to the carpenters, to the builders, to the masons; and let them use it to buy timber and quarried stone to repair the house. 7 But no accounting shall be asked from them for the money that is delivered into their hand, for they deal honestly.' 8 The high priest Hilkiah said to Shaphan the secretary, 'I have found the book of the law in the house of the Lord.' When Hilkiah gave the book to Shaphan, he read it. 9 Then Shaphan the secretary came to the king, and reported to the king, 'Your servants have emptied out the money that was found in the house, and have delivered it into the hand of the workers who have oversight of the house of the Lord.' 10 Shaphan the secretary informed the king, 'The priest Hilkiah has given me a book.' Shaphan then read it aloud to the king. 11 When the king heard the words of the book of the law, he tore his clothes.

Judah in exile

Josiah became king of Judah in 641/640 BCE, after the assassination of his father, Amon (see Sweeney 2001). The general argument is that because came to throne at eight years old, and because these were turbulent times, he was easily tutored and held under the sway of temple priests and scholars from the beginning. The consensus for some time (Dever 2001; Finkelstein and Silberman 2001) has been that when Josiah reached adulthood, the priestly faction duped him with a pious fraud. That is, they wrote an early version of Deuteronomy (called the Book of the Law), hid it in the temple, and then 'discovered' it during renovations (which they had urged upon the young king in the first place). Josiah, completely fooled by the ruse, then set about a massive programme of reform based on this Book of the Law. He repaired the temple in Jerusalem and dedicated himself and his people to the 'old' covenant of the law. Then he went on a rampage. The list of cultic objects he burned, broke, ground up, and otherwise destroyed is staggering. 2 Kings 23 reads like a catalogue of every imaginable Near Eastern religious practice. Here is a small sample:

> 4. The king commanded the high priest Hilkiah, the priests of the second order, and the guardians of the threshold, to bring out of the temple of the Lord all the vessels made for Baal, for Asherah, and for all the host of heaven; he burned them outside Jerusalem in the fields of the Kidron, and carried their ashes to Bethel.
>
> 5. He deposed the idolatrous priests whom the kings of Judah had ordained to make offerings in the high places at the cities of Judah and around Jerusalem; those also who made offerings to Baal, to the sun, the moon, the constellations, and all the host of the heavens.
>
> 6. He brought out the image of Asherah from the house of the Lord, outside Jerusalem, to the Wadi Kidron, burned it at the Wadi Kidron, beat it to dust and threw the dust of it upon the graves of the common people.
>
> 7. He broke down the houses of the male temple prostitutes that were in the house of the Lord, where the women did weaving for Asherah.
>
> 8. He brought all the priests out of the towns of Judah, and defiled the high places where the priests had made offerings, from Geba to Beer-sheba; he broke down the high places of the gates that were at the entrance of the gate

of Joshua the governor of the city, which were on the left at the gate of the city.

(2 Kings 23:4–8)

Josiah killed all the priests who followed other religions and dug up the bones of the apostates and burned them. He scoured the length and breadth of Judah and large areas of the former kingdom of Israel for anything remotely alien to the Israelite identity or that smacked of assimilation to other cultures. He destroyed what he found. Finally, he held a massive Passover ceremony in Jerusalem. According to 2 Kings 23:21–3, no such Passover had been held in Jerusalem since the beginning of the monarchy.

What Josiah did through these sweeping reforms was to establish Judean cultural identity on a new and purified footing. In place of an eclectic medley of practices from here and there, he promoted simple symbols of Judean ethnicity. First and foremost, he reaffirmed the old tradition that the Judeans were the descendants of people who had been liberated from Egyptian slavery by Moses. Their destiny was not, therefore, to be in bondage to the pharaohs or any other empire as had been so common in their long history. They were a free people. Josiah's great Passover, a ritual that symbolically recreates the exodus from Egypt, signified that freedom. Second, they were the inheritors of the thrilling military dynasty of David, signified most especially by the city that David had supposedly conquered – Jerusalem – and by the glorious building works of his son Solomon. They were to be a nation reborn. Josiah would rule as David had done, and all would bow before him.

Unfortunately, things did not go as planned. In 609 BCE the Egyptians under Necho II marched north in the hopes of allying themselves with the remnants of the fading Assyrian empire against the rising star of Babylon. To get to Assyria they had to take the usual route through Judean and Israelite land. Here was Josiah's great test. Was he the new David? Could he find a new ascendancy for Judah centred on a resurrected Jerusalem? Sadly, not. He met the Egyptian army on the plain of Megiddo in a great and final battle marking the end of his revitalization efforts (and whose location gives us the Hebrew word for a great cataclysmic battle: Armageddon). He died of wounds suffered in battle, and Judah became a vassal of Egypt. In 605 BCE, when Babylon conquered Egypt, Judah was forcibly switched to being a tributary client state of the rising neo-Babylonian empire.

The destruction of Jerusalem and the Babylonian exile

One after another of Josiah's heirs brought enormous misfortune on Judah. In 601 BCE his son Jehoiakim tried to partner with Egypt in an attempt to overthrow Babylon's rule. This was a very costly political mistake. Initially the Babylonian ruler Nebuchadnezzar II (more correctly, Nebuchadrezzar) sent warrior bands from neighbouring tribes of Moabites, Ammonites, Arameans and such to harass the Judeans and make them aware that he would not tolerate the situation. Meanwhile Jehoiakim died and his son Jehoiachin took the throne around 598 BCE. Records are not clear as to whether he was eight or eighteen years old when he began to reign, but he was certainly in an extremely weak position due to lack of experience and the constant guerrilla warfare and imperial turbulence. Mere months into his reign he was beset by Babylonian troops who defeated Judah and deported the entire royal household to Babylon. They also robbed the temple and carried off a large number of Judeans into exile. These acts are described in the book of Kings (2 Kings 24:12–16):

> 12. King Jehoiachin of Judah gave himself up to the king of Babylon, himself, his mother, his servants, his officers, and his palace officials. The king of Babylon took him prisoner in the eighth year of his reign.
>
> 13. He carried off all the treasures of the house of the LORD and the treasures of the king's house; he cut in pieces all the vessels of gold in the temple of the LORD, which King Solomon of Israel had made, all this as the LORD had foretold.
>
> 14. He carried away all Jerusalem, all the officials, all the warriors, ten thousand captives, all the artisans and the smiths; no one remained, except the poorest people of the land.
>
> 15. He carried away Jehoiachin to Babylon; the king's mother, the king's wives, his officials, and the elite of the land, he took into captivity from Jerusalem to Babylon.
>
> 16. The king of Babylon brought captive to Babylon all the men of valour, seven thousand, the artisans and the smiths, one thousand, all of them strong and fit for war.

Harsh though this sounds, much worse was to come, and by comparison this so-called 'first deportation' which began the Babylonian Exile may seem mild. Jehoiachin was apparently cared for reasonably well in Babylon, and his uncle, who was given the name Zedekiah when he became king, was allowed to maintain the Davidic line in Jerusalem. For the time this was rather tame treatment for rebels. Maybe, too, this is why Zedekiah had the courage to resist Babylon. He made the seemingly perpetual mistake of trying to rely on an alliance with (a much weakened) Egypt against his enemies, and this time the full wrath of Nebuchadnezzar was unleashed on him. The Babylonian army laid siege to Jerusalem and, after nineteen months of starving the city, they captured it in 587 BCE. The results were catastrophic. The slaughter was hideous and cruel. They butchered Zedekiah's sons before his eyes, and then blinded him so that this was the last thing he saw before being taken in chains to Babylon. They destroyed the temple, they set the city ablaze, they razed the palaces and fine buildings, and they tore down the city walls. Jerusalem was a smoking ruin. The few people of any substance who were still alive were taken to Babylon, with only the most wretchedly poor left behind.

This time Nebuchadnezzar did not trust Judah to be an independent state under a Davidic king. Instead he appointed a governor to rule the land as a direct province of Babylon. The new governor was pretty well universally viewed as a traitor, so it was not long before yet another rebellion was fomented under a nationalist named Ishmael (whose origins and lineage are rather obscure). The loyalists killed the governor and the Babylonian guard. It is not certain what followed, although in the book of Jeremiah we read (Jeremiah 52:30):

> 30. in the twenty-third year of Nebuchadrezzar, Nebuzaradan the captain of the guard took into exile of the Judeans seven hundred and forty-five persons;

This reprisal would have been typical for a rebellion of the sort led by Ishmael. It was the third and last of the deportations to Babylon and occurred around 582 BCE. Thus began the great Babylonian Captivity, which is the background of the analysis in this book.

Little is known about the physical conditions of the exiles in Babylon. There are no direct accounts from extra-biblical sources, either narrative or archaeological, and the meagre scraps within the Bible are little help. Some people might think that the book of Daniel with its tales of Nebuchadnezzar's treatment of the captive Daniel and his colleagues might supply the necessary information, but scholars generally agree that this book was crafted during the reign of Antiochus Epiphanes (175–163 BCE), and was set back in the exilic period for political reasons (Collins 2002). So, it cannot be relied upon as genuine history.

The flimsy evidence from biblical sources suggests that most of the exiles were relocated into camps such as Tel-abib, Tel-melah, Tel-harsha, Cherub,

Addan and Immer, probably situated a small distance south of Babylon, although the exact locations are now unknown. Here they were able to build their own communities. They were not prisoners or slaves; neither were they completely free. They had to make do with the situation as it was given to them, and how they responded to their condition as exiles is of paramount importance to the argument of this book.

The Judeans at the beginning of the Exile had no idea what their ultimate fate would be. Without the express decree of the Babylonian ruler they could not return to Jerusalem, and there was little reason to suppose that such a decree would ever be given. The prophet Jeremiah was offered the option of going into exile in Babylon or staying in Judah, and he chose the latter. In a letter to the exiles from Jerusalem he recommended that they build houses, plant farms, marry, have children and get on with life (Jeremiah 29:5–7), and the evidence suggests that this is precisely what they did. The big question facing the exiles was whether they could survive as a people being separated from their homeland in general and from Jerusalem in particular. It was not just that Jerusalem had been their capital city for over 400 years. Jerusalem represented symbolically just about everything that it meant to be Judean, especially after the powerful reinvigoration it had received under Josiah and the Deuteronomists. So, now what? The pitiful lament found in the first verses of Psalm 137 sums up the situation poignantly:

1. By the rivers of Babylon—
    there we sat down and there we wept
    when we remembered Zion.
2. On the willows there
    we hung up our harps.
3. For there our captors
    asked us for songs,
    and our tormentors asked for mirth, saying,
    'Sing us one of the songs of Zion!'
4. How could we sing the Lord's song
    in a foreign land?
5. If I forget you, O Jerusalem,
    let my right hand wither!
6. Let my tongue cling to the roof of my mouth,
    if I do not remember you,
    if I do not set Jerusalem
    above my highest joy.

(Psalm 137:1–6)

The true tragedy of their situation is borne out in these lines. They sought to remember Jerusalem at all costs. However, lamenting and remembering alone would not ensure their survival.

They had to replace temple worship with something. They had to find a way to relate to God without temple worship, and, most especially, without temple sacrifices. They asked difficult questions. The greatest of all of these was whether their god had come with them from Judah or whether he had stayed behind in Jerusalem because that was his home. They had conceived of his temple (and the Ark of the Covenant) as quite literally his dwelling place, so could he – would he – move from his home to be with his chosen people in exile?

The Judeans thought of their god – Yahweh – as the most powerful of the gods, but not as the only divine being by any means. They accepted that the gods that the Assyrians and Egyptians and Babylonians worshipped were real, just inferior to Yahweh. The first commandment of Exodus 20:2 and Deuteronomy 5:7 declares, 'you shall have no other gods before me'. It is saying simply that you must worship Yahweh as the supreme god, not that he is the only one. There was, therefore, the clear danger that the exiles could succumb to the temptation of believing that Yahweh was not as all powerful as they had once believed. After all, his city and temple were in ruins. Might that not mean that the Babylonian gods were now superior? These were dangerous questions. If they were to survive as a people, they had to find convincing answers.

The story of the exodus from Egypt that had been brought to the fore under Josiah's temple reforms would be of some help in answering these questions, and it is likely that the narrative reached its final shape during the Exile (Dozeman 2010; Fretheim 1991). The exiles could comfort themselves with the thought that they were in terrible bondage under the pharaohs long ago, and Yahweh had liberated them. He had been with them in Egypt during their slavery there and had led them out across the Red Sea, through the wilderness, and into the promised land. So, he could do it again, couldn't he? Certainly, that is the message that the exiles wanted to hear, but it was not a flawless argument.

Suffering servants

Deuteronomic history, of which the exodus narrative is a part, argued that Jerusalem was the final destination of the Israelites. Yes, Yahweh travelled with them in the desert and guided them on their journey. But back then he was on his way home. Would he want to leave home once he had arrived? The whole point of Josiah's glorious Passover (whose essence is the reliving of the exodus story), was that the people gathered in Jerusalem and celebrated the

Judah in exile

fact that they were finally home and had been purified by their journey to get there. Josiah and the Deuteronomists stressed the vital importance of meeting in Jerusalem for major ritual occasions – especially Passover. As that was now impossible, the strategy had to be rethought.

Many biblical scholars argue that classic Judaism developed during the Exile as the exiles posed questions about their conditions and sought answers to them, and, importantly, as they developed new ways of practising their faith 'out of place' (see, for example, Middlemas 2005). Without the ability to make physical sacrifices of animals in the temple in Jerusalem, it was necessary for them to shift their religious ideology away from the material plane into the spiritual realm. In this displaced spiritual zone, people could make symbolic sacrifices of themselves. It was possible to be the perfect sacrificial object through one's personal conduct in the world. Textual support for this new notion of self-sacrifice comes from a large portion of the book of Isaiah, roughly chapters 40 to 55, and usually referred to as Deutero-Isaiah (or Second Isaiah). These chapters were probably written by an exiled poet/prophet living in Babylon (Blenkinsopp 2002). The tone and style of these chapters are radically different from both earlier and later parts of Isaiah. The image of the 'suffering servant' appears in these chapters, as someone who is the loyal follower of Yahweh purified through suffering in the form of personal self-sacrifice:

> 4. Surely he has borne our infirmities
>   and carried our diseases;
>   yet we accounted him stricken,
>   struck down by God, and afflicted.
> 5. But he was wounded for our transgressions,
>   crushed for our iniquities;
>   upon him was the punishment that made us whole,
>   and by his bruises we are healed.
> 6. All we like sheep have gone astray;
>   we have all turned to our own way,
>   and the Lord has laid on him
>   the iniquity of us all.
> 7. He was oppressed, and he was afflicted,
>   yet he did not open his mouth;
>   like a lamb that is led to the slaughter,
>   and like a sheep that before its shearers is silent,
>   so he did not open his mouth.
>
> (Isaiah 53:4–7)

Most people with a Christian background or who know Handel's oratorio *Messiah*, will recognize this message as one that conveys a Messianic vision, in which the Messiah is cast as the perfect sacrificial victim. But Christianity and Handel come much later: we need to focus on the Exile. What this passage is saying is that the true believer becomes the sacrificial lamb of Yahweh, and that therefore a real lamb is no longer needed. Furthermore, the suffering servant does not have to be in Jerusalem for the sacrifice to have an effect. In fact, being away from Jerusalem is critical to the whole theological position: it is the loss of Jerusalem that is the immediate cause of all the suffering. Beyond that, the deeper, ultimate cause of the suffering is people's disobedience to Yahweh. Babylon did not defeat Yahweh; Yahweh let Judah be defeated as a penalty for the people's sinful behaviour.

Yet there is also good news here too. If disobedience leads the people away from Yahweh and Jerusalem, then obedience and self-sacrifice are opportunities to get closer to God in a new way. Once the suffering servants have proven their worth, Babylon will be defeated, and the people will be returned to Jerusalem in a new and brighter exodus (Isaiah 48:14–21). Real flesh-and-blood, bleating sacrificial lambs are irrelevant, at least for the time being.

In this transitional context, then, what is obedience to Yahweh? What is right action if it is not temple sacrifice? It may sound unhelpful to say that 'right action' means being 'holy', but, in fact, the concept of holiness that developed in the Exile is important and is the crux of my argument. To understand it we need to explore the Hebrew word for 'holy', *qadosh* (קדוש). The etymological root of this word means 'set apart' or 'kept distinct'. Things are made holy by separating them from other things; people are made holy by separating them from other people. Here is the simple solution to the whole puzzle facing the Judeans about how to survive in exile and maintain their identity. They had to be different (that is, separate) from everyone around them in the Babylonian empire: they had to keep themselves to themselves. According to the logic of holiness, they had to vehemently avoid assimilation as their ticket back home to Judah. Holiness and cultural isolation were the same thing. These qualities would get the exiles closer to Yahweh – more so than old, outmoded sacrifices of animals in the temple.

The scholars and priests in Exile had to figure out exactly what form this holy distinctiveness should take. They also had to ground this distinctiveness in a theologically sound blueprint in order to legitimize it. In addition, they needed a new focal point for ritual and worship that would reinforce and reinvigorate the people as they waited for their release from bondage. It is my contention that the crafting of a version of Genesis (not the final version) in the Exile was the crowning achievement of the Judean intellectuals in responding to these challenges. The book of Genesis laid out the essential theological foundation for the exiles. It taught them how to be distinct and why. Let me stress again at this point, my hypothesis that Genesis was initially redacted into a book during the Exile is not the current consensus among biblical scholars, who generally treat it as a post-Exilic creation (with conflicting reasons for justifying this point of view – see Carr 2014). My reading of the text as a work of scholars in exile, as exemplified in the following chapters, is a point I am sure I will have to defend vigorously in future.

I admit that my argument is cultural, and slightly tautological. But tautologies are not logically invalid. I reached the conclusion that Genesis was initially redacted during the Exile by looking at the multiple themes I explore in depth in this work, and asking, 'What makes them a coherent whole?' The notions of separation and segregation as key strengths are repeatedly hammered home. Then I asked at what point in their history would separation and segregation be of the utmost importance to the Judeans? Exile or post-Exile? A good case can be made for both. After returning from Babylon, the post-Exilic historians and prophets were painfully aware of the many temptations of the returnees to drift back into old syncretic habits (see Ezra-Nehemiah and Chronicles). The dangers of assimilation and the loss of Judean identity were certainly a present danger. But they were at home in Jerusalem and had the ability to rebuild the temple. In exile in Babylon the Judeans were completely adrift. Without the physical trappings of ethnic identity – Jerusalem, the temple, the Jordan river etc. – to hold on to, they needed an ideology that was not rooted in the world they could see around them, but that was transcendent. Genesis provided that ideology.

Biblical scholars in the past have pointed to three Jewish practices as keys to avoiding assimilation in exile: male circumcision, Sabbath observance and strict dietary laws (Alstola 2020). Circumcision is a clear and permanent physical mark on every male that says, 'I am different.' This was not a new practice for the Judeans, but it took on added significance as a marker of ethnic distinctiveness for the exiled population in Babylon. Sabbath observance would also have made the exiles stand out while they lived in Babylon. Most of us are so used to the idea of a seven-day week that we tend to forget that it is simply a cultural invention, and quite arbitrary. Unlike the day, month and year, it is not based on any astronomical phenomenon. Different cultures throughout history have had 'weeks' that comprise varying periods of time, and one day of rest is not necessarily involved. What was important in the Exile was that the Sabbath became a special day on which all Judean people took a day off from work and also affirmed their collective ethnic identity in corporate worship. They may also have used the day to study scripture and expound upon precisely what Judean identity was all about.

It is possible that the Babylonians had a seven-day week, and some scholars argue that the Judeans copied the cycle from them (Zerubavel 1985). It is also possible that the Babylonians took every seventh day off from work because they thought the day was unlucky, hence any work done that day would be worthless or even dangerous. But what the Judeans did was completely different. Their seventh day was not just a day of rest. It was a day for positively asserting their ethnic identity. Setting aside a day devoted specifically to public worship may well have been their innovation.

Last, having strictly distinct dietary practices is an ironclad way of remaining culturally separate. Eating and drinking together is an enormously important way of creating and maintaining bonds between kin and friends. Conversely, if you are forbidden from eating and drinking with others whose food habits are deemed 'unclean', then it is difficult to befriend them or assimilate to them. Strict dietary laws make you look inwards to your own community, and eating becomes a daily ritual act of separation from others. The pork taboo is an important case study in this regard.

Many scholars have argued that Judaic dietary laws were God's way of keeping his chosen people healthy (Brondz 2018). The discovery of trichinosis in the nineteenth century was seen at one time as adequate evidence to validate the hypothesis. No pork, no trichinosis. Following this logic, though, we would have to add a taboo on chicken (salmonella), and on cattle, sheep, and goats (anthrax). Yet none of these animals are taboo, and lamb is the prized meat of the Passover, the quintessential Judaic ritual meal. Rather, the point of the taboo against pork, which includes not even eating from plates on which pork has been served in the past, is that you cannot eat with anyone who is a pork lover. All the non-Judean peoples of the plains of Mesopotamia were pork lovers (Grossman, Paulette and Price 2017; Guillaume 2018).

While these three practices were all good ways to keep the Judeans in exile separate from others, there is much more to the story than that. What happened in Babylon was not just the invention and practice of a group of traits that made Judeans distinct and separate. They were already a small, oppressed minority who spoke a strange language. What is fascinating about these exiles is that they turned their situation completely on its head. They transformed their weaknesses into their greatest strengths. They made their marginality work for them, not against them. They did this by having an incredibly powerful social theory to underpin and explain their distinct behaviour, so that their ethnic markers were not just arbitrary symbols. Separate is good, mixing is bad.

In fairness, I must stress that even with the most rigidly enforced rules against mixing and assimilation, oppressed ethnic groups inevitably end up adopting some 'foreign' traits from their oppressors, for all kinds of reasons. There is no question, for example, that some sections of Genesis are attributable to Babylonian sources – though radically altered. In subsequent chapters I take up the issue of how and why these sources entered Judaic culture, given that assimilation was a critical threat to their ethnic identity.

Further reading

Anthony F.C. Wallace pioneered the study of revitalization movements in anthropology; see his classic study, 'Revitalization movements' (1956). A more recent work is *Reassessing Revitalization Movements*, edited by Michael E. Harkin (2004).

The best archaeological overview of the latter period of the Judean monarchy is *The Archeology of the Land of the Bible Volume II* by Ephraim Stern (2001). For concise and readable accounts of the discrepancies between the findings of contemporary archaeology and the biblical historical narratives I recommend *The Bible Unearthed* by Neil Asher Silberman and Israel Finkelstein (2002), *Beyond the Texts* by William Dever (2017), and *David and Solomon* by Israel Finkelstein and Neil Asher Silberman (2007). Some of the flavour of the battles between archaeologists over the interpretations of their finds can be discerned in *The Rise of Ancient Israel* by Hershel Shanks, William Dever, Baruch Halpern and Kyle McCarter (2012).

The investigation of the Exile by biblical historians making the best of limited primary data has produced hundreds of texts. Start with Peter Ackroyd's *Israel under Babylon and Persia* (1970). This is a good basic (although severely dated) overview of the relevant biblical sources, and deals with the entire period of the Exile from a literary and ideological standpoint. Some others with different points of view are put forth by Hans M. Barstad, *The Myth of the Empty Land* (1996), Philip R. Davies, *In Search of 'Ancient Israel'* (1992), Lester L. Grabbe (ed.), *Leading Captivity Captive* (1998), and Daniel L. Smith., *The Religion of the Landless* (1989).

Many anthropologists have explored the dietary laws of Jews to try to figure out what they are all about. Most conclude that food laws are symbolic of deeper cultural values. A well-known anthropological analysis of the Old Testament pork taboo can be found in Mary Douglas's classic *Purity and Danger* (1966). A contrasting point of view is presented by Marvin Harris in *Cows, Pigs, Wars, and Witches* (1974). Harris also looks at revitalization, Messianism, witchcraft and other practices from a materialist perspective. Treat Harris with much more than a grain of salt, however. His knowledge of the ancient Near East is tenuous at best, and recent archaeological investigations have shown that the settlements of Israel and Judah had a complex history of eating domesticated pigs – e.g. 'Pig husbandry in Iron Age

Israel and Judah' by Lidar Sapir-Hen, Guy Bar-Oz, Yuval Gadot and Israel Finkelstein (2013). This article substantially undermines Harris's speculation.

The subject of the lost tribes of Israel continues to generate interest, both scholarly and non-scholarly. For a good overview of the subject, read Tudor Parfitt's *The Lost Tribes of Israel* (2002), or Rivka Gonen's *The Quest for the Ten Lost Tribes of Israel* (2002).

Recordings of modern versions of Psalm 137 show how the poetic theme of exile has been re-worked by contemporary marginalized peoples. My favourite reggae version, called 'Rivers of Babylon', is by the Melodians (whose members Brent Dowe and Trevor McNaughton wrote it). It can be found on the movie soundtrack album *The Harder They Come* by Jimmy Cliff. It was covered in 1978 by Boney M and stayed no. 1 on the English pop charts for 5 weeks, going triple platinum. There is also a round in three parts called 'By the Waters of Babylon' that crops up in modern Christian and Jewish song books and hymnals. It can also be found on *American Pie* by Don McLean, where the track is titled simply 'Babylon'.

3

What's in a word?

Genesis is, above all, a book about the power of words and that fact is impressed on the reader from the very beginning – the beginning of the book and the beginning of time. Until the Exile, the Judeans did not have a canon of sacred texts. They did not need one. Temple worship was not about reading scripture; it was about actions such as sacrifices. They would certainly have had all manner of texts that had specific uses, such as histories, legal codes and collections of prophetic sayings, but they did not have a canon such as the Torah. The Torah eventually grew out of the Exile – perforce – and Genesis is its foundation stone.

To create the world, according to the first chapter of Genesis, God used *words*. This is a most unusual form of creation in cosmogonic narratives. For a thorough survey of creation stories, you could consult a source such as *A Dictionary of Creation Myths* (Leeming and Leeming 2009). There you will discover all manner of narratives, classified by various scholars into types (e.g. Leonard and McLure 2004), including creation *ex nihilo* (from nothing), bringing order out of chaos, dismemberment of a primordial being, diving in a primeval ocean for land, and the emergence of humans from other worlds. Genesis stands unique in describing the creator as doing all the creative work by speaking – by using words. Every creative act begins 'And God said...' (see Chapter 4).

Thus, a cultural exploration of Genesis requires careful attention to the language of the text, which can help expose critical aspects of the thought of the people of ancient Judah. We need to look closely at words in the original Hebrew, their meanings and how they were used, particularly in personal names, the names of God, and sacred words overall. For the Judeans in exile, words were direct windows on to the sacred. Books and literacy were vital to the cultural survival of the exiles. In the absence of the temple and its sacrificial rituals, books became the way to get close to God. This chapter examines the spiritual power of Hebrew words and texts.

Personal names

To the modern eye, Hebrew names in the Bible can look quite plain and common, such as David and John, or more unusual, like Zerubbabel and Habakkuk, or somewhere in between, as with Josiah or Simeon. This situation arises because modern English speakers generally have a completely different concept of naming from that of ancient Judean peoples. Admittedly naming practices vary considerably in the modern world and are dependent on a host of factors. It is typical, though, for parents to pick names out of a common pool of possibilities. For example, Adam, Jacob, Joseph, Esther and Ruth are names that anyone might be given. Parents may have some sense that the names have underlying meanings and that they are biblical, but the etymological significance is unlikely to have a huge influence on the choice. In the United States, it is just as common for a child to be named for a pop icon or movie star as for any possibly more significant reason. In England, the name Keira became popular in the early part of the twenty-first century because of the fame of actress Keira Knightley.

In ancient Hebrew thought, however, personal names were individually significant, and did not respond to popular trends. In most cases in the Hebrew Bible, a person's name was unique to him or her and was also complexly symbolic. There was no long line of kings named Solomon I, Solomon II... and so forth. The implication is that there could be only one Solomon and that was it. Neither was there a slew of little boys named Moses in honour of the great leader. Yes, in the later historical period names do start to repeat. There was a Jeroboam II, for example, but this was a new era.

In Genesis, names are unique to each individual and have the greatest importance. A person's name is, in a sense, a summation of that person's essence. Nowadays we miss this point when we read the Bible in translation unless we also understand Hebrew and have some familiarity with Hebrew linguistics. Look, for example, at the names of the sons of Jacob's first wife Leah, who Jacob was much less keen on ('unloved') than her younger sister Rachel, his second wife:

> 31. When the Lord saw that Leah was unloved, he opened her womb; but Rachel was barren.

> 32. Leah conceived and bore a son, and she named him Reuben; for she said, 'Because the Lord has looked on my affliction; surely now my husband will love me.'

33. She conceived again and bore a son, and said, 'Because the Lord has heard that I am hated, he has given me this son also'; and she named him Simeon.

34. Again she conceived and bore a son, and said, 'Now this time my husband will be joined to me, because I have borne him three sons'; therefore he was named Levi.

35. She conceived again and bore a son, and said, 'This time I will praise the Lord'; therefore she named him Judah; then she ceased bearing.

(Genesis 29:31–5)

To the average English-speaking reader, the naming segments of this passage makes no linguistic sense whatsoever. What is important is that each boy's name has a linguistic relationship to the phrase that Leah utters at his birth. Take the first one. The name Reuben can be read (and spoken) in Hebrew as something like 'behold a son'. As such, he is Leah's great hope. She hopes that now that she has a son and heir out of her womb, Jacob will start to love her. Through the boy's name Leah is perpetually reminding Jacob, 'Look, I gave you a son.' Every time Jacob uses the boy's name he must remember. Furthermore, the name symbolizes Reuben as the firstborn son and therefore the senior brother. That means that the tribe of his descendants which bears his name will be senior to all the other 'brother' tribes in perpetuity. All that dense meaning, and more, is wrapped up in the name Reuben. The name cannot be given to anyone else because it is unique to Reuben's birth and circumstances.

Another important point is that significant people are frequently given new names when something about them changes drastically. The classic case is Jacob. His original name comes from the nature of his birth. He was the second born of twins as follows (Genesis 25:24–6):

24. When her time to give birth was at hand, there were twins in her womb.

25. The first came out red, all his body like a hairy mantle; so they named him Esau.

26. Afterwards his brother came out, with his hand gripping Esau's heel; so he was named Jacob.

The name Jacob can be read in Hebrew as something like 'the one who grabs the heel', which is a metaphorical way of saying that though he was junior to his brother he would harass him and ultimately supplant him. Jacob was father to the Israelite nation and Esau to the Edomites. The latter were indeed the older culture, but they were eventually supplanted by Israel.

As a mature man Jacob gets a new name as the result of a remarkable incident (Genesis 32:22–32). While on a journey he is accosted by a stranger, who wrestles with him over the course of an entire night. The match is a draw until daybreak, when the stranger tries to get away, and has to magically cripple Jacob to do so. At this point the stranger gives him a new name: Israel, which can be read (punningly) in Hebrew as 'the man (*ish*) who wrestles (*ra*) with God (*el*)', leaving us to ponder the stranger's exact identity. Jacob's birth name gave him the character of someone who is constantly striving to be the best, and this characteristic is still present in his new name. But he has been given an added dimension. He is now the one who contends with God himself, not simply his brother. Furthermore, the nation that he will beget through his twelve sons will maintain that personality in perpetuity. Israel's relationship with God will never be easy; it will never be one of simple and blind obedience. Israel will always be wrestling with God, sometimes getting crippled into the bargain. Likewise, brother will always be competing with brother for supremacy, with the younger often winning over the older (see Chapter 9).

Getting a new name is common in Genesis and signals a new phase in a man or woman's life. As with the case of Jacob, the new name does not indicate a radical change in the person's character; rather, the name highlights a significant addition to, or enhancement of, existing traits. Thus, when God expels the human couple from the garden in Eden, Adam gives his companion a new name (Genesis 3:20). Up to that point the text refers to her as simply 'the woman' (*ha-ishshah*):

> 20. The man [*ha-adam*] named his wife Eve [*havvah*], because she was the mother of all who live.

The Hebrew word *havvah* sounds like, and may be cognate with, the verb 'to live', (*hayyah*), hence the commentary that the name means 'the mother of all who live'. She is no less of a woman because she is now the mother of all humanity. Motherhood has been added to her womanhood. All significant name changes in Genesis have this quality. Interestingly, Adam does not get a new name. He is always called simply *ha-adam*, the man. Eve's transformation from woman to mother is immensely more powerful (see Chapter 10).

Names in the Hebrew world set up patterns of interlocking behaviors and meaning that continue down through the generations. Whatever traits a father or grandfather or distant forebear had, good or bad, are passed down through the generations, and it takes an act of God to change that pattern. If a mere mortal were to ignore the pattern, or try to change it, nothing but trouble would result. Genesis is all about patterns. As crystallized in naming practices, Genesis establishes the grand pattern of the world, and of the nations of the world, most especially so that the Judeans can see their place in it all. People's names, place names and the names of common objects, are all traces of that pattern for the Judeans to see and work with on a daily basis. They are a reminder that the pattern is always there.

Personal names and names of objects imply the existence of a kind of permanent essence in people and in things, a way of thinking that is quite the opposite of the way that modern secular people think (Alford 1988; vom Bruck and Bodenhorn 2006). Modern people tend to view the world as constantly changing and evolving, and see themselves as active agents in the making and remaking of themselves. For the Judeans in exile the last thing they needed was a philosophy of evolution. Given their insecure situation during the Exile, they needed a philosophy that allowed them to rest secure in a world that was at its deepest levels unchanging and in which they had a well-defined role. Within this view, they were suffering only a temporary setback because they had been disobedient; they had strayed from their predestined path and so were being punished. If they returned to the right path, however, their glory as a nation would be restored. For them the idea of a changeless undergirding pattern of supreme order was vitally important. Success for them was not achieved by evolving and moving forward in linear fashion, but in cycling back to their beginning point. Genesis is both their beginning and their ultimate goal.

The name of God
The exiles saw the name of God, Yahweh, as completely entwined with this sense of the world as permanently ordered. The great exilic prophet Ezekiel makes it abundantly clear that when you misuse God's name you are making big trouble for yourself, because what you do to his name you are essentially doing to him. God and his name are one and the same thing:

> 22. Therefore say to the house of Israel, Thus says the Lord God: It is not for your sake, O house of Israel, that I am about to act, but for the sake of my holy name, which you have profaned among the nations to which you came.
> (Ezekiel 36:22)

Because Ezekiel was an active voice among the Judeans in Babylon, his thoughts give us insight into the thinking of the redactors of Genesis. He tells us expressly that God's name is much more than a representation of his nature: it is his nature. There is considerable debate concerning the exact etymological meaning of the name of God: Yahweh – written as four consonants (יהוה) YHWH, with no vowels in the oldest manuscripts. Some argue that the word means something like 'eternal being' or 'the one who causes things to be' or some other modification of the verb 'to be'. Such problems need not delay us here (see, for example, Wilkinson 2015). It is sufficient to understand that God acts because of his name and that the Judeans had a great privilege in knowing his name.

Ezekiel constantly stresses that Yahweh acts because he *is* Yahweh, not because he is *called* Yahweh. When God acts, Ezekiel repeatedly says that he does so to let the people 'know that I am Yahweh'. For example, in Ezekiel 20:12 he demonstrates that by the act of separating (making holy) his people he is demonstrating his nature as Yahweh:

> 12. I also gave them My Sabbaths, to be a sign between them and Me, to *know that I am Yahweh*, who sets them apart. [emphasis added]

The fact that a person's name and essence are one and the same means also that if you know a person's name – if you know God's name – there is a very powerful relationship between the two of you. You can call upon that person – or God – to act for you because you know the innermost workings of that person. When God revealed his name to Moses at the burning bush (Exodus 3) he was empowering Moses (and his people) in a very special way. He was opening up his nature to him and thereby entrusting him with considerable power. That is also why the third commandment is that the name Yahweh is not to be abused (Deuteronomy 5:10). One conundrum that I will leave unresolved for now is how Genesis could consistently use the name Yahweh for God when it was not revealed to Moses until much, much later (in a completely different book).

Many Hebrew personal names incorporate prefixes or suffixes that stand for the divine name, Yahweh, and in so doing create an even tighter bond between the individual and God. In English transliterations the prefixes are usually 'Jo-' as in Jonathon ('whom Yahweh gave') or John ('Yahweh is merciful') or 'Jeho-' as in Jehoiakim ('whom Yahweh has established') or Jehoshaphat ('Yahweh is judge'). The usual suffix is '–iah' as in Jeremiah ('Yahweh will raise') or Isaiah ('salvation of Yahweh'). It is an enlightening exercise to count how many biblical names use these prefixes or suffixes.

These prefixes and suffixes are only suggestive of the sound of the name Yahweh because it was taboo to say the actual name out loud. In fact, the misreading of the divine name as 'Jehovah' comes from a misunderstanding of the Hebrew text of the Torah, which contained a code to prevent accidental reading of the name out loud. The full story is really quite fascinating and helps us deepen our analysis of naming and words in the Bible.

The earliest Hebrew texts consisted of consonants only and readers filled in the vowels for themselves (and to make life more difficult there were no spaces between words). Mostly there were not too many problems in reading the language because the context was usually adequate to explain what a potentially ambiguous word was. Take an example in English. The consonants C-R-N could be 'corn' or 'crane' or 'crone' or 'acorn' or 'corny' or others, when you add vowels. In the following sentence, though, there should be no ambiguity:

I saw a C-R-N fly across the lake. (crane)

Even the following is unlikely to be ambiguous:

I ate C-R-N for dinner. (corn)

It could just barely be crane (or acorn) you ate, but highly unlikely. What about this one, though:

C-R-N is good.

Now we have a problem. As it happens, in many analogous cases in the Hebrew text the ambiguity is deliberate. It is all part of the magic of words. The ambiguity helps you to see connections between things. Punning and word play are a vital element of the text. Many of the personal names in Genesis are not straight or literal phrases; rather, they are complex puns, as in the case of the names of Jacob's sons. Some names are so complicated that scholars still fight over their meaning. Take Adam as an example. The word Adam literally means 'human', but it is very close to the word *'adamah*, which means 'earth' or 'soil' (an English equivalent might be 'human' and 'humus'). So, Adam is not just a human being: he was fashioned from the soil of the earth (Genesis 2). Furthermore, God commands that when Adam dies he will return to the soil whence he came. So, his name contains his nature, and also his origin and his destiny. What is more, Judeans reading this passage in Genesis saw themselves as Adam's descendants, and, therefore, saw themselves as sharing in his destiny.

A group of scribes known as the Masoretes, who were active in the Near East from roughly the seventh to the tenth centuries CE, attempted to clean up the sacred Hebrew texts by adding diacritical marks known as 'points' to indicate the exact vowels to be used (see, for example, Tov 1992). This practice had become necessary because by the Middle Ages biblical Hebrew was a long dead language used only in religious contexts (much as Latin was used at that time by priests and scholars). Without help with the vowels, most people could barely read the text at all. Adding vowels was a decided benefit, but it also raised problems. Sometimes the Masoretes got it wrong and, in the process, triggered theological disputes that continue to this day.

The divine name in the text was never to be spoken. One reason for this rule is that saying God's name was to invoke him to come into your presence. Such is the power of names. Invoking God was not a wise move, given the explicit warning against such abuse found in the third commandment. So, euphemisms for God had to be used. One common replacement for God's name is *ha-shem*, which is Hebrew for 'the name'. Another was '*adonai*, meaning 'my Lord'. In fact in many translations of the Bible, including the Authorized Version, 'the Lord' is the preferred reading when Yahweh appears in the original. The Masoretes apparently chose to replace 'Yahweh' with 'Lord' when reading the text out loud, and signalled this fact by replacing the correct vowels with the vowel points for '*adonai* under the consonants of Yahweh in the body of the text. The resulting 'word' was actually grammatically impossible in Hebrew and that was the signal to the reader that you had to say something else.

Here the problems of transliterating the consonants of Hebrew letters into English letters get complicated, and I will simplify things at the expense of absolute accuracy. Normally, the consonants of the divine name are transliterated into English as YHWH (which, of course, with vowels, gives us Yahweh). There is also, however, a Germanic transliteration which is more like JHVH. Take the latter consonants and add the vowels from '-a-D-o-N-ai and you get something like JaHoVaiH. With a little bit of imagination, you can see how this could come to be read as Jehovah. The word was never meant to be read this way at all, but the mistake stuck and thus many Christians wrongly believe that the divine name is Jehovah. In fact, we don't know how YHWH was pronounced, because we don't know the vowels. Yahweh is the best guess, and most scholars accept it. If we knew the vowels for certain we would have a better chance of figuring out what the name meant (although we do have to be careful not to put all of our confidence in etymology alone).

This idea that names are supremely powerful and can be used supernaturally to invoke a person or a god (and can also be used in spells and incantations for good or harm) is common in cultures throughout the world to this day. The Yąnomamö of the Amazon basin, for example, will not speak aloud the name of a dead person and are very reluctant to reveal their personal names to strangers lest they be used against them. The anthropologist Napoleon Chagnon had enormous difficulty doing kinship studies among them because they would constantly provide made-up, ridiculous names for their living and dead relatives in order to avoid using their real names (Chagnon 1968). Modern Jews will often name a child in honour of a dead relative but will not use the exact name. Instead they will choose a name that has some phonetic relationship, such as an initial sound or syllable – Moshe might become Morris, for example.

The supernatural properties of Hebrew personal names apply equally to place names, and even to words and phrases in general. Reading Genesis you will note frequently that places are named or renamed because of significant events that have happened there. Jacob, for example, names the place where he has had a vision of a stairway to heaven Bethel ('the house of God'), the spot being a gateway between heaven and earth (Genesis 28). The prophet Ezekiel foretells that the exiles will eventually return and rebuild Jerusalem, and that the city will be renamed Yahweh-shammah, that is, 'Yahweh is there' (Ezekiel 48:35).

The sacredness of Hebrew words

Seemingly ordinary words in Hebrew can carry the same supernatural power as proper nouns. Hebrew is a language in which one can spend endless amounts of time ruminating about the interplay of etymological relationships and what they mean. Hebrew words are made up from a relatively small stock of roots that have very basic meanings. These roots are typically made up of clusters of three consonants. By adding vowels and by tweaking, twisting and poking the roots, the core meaning melds into verbs, nouns and adjectives that are all variations on a theme.

Take as an example the three Hebrew letters Q (Qof) D (Daleth) M (Mem) that form the root Q-D-M. The underlying meaning of the root is 'preceding'. Add some vowels to the root to get QeDeM and you have the word for 'old times', that is, times preceding current time.[7] The word also means 'east', because the sun rises in the east and, therefore, the east represents the earliest part of the day (the part that precedes the rest). The word 'early' is derived by adding a prefix and adjusting the vowels to produce muQDaM, while different vowels produce QoDeM, 'first'. If you want to get to a place early you must 'hasten' QaDaM, and those who are constantly striving to be first (to precede all others) can be called maQDiMim, 'the diligent'.

---

7   This method of transliteration of Hebrew into Roman characters is unorthodox/idiosyncratic to make the point that Hebrew word formation is strongly dependent on inflexions of tri-literal roots. The upper-case letters preserve the tri-literal root, while the lower-case letters add vowels (and sometimes consonantal prefixes or suffixes) to the root.

Something analogous can be seen if we take the English root CARN- from a Latin root meaning 'flesh'. The following list of words all contain the root and you can see how it can be shaped and turned into all manner of meanings but with flesh somewhere in the background:

- CARNivore – flesh eater
- CARNival – festival just before Lent after which flesh is forbidden (etymologically it literally means 'take flesh away')
- CARNation – flesh-coloured flower (in the wild)
- CARNelian – flesh-coloured stone and a flesh-coloured shade of red (the colour of Campbell's soup cans and one of the official colours of Cornell University)
- CARNelain – flesh-coloured (red) grape variety
- inCARNation – taking on flesh, becoming substantial, taking human form, and hence reinCARNation, taking flesh/human form again.
- CARNal – knowledge of the flesh, hence sexual knowledge (from an equation of flesh and sin)
- CARNage – destruction of flesh, hence general brutal destruction
- exCARNate – to strip of flesh, as is common in some Asian burial practices
- inCARNadine – to turn red (flesh coloured)

Speakers of the English language tend not to treat such confluences of meaning as terribly significant. The fact that Campbell's soup cans share a colour with a flower, a stone, a university and a grape does not set us scratching our heads to find the hidden messages latent in the words (although the soup and the university are actually related). But classical Hebrew scholars considered such semantic interplay to be vitally important for decrypting the deeper implications of their sacred texts. These powerfully and complexly interlocking meaningful words took on a mystery and a symbolic meaning for them (and continue to for orthodox rabbinical scholars).

The words of the sacred texts were not just the words of God, they were pieces of God himself. Probe the words and you probe the mind of God directly. Here then is the answer to the questions 'is God with us?' and 'what shall we do without a temple?' The answers are that God is always with us when we have his words with us, and because he is present in his words (as he was present in his temple), the sacred text can become our new 'temple'. The Word and God become synonymous.

Furthermore, it is clear from Genesis 1 that God's word is supremely powerful. All his acts of creation are acts of speech. Everything happens because God speaks. He says, 'let there be light' and light comes into existence. Words, especially the sacred word of God, make things happen and reveal the very inmost workings of God. What is more, when words have been used to effect action they must be used carefully because they cannot be retracted, nor can what they have done be undone. Jacob tricks the blind Isaac into thinking that he is his elder brother Esau and so receives his father's verbal blessing (Genesis 27). When the trick is discovered Isaac laments:

> 35. 'Your brother came deceitfully, and he has taken away your blessing.'

The words of the blessing are real things of value every bit as much as coins or goats. You can take them and keep them and use them for your own needs. If you give them away you cannot take them back. If you abuse them, the damage is real.

Hence the shaping of a permanent, eternal, mysteriously potent sacred text, the Torah, became one of the most pressing needs of the priests and scholars in exile. They were creating an artefact that was in essence to be the new house of God. It could go anywhere they went, and in the course of time it could – under the right conditions – be copied so that if the people divided, God would still be with them all.

The power of specifically written texts becomes evident in the works of the exilic prophets. Ezekiel is the first prophet to receive God's word in written form. All the other prophets heard the voice of God directly:

> 2:9. I looked, and a hand was stretched out to me, and a written scroll was in it.
>
> 10. He spread it before me; it had writing on the front and on the back, and written on it were words of lamentation and mourning and woe.
>
> 3:1. He said to me, O mortal, eat what is offered to you; eat this scroll, and go, speak to the house of Israel.
>
> 2. So I opened my mouth, and he gave me the scroll to eat.
>
> 3. He said to me, Mortal, eat this scroll that I give you and fill your stomach with it. Then I ate it; and in my mouth it was as sweet as honey.
>
> (Ezekiel 2:9–3:3)

Ezekiel 9 also contains a curious passage concerning the execution of God's justice. He is narrating a vision of a time when God will bring down vengeance on idolaters. He sees six men with weapons in their hands, and then a seventh, dressed in fine clothes, who carries writing equipment. This scribe is instructed to write on the foreheads of the faithful. The six men with weapons are instructed to kill everyone, and spare only those with writing on their foreheads. So, inscription itself becomes a magical means of survival. In the days of slavery in Egypt the blood of a sacrificial lamb was a suitable warning sign for an angel of death, but by the Exile warnings were written words.

The great prophecies of the Exile, specifically Ezekiel and Second Isaiah, are very clearly written prophecies, an indication that writing and sacred words took on special significance in the Exile. The earlier prophets spoke their pronouncements to the nations around them, and their words were subsequently written down and collected into finished texts by scribes. But much of the work of the exilic prophets began life as written texts. These works contain, for example, carefully crafted poems of high literary quality. The written word was taking on a new-found importance in the lives of the exiles.

Embodied language

This discussion of the sacredness of words leads to one more point about Hebrew culture before moving on to look at Genesis itself. Hebrew language and culture are 'embodied', that is every action, idea and object is ultimately based on the bodily experience of it. All abstractions are grounded in concrete experiential images. Go back to the analysis of the root Q-D-M. The word *miq·qe·ḏem* (מקדם) can mean both 'in the past' and 'in the east'. The concepts of 'east' and 'past' are essentially the same. Likewise, the west represents the future. If you are standing facing east at midday, the place where you are looking represents where the sun rose in the past, and the point behind you represents where the sun will set in the future. The passage of the sun is our visible, experiential, embodied sense of time. The end points of that (physical) passage are the end points of time itself. So, the abstractness of time is realized through the concreteness of physical space as we experience it.

It is fairly common knowledge that the Genesis text uses the verb 'to know' (ידע) as a verb referring to sexual activity – 'Adam knew his wife Eve and she conceived...' (Genesis 4:1). Modern readers tend to think of this usage as some kind of translator's euphemism to avoid unmentionables in a sacred book. However, the Hebrew word is quite explicit and reveals something very important. Knowing is a physical, embodied activity. Up until the point that Adam had sex with Eve he did not *know* her because he had not experienced her flesh in a physical way. It was not possible for him to 'know' her in the abstract.

This point brings us to the forbidden tree in the garden. Most Christians through the ages have been taught via art and poetry that this was an apple tree, and this notion has filtered into popular culture. But the text says no such thing. It is called the tree of the knowledge of good and evil. Anyone who eats of the fruit of this tree will cease to be innocent, and instead will know the difference between good and evil. Perhaps this is some kind of magical fruit that dispenses wisdom upon eating it? I think the reason that eating the fruit dispelled innocence is better understood by extending our analysis of Hebrew thought and action.

The text says that the tree's fruit was forbidden, yet it was very attractive. So, there was a temptation to eat from the tree because the fruit looked so delicious. What the actual fruit was does not matter, what mattered was that it was temptingly delectable. And it was taboo. Eventually, Eve and Adam could not resist; they succumbed to temptation and ate the fruit. By so doing they had been disobedient: they had sinned because they were told not to eat the fruit. Hence, they now 'know' sin. They know sin because they have experienced it. Before they ate the fruit they could not know the difference between good and evil, because they had no experience of it. Subsequently they knew perfectly well – with their lips, tongues, teeth and stomachs. They knew sin with their bodies.

Names, words and morality

Because ancient Hebrew was a concrete, embodied language, Genesis is a concrete, embodied book. The patterns of history and the lessons to be learned from history are cast in the specific behaviours of real individuals, rather than in abstractions or general moral commandments and principles. These individuals' narratives provided the models for the behaviours of the exiles in very tangible form. There are no long philosophical discourses. Instead, there are exemplars of right action described through vivid storytelling. We learn about strict obedience, for example, by hearing about Abraham's willingness to sacrifice his son and heir at the command of God. We learn about brotherly rivalry and jealousy, and their consequences, via the story of Cain and Abel.

Each narrative contains a point that is exemplified. The characters in one story may do something that flatly contradicts something that has occurred in another. This fact is of no consequence. Each story is a self-contained unit illustrating a point. When you have grasped the point, you move on. It is ethnocentric of us to complain that Abraham says one thing in a certain story, and the exact opposite in the next. That is a modern, secular sense of logical consistency that is not applicable to the biblical text and the culture behind it.

Above all, Genesis is a book of contrasts. It shows its readers examples of right action and wrong action and leaves them to draw their own conclusions, aided by graphic images of what can happen when people make bad choices. Because it is a book of stories, Genesis has also inspired countless great works of art, music and drama over the centuries. In some respects, the lessons are timeless. I have a specific purpose here, however. My interest in the text concerns its place in the lives of the Babylonian exiles. We should begin at the beginning.

Further reading
To learn about linguistics and anthropology, you might start with *Language, Culture, and Society: An Introduction to Linguistic Anthropology* by Zdenek Salzmann (2004). For the lighter side of things, and yet still scholarly, see *Word Play: What Happens When People Talk* by Peter Farb (1975).

The study of classical Hebrew language is often very dry and technical. But word play, puns and roots are a constant source of academic study. A couple of works to dip into are *Puns and Pundits: Word Play in the Hebrew Bible and Ancient Near Eastern Literature*, edited by Scott B. Noegel (2000), and *Biblical Names: A Literary Study of Midrashic Name Derivations and Puns* by Moshe Garsiel (1991). A good parallel translation of the Hebrew text of Genesis, with abundant footnotes to help you understand the word play in the original language, is Nahum Sarna's *The JPS Torah Commentary: Genesis* (2001).

Two dictionaries explore the complex connectedness and interplay of English words based on their etymological roots in rich detail: *Origins: A Short Etymological Dictionary of Modern English* by Eric Partridge (1983) and *The Origins of English Words: A Discursive Dictionary of Indo-European Roots* by Joseph T. Shipley (1984).

The history of writing is fascinating. Two books that will get you started are Steven Fischer's *The History of Writing* (2001) and Anne-Marie Christin's *A History of Writing: From Hieroglyph to Multimedia* (2002).

4

The creation formula

The story of the seven days of creation that opens the book of Genesis is rightly famous. It has figured in poetry and art down the ages, such as the magnificent frescoes by Michelangelo on the ceiling of the Sistine chapel. It is also a vast ideological and intellectual battleground. It figures explicitly and implicitly in philosophical, political and ethical debates. It was, for example, the centrepiece of the famous Scopes 'monkey' trial in 1925 in Dayton, Tennessee, and is used in the ongoing debate in the USA over what does and does not belong in high-school science textbooks. Although the precise details of the creation story are not well known to most people, this short passage, which occupies scarcely a page of text, has been written about more often and in greater detail than any other section of the Bible. In fact, long articles have been written about single words in it, and whole books have been written about just one or two of its verses (for example, Tsumara 2005).

Let us start by reviewing the actual text of the story. Several aspects of the text suggest that it was originally a poem designed to be recited aloud in public. For your convenience I give you the entire text of the creation story here. I use italic to indicate certain repetitious aspects of the text which I will discuss. I divide the story up into stanzas representing the individual days of creation so that the poetic structure can be appreciated.

> 1:1. In the beginning when God created the heavens and the earth, 2. the earth was a formless void and darkness covered the face of the deep, while a wind from God swept over the face of the waters.
>
> 3. *And God said*, 'Let there be light'; and there was light. 4. *And God saw that the light was good*; and God separated the light from the darkness. 5. God called the light Day, and the darkness he called Night. *And there was evening and there was morning*, the first day.

6. *And God said*, 'Let there be a dome in the midst of the waters, and let it separate the waters from the waters.' 7. So God made the dome and separated the waters that were under the dome from the waters that were above the dome. *And it was so.* 8. God called the dome Sky. *And there was evening and there was morning*, the second day.

9. *And God said*, 'Let the waters under the sky be gathered together into one place, and let the dry land appear.' *And it was so.* 10. God called the dry land Earth, and the waters that were gathered together he called Seas. *And God saw that it was good.* 11. *And God said*, 'Let the earth put forth vegetation: plants yielding seed, and fruit trees of every kind on earth that bear fruit with the seed in it.' *And it was so.* 12. The earth brought forth vegetation: plants yielding seed of every kind, and trees of every kind bearing fruit with the seed in it. *And God saw that it was good.* 13. *And there was evening and there was morning*, the third day.

14. *And God said*, 'Let there be lights in the dome of the sky to separate the day from the night; and let them be for signs and for seasons and for days and years, 15. and let them be lights in the dome of the sky to give light upon the earth.' *And it was so.* 16. God made the two great lights – the greater light to rule the day and the lesser light to rule the night – and the stars. 17. God set them in the dome of the sky to give light upon the earth, 18. to rule over the day and over the night, and to separate the light from the darkness. *And God saw that it was good.* 19. *And there was evening and there was morning*, the fourth day.

20. *And God said*, 'Let the waters bring forth swarms of living creatures, and let birds fly above the earth across the dome of the sky.' 21. So God created the great sea monsters and every living creature that moves, of every kind, with which the waters swarm, and every winged bird of every kind. *And God saw that it was good.* 22. God blessed them, saying, 'Be fruitful and multiply and fill the waters in the seas, and let birds multiply on the earth.' 23. *And there was evening and there was morning*, the fifth day.

24. *And God said*, 'Let the earth bring forth living creatures of every kind: cattle and creeping things and wild animals of the earth of every kind.' *And it was so.* 25. God made the wild animals of the earth of every kind, and the cattle of every kind, and everything that creeps upon the ground of every kind. *And God saw that it was good.*

26. *And God said*, 'Let us make humankind in our image, according to our likeness; and let them have dominion over the fish of the sea, and over the birds of the air, and over the cattle, and over all the wild animals of the earth, and over every creeping thing that creeps upon the earth.'

27. So God created humankind in his image, in the image of God he created them; male and female he created them.

28. God blessed them, and God said to them, 'Be fruitful and multiply, and fill the earth and subdue it; and have dominion over the fish of the sea and over the birds of the air and over every living thing that moves upon the earth.' 29. God said, 'See, I have given you every plant yielding seed that is upon the face of all the earth, and every tree with seed in its fruit; you shall have them for food. 30. And to every beast of the earth, and to every bird of the air, and to everything that creeps on the earth, everything that has the breath of life, I have given every green plant for food.' *And it was so.* 31. *God saw everything that he had made, and indeed, it was very good. And there was evening and there was morning*, the sixth day.

2:1. Thus the heavens and the earth were finished, and all their multitude. 2. And on the seventh day God finished the work that he had done, and he rested on the seventh day from all the work that he had done. 3. So God blessed the seventh day and hallowed it, because on it God rested from all the work that he had done in creation.

(Genesis 1:1–2:3)

The text has a loose poetic pattern which is formulaic, and this suggests that the language contained here was once part of oral tradition. The basic structure of each stanza (with some exceptions) is as follows:

And God said let... [creative act]
And it was so.
And God saw that it was good.
And there was evening and there was morning, the [xth] day.

Such formulaic structures are typical of oral tradition: they make it easier to remember the whole narrative because they provide an easily memorized framework within which to plug the different actions on the different days. This type of schema, known as incremental repetition, is also seen in well-known traditional songs such as 'The Twelve Days of Christmas' and 'Old MacDonald'. Besides being an aide-memoire, though, this organizational scheme also provides a poetic sense of order and that is what this narrative is all about. The world is deeply ordered, and order is good. The narrator says that God methodically went through an almost mechanistic sequence of repeated actions to create order: he speaks, action flows from his command, the result is good, the day ends – and so on to the next day when the process repeats.

Narrative order and world order

Let us recall a point I raised in the previous chapter: God's acts of creation are all verbal. His words produce order and creative action: words are power. The creation tale suggests that the physical world is the material manifestation of God's word. God's word is inherent in everything we can see and touch. His word made everything there is. That is how solid and real and powerful words are. When you have God's words in a book, including the actual words of creation, you have all of God's energy at your disposal. As God creates things, he also names them, and this naming signals his dominion over them.

In this narrative, God's words are carefully organized into a verbal pattern that reveals the orderly pattern of the world. The narrative is an actual model of the schema it is relating. The main thread of the story is simple: God takes disorder and through his creative word turns it into supreme order. Physical matter exists alongside God before the beginning of time, so he is not entirely creating something out of nothing. The text clearly states that there was water and there was darkness with him from the start. To the ancient Judeans darkness was not merely the absence of light as we conceive of it in our modern scientific world-view. For them darkness was a real tangible thing, here described as something like a blanket covering the primeval waters. When God created light on the first day, he had to make sure it did not mix with the darkness, otherwise there would be chaos. So, separation becomes as important a creative act as the fashioning of new things.

The story of creation certainly involves the making of new things such as light and plants and people. But, more importantly, the story of creation is a parable about the sheer joy and beauty that emerges from acts of separation and organization. Genesis offers much less emphasis on how things came into being and much more on how God found a perfect place for all things once they had come into being. God created order through separation. God is supremely organized.

When it comes to the orderliness of the narrative of the creation itself, we have a small problem, though. On four of the days of creation God works on one basic creative act organized within the standard poetic framework I have outlined. On the third and sixth days, though, there are two distinct creative acts per day, with the formula (except for the last phrase that indicates what day it is) being duplicated. On day three, for example, we have this pattern:

(a) *And God said* – let the sea and dry land be separated.
And it was so.
And God saw that it was good.

(b) *And God said* – let the earth bring forth vegetation.
And it was so.
And God saw that it was good.
And there was evening and there was morning, the third day.

A similar, although slightly more complicated, duplication occurs on day six. If the tale were entirely logically and poetically consistent, day three would end after the separation of sea and dry land. The creation of vegetation would then have taken place on the following day. But if the creative acts for days three and six are split up into two days each, you then have eight days of creation, plus a day of rest, making a nine-day week. Was that possibly how the original poem was? Did the earliest Hebrew cultures have a nine-day week? Did the final editors squash eight creative acts into six days in order to accommodate a shift from a nine- to a seven-day week? Scholars have pursued both sides of all these questions with little resolution (see Richards 2000).

Time as a cultural construction

There is strong evidence that the ancient Babylonians had a seven-day week (Zerubavel 1985). They were fascinated with astronomy and astrology, and linked bodies in the solar system with their pantheon. They recognized five planets, Jupiter, Venus, Saturn, Mercury and Mars, and connected them, along with the sun and moon (which they also conceived of as planets), with their most powerful deities. Apparently, they also found a correspondence between these bodies/deities and the days of the week – hence a seven-day week. Since the beginning of the twentieth century, some scholars have argued that the Judeans adopted the seven-day week from the Babylonians while in exile, as part of a larger thesis that much of the so-called 'mythic' portions of Genesis is derivative of Babylonian lore.

Friedrich Delitzsch, an Assyriologist, gave a much-discussed lecture in 1902 titled 'Babel and Bible' in which he argued that many Genesis tales, including those of the creation and flood, derived from Babylonian sources. Subsequently, Delitzsch's thesis became part of a significant school of thought known as the Bible-Babel hypothesis, as well as the core of a major controversy (see, for example, Hanson 2011). The Bible-Babel speculations have some merit and are still espoused in some quarters (with major critical adjustments). A cataclysmic and global flood tale is unlikely to have arisen indigenously in the temperate mountains and desert wildernesses of Judah, where lack of water was much more relevant to daily life than flooding. The riverine plains of Mesopotamia, which experienced periodic flooding, are a more obvious breeding ground for such tales. But, if the exiles' biggest fear was assimilation to the dominant culture, they were much more likely to do everything possible to distance themselves from Babylonian practice and belief than to accommodate to it. That is my main thesis here. Nonetheless, just because a culture bent on nativistic purism vehemently resists foreign influences, does not guarantee that those influences will not creep in regardless. I am sure that some aspects of the creation and flood stories in Genesis had their roots in Babylonian narrative, although it was not a matter of straight borrowing.

The concept of the 'origins' of customs – what counts as an origin, and why people value them – has long fascinated me (Forrest 1999:chap. 1). That is why I am drawn to Genesis, the book of origins. Origins are obviously crucial to nativists also. But, as I have been at pains to point out repeatedly elsewhere, how a culture acquires a tale or custom and what happens to them subsequently is a long and complicated story. Cultures are adept at absorbing 'foreign' habits and in the process bending and reshaping those habits to fit pre-existing cultural norms and expectations (see, for example, Forrest and Forrest-Blincoe 2018). That is almost certainly what happened with the Judean seven-day week and the flood narrative.

In tone and substance, the days of the week of the Biblical creation story are the diametric opposite of what we find in Babylonian narratives. In the Biblical story, for example, the sun and moon – potent gods in so many ancient belief systems – are not deities or even living entities. They are no more than lanterns created by God and hung in the sky to mark the passage of time. Likewise, the story of creation occurring over seven days in Genesis does not link each day to an astral body or deity as in the Babylonian world-view. Instead, each day is associated with a creative act by a single god. That is one of the main lessons of the story, namely, everything that exists was made by God and he is in control of it all (and of equal importance to the exiles, this fact also means he is always everywhere, and not just confined to a temple in Jerusalem). The story of the seven-day week in Genesis supports a uniquely Judaic world-view. Thus, the seven-day week, while certainly a Babylonian concept, could have been independently invented by the Judeans. The seven-day week is found in many ancient cultures, and was probably separately invented in a number of them rather than being the result of diffusion from one single point of origin. Many ancient cultures used a lunar calendar with months of twenty-eight days. Dividing that month into four quarters to make seven-day weeks is perfectly rational.

Because the story of creation in Genesis has eight distinct acts of creation in it, I am inclined to believe that the Judeans, at one point in very distant history, had an eight- or a nine-day week (nine with a day of rest). Along with that, they had a narrative that recounted, through orderly incremental repetition, the acts of creation over eight days. They may or may not have had an extra day of rest at the end. Somewhere along the line they adopted a seven-day week, and so the narrative had to be truncated to accommodate the new situation. It is also possible that the original narrative did not connect the acts of creation to the days of the week at all, and that when this connection was made the narrative had to be modified. Whatever the case, this transition could have taken place well before the Exile. It is also possible that the Judeans always had a seven-day week and at some point merged their creation narrative with the days of the week, having to make the pieces of the creation story fit somehow. We cannot know for sure, but we must always remember that their logic is not our logic. Days three and six break a pattern of one act of creation per day, but that pattern (my pattern) is a superimposition on to the story and is not the only analytic pattern we might discern.

Eight days a week

For most cultures, ancient and modern, the week is an urban commercial phenomenon (Richards 1999; Zerubavel 1985). Hunters and gatherers do not need to count weeks. They are more interested in the seasons. They need to know when to shift camp to follow migrating animals, to know what plants are available at different times of the year, and to be certain of finding a source of drinking water. Subsistence food producers (people who grow food for their own use and not for sale), and nomadic pastoralists (people who herd animals as their main mode of subsistence and who migrate seasonally) are also more in tune with seasonal changes, than with smaller units such as weeks. They follow the seasons for planting and harvesting, or for moving herds to find fresh pasture and water. Intensive agriculturalists (people who grow crops for sale and who use markets for trade, and barter), in contrast, need more narrowly defined and fixed cycles of days for commerce. For them, daily is too often to hold markets, while monthly is not frequent enough. Since the rise of agriculture, weekly markets have become the norm worldwide. As mentioned, the seven-day week was common historically because it neatly divided the lunar month of twenty-eight days into four equal parts. But eight- and nine-day weeks were known and persist in some modern cultures alongside the ubiquitous Gregorian seven-day week. In ancient calendars the most significant day of the week was often designated specifically as 'market day'. The fact that the Judeans transformed a commercial practice into a cultic one, tied to their national and ethnic identity, is supremely important: they took something that was common practice among all the peoples around them and transformed it into something that was uniquely theirs and made them special.

Order in creation

It is possible to plot the scheme of the Genesis creation by listing the days and the acts associated on those days in a linear sequence:

    Day 1   light (day and night)
    Day 2   dome (seas and sky)
    Day 3a   dry land
    Day 3b   vegetation
    Day 4   sun, moon, and stars
    Day 5   fish and birds
    Day 6a   wild animals
    Day 6b   humans
    Day 7   rest

However, such a simple linear sequence fails to reveal vital aspects of the narrative. There is a symmetry inherent in this organization of these creative acts that a daily enumeration misses. From an ancient Judean perspective (Fontaine 1986; Lange and Meyer 2011), a clear parallelism exists when days one to three are paired with days four to six. They thought of the first three days as those in which God created environments and the second three days as the time when he populated each of those environments in turn. For modern readers the pairing of 2/5 and 3/6 needs little explaining. On the second day God created the seas and the sky and on the fifth he created the fish and the birds. Very simple. On the third day he created the dry land and its vegetation and on the sixth he created land animals and humans (the latter being a bit of a special case to which I return in a moment). The pairing of 1/4 is odd to the modern mind, though, because we do not treat light and darkness in the same way as the ancients. For them, light and dark were tangible entities in their own right (darkness was a thing). Furthermore, light and dark were completely synonymous with day and night, and for them, the sun and moon were not the sources of the light at those times. They were 'inhabitants' of the day and the night: they were signposts existing within the day and night. In the Judean world-view the sun lived in the day in much the same way as fish live in the seas.

There are two axes of symmetry inherent in the story of creation: one based on the physical realm, the second on the temporal realm (Figure 4.1). The beginning verses of the narrative make it clear that while 'the earth' existed along with primal water and darkness it had no form. Matter was completely

The creation formula   63

disorganized. Entropy was at its maximum. Piece by piece God created order out of the disorder, so that by the end of his creative activity he could rest and contemplate that the order was not just good, it was 'very good'. The world was perfectly ordered. To give some visual sense of these two lines of symmetry we can re-order the days thus (adding a day zero to mark the 'time' before time).

Day 0 watery abyss (utter disorder)

⬆

Day 1 light (day and night) ⟷ Day 4 sun, moon, and stars
Day 2 dome (seas and sky) ⟷ Day 5 fish and birds
Day 3a dry land ⟷ Day 6a wild animals
Day 3b vegetation ⟷ Day 6b humans

⬇

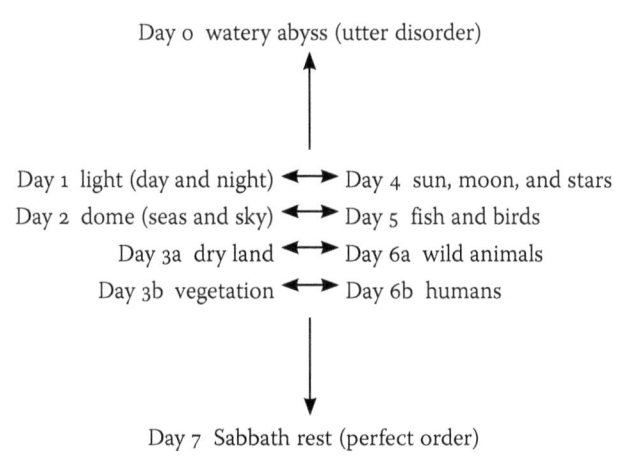

Day 7 Sabbath rest (perfect order)

Figure 4.1 Symmetry in the acts of creation.

At this point most commentators stop. But an anthropological analysis can go a lot deeper. The creative acts of the first three days are concerned with the creation of opposites, such as night and day, or sea and dry land. Dualities like this are called binary oppositions, and for some anthropologists (generally known as structuralists) they are the building blocks of all human thought. A binary opposition is a pair of terms that are the exact opposite of each other, for example, good/bad, black/white, day/night, raw/cooked. Which oppositions are powerful and which insignificant, and even what counts as a binary opposition, varies from culture to culture, but structuralists argue that the opposition of culture and nature, and, by extension, order and disorder, is fundamental to all cultures (Lévi-Strauss 1963). According to this paradigm, these binary oppositions structure all human thought processes, conscious and unconscious. Structuralism as an overarching anthropological theory of human culture and behaviour has long exceeded its shelf life, and anthropologists often speak of us living in a post-structuralist academic world (for example, Harrison 2006). Structuralism certainly suffered from chronic overreach, but in the case of the Genesis creation story, it has some value for analysis.

It should be obvious that the creative acts on the first three days are essentially the creation and separation of binary opposites: light and darkness (day one), above and below (day two), sea and dry land (day three). On the first day God creates light. That is not enough of a creative act, however. If the light mixes with the darkness, the result is a grey mess that has no use. So, God separates the light from the darkness and sets in motion the alternation between the two. In so doing he sets time in motion. This conception of time is essentially cyclic: light (day) follows darkness (night) and darkness (night) follows light (day) in an endless pattern. Without these binary opposites and their alternation there can be no time. The creation of cyclic time is the beginning of order. Light and darkness must be kept separate in order for time to continue to exist and for a general sense of order to prevail. Most of the time they are indeed separate, and order reigns. But twice in each total diurnal cycle – at dawn and at dusk – they overlap for a short period: light and dark commingle so that it is not quite day and not quite night.

Anthropologists call the betwixt and between state that merges opposites, the liminal state, from the Latin word *limen*, meaning a threshold (van Gennep 1909). Dawn and dusk are liminal times between day and night: they are both and neither. They are the seam lines where the fabric of day and night join: they are moments when the nature of creation is unveiled to us by its brief undoing. Dawn and dusk are times when the primordial mixing of light and darkness at the beginning of creation briefly returns. Generally speaking, cultures worldwide find liminal things to be both powerful and dangerous (Douglas 1966). Because they threaten our much-needed sense of order they are dangerous, yet dangerous places can be exhilarating, and they can empower the people who venture into them. Dawn and dusk were especially liminally potent and sacred times to the Judeans: daily reminders of God's work at the beginning of creation, as well as cautionary moments suggesting what might happen permanently should God choose to undo his work.

The New Revised Standard Version of the Bible, which I use here, translates the daily formula as 'And there was evening and there was morning...' but the literal translation of the Hebrew ought to be 'And there was dusk and there was dawn...' Translators tend to shy away from using the latter terms because they are associated in the modern mind with the setting and rising of the sun (which was not created until day four). It looks anachronistic to have dawn and dusk for the first three days with no sun. This interpretation is an ethnocentric mistake. Dusk and dawn in this narrative are key turning points of the day, when light gives way to darkness and vice versa, to be especially noted because they reveal God's handiwork. For the Judeans the sun appeared at dawn, the time when light emerges from darkness. It did not make the dawn, nor the light – it was a sign of the light; it lived in the light. Because people can be particularly aware of God's creation at these liminal moments they become ideally suited as times for worship. They are also the physically tangible, embodied turning points of the day that you can see and feel; unlike midnight, which is an arbitrary middle point that has no outward physical manifestation. Jews, even now, begin a new day and begin worship at dusk.

Having given order to the primeval darkness, God turns his attention to the watery abyss on day two. He separates the water into two components: the waters above and the waters below, using a dome he has called into being – the sky – to keep them separate. In the process God takes the first step in ordering physical space, that is, he creates a sense of up and down. The waters above are stored behind the dome of the sky (and make it appear blue), and can rain down on the lower level when God opens portals in the dome. The waters below, for the moment, remain in a semi-disordered state in the lower region.

On day three, God completes his acts of physical and temporal separation. He collects together the waters below into seas, and delineates them clearly from the dry land, which emerges once the water is amassed into large bodies. Days two and three together, therefore, demarcate three physical zones: the air, the seas and dry land. These three zones are the result of two intersecting binary oppositions, namely, up and down, and sea and dry land (see Figure 4.2).

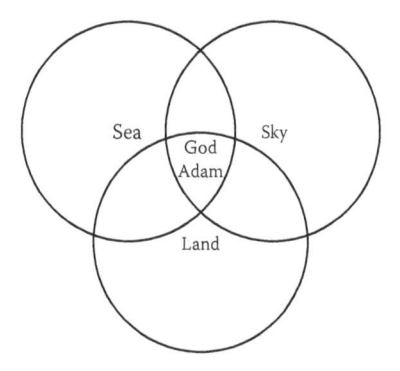

Figure 4.2   The three zones of creation.

While each zone is quite distinct, there are margins, or liminal zones, where each intersects with the others. The dry land and the sky are quite separate, but they meet on mountain tops. The dry land and the sea have marginal zones at the seashore. The sea and the sky meet in water spouts and storms. Like dawn and dusk, which are temporally sacred, these liminal zones are physically sacred. Here are the places where God's presence can be felt most keenly. Combine the two and you have a locus of great spiritual power, such as a mountaintop at dawn or a seashore at sunset. A perfect spot, now much valued by trekkers, is the Sinai (home of Mount Sinai). Here many mountain peaks overlook the northern arms of the Red Sea and create inspiring views at dawn, when the sight of land, sea and sky come together.

This is the ideally liminal place for Moses to receive the law that was to be the foundation of Jewish culture for all time.

Most people shy away from these marginal zones because of their danger. Only priests and those especially close to God would be brave enough to venture into these areas. So, while Moses scaled Mount Sinai to receive the law from God, the rest of the people preferred to stay safely grounded away from the mountain. But mark how many times in the Bible people get closer to God by ascending mountains. Likewise, there are powerful moments in the history of Israel when God replicates the separation of sea and dry land, such as at the Red Sea during the exodus and at the Jordan River when the people first enter the Promised Land.

On days four to six, God populates the zones he has created by creating appropriate creatures to fill them. We have already seen that the sun, moon and stars are the inhabitants of the temporal zones of day and night. On day five God fills the seas with fish, and the sky with birds. On day six he fills the land with animals. This schema becomes fundamentally important later in the law, when God decrees what is clean to eat and what is not. Ultimately this too comes down to a sense of orderliness. Animals that are clean to eat are those that stay in one physical zone and which, in a symbolic or archetypal sense, fit that zone perfectly. Fish with fins and scales are the best example. They live in the sea and they live in complete harmony with that element. They are excellently crafted to swim in the water and to treat the whole ocean as their home. They are the model of water dwellers. Lobsters and crabs by contrast are not so perfectly in harmony with their chosen zone. They have legs, and often walk like land animals on the bottom of the ocean. It is as if they are categorically mixed up. They are behaving like land animals yet live in the sea. Crabs can also come out on to the land, confusing the zones even further. These shellfish confound the orderliness of the physical zones and are therefore ritually unclean. Flightless birds suffer the same fate. A bird is supposed to dwell in the sky, but if instead it stays on the ground and walks around like a land animal, then it is confusing categories also and is, hence, unclean. If you eat the unclean you help support the confusion by bringing the disorder into your own body. You begin to know disorder in a bodily sense.

Mary Douglas argues that the concepts of clean and unclean are more about a sense of orderliness than anything else. According to Douglas, animals that are unclean to eat are those that are 'out of place'. Birds that walk, amphibians, sea creatures that cling to rocks and so forth live in the wrong zones for their features, or fail to fit their zone ideally, or have some physical ambiguity. Something in its right place is clean, and something out of place is unclean. This kind of interpretation has relevance for our lives also (Douglas 1966). English speakers use the terms 'soil' and 'dirt' to signify the ground in which we plant things, and we do not consider the earth to be inherently dirty when it is in its place. Dirt on farmland is not dirty. But if you get it on your hands or your shirt, they become dirty (or unclean) because, according to the cultural code, the physical substance of the earth does not belong on your hands or your shirt.

The sense of what 'fits' its environment and what does not is culturally defined and, to a degree, arbitrary. For the Judeans the archetype of the land animal that fits its environment perfectly is the ruminant (an animal that eats grass and chews its cud) with a split hoof. But why are ruminants more ideally suited to land dwelling than the pig? There are no easy answers. Many cultural constructions are arbitrary and that's the end of it. It could be argued, as does anthropologist Marvin Harris, that ruminants are more efficient in some environments than pigs because they can turn grass and other material that is inedible to humans into high-grade protein. (Harris 1975) They can survive in poor environments, such as Near Eastern wastelands, thus making every scrap of land profitable. In urbanized environments where there is plenty of food waste, pigs thrive because they turn trash into delightful fat and protein. Could it be that the pig symbolized what the Judeans saw as wanton, gluttonous cities like Babylon, while sheep, goats and cattle represented the purifying openness of the wilderness and the rugged mountains of Judah? Could it also be that the Judeans, seeing the exodus as their great defining moment, idealized themselves, in some legendary way, as pastoralist nomads and therefore saw the classic migratory herds – cattle in the generic sense – as 'good' animals; and animals that could not be herded – pigs – as 'bad' animals?

When God creates the land animals he gives them 'every green plant for food' (Genesis 1:30), making the herbivore (typified by the ruminant) the ideal land animal by simple designation. Pigs cannot eat grass, but they can eat flesh. Animals that kill, or that eat carrion or flesh fed to them, undo the commandment to 'be fruitful and multiply'. In their original state of grace the animals were all herbivores. When humans ruined primordial perfect order through their disobedience, the world became more deadly and some of the animals started killing and eating other animals. That is the main problem with humans undoing God's work: everyone and everything, including the innocent bystander, is affected. Humans at the outset, too, were vegetarians according to Genesis. When they learned to know, with their own hands, about death and killing, after the expulsion from the garden, they became carnivores. Even so, it was never acceptable for them to eat carnivores, because that would be doubly undoing the commandment to 'be fruitful and multiply'. They would be adding one killing on top of another: they would be killing killers.

Order and separateness

The notion of order that permeates this narrative is ingrained in the concept of separation: opposites should be kept separate; things that are unlike should be kept separate. In the precisely legalistic iterations of the law found in Leviticus, there are clear commandments to keep all things distinct and separate. You may not breed hybrid animals (animals with different kinds of parents, such as the mule), you may not make cloth from mixed materials, you may not plant two different species of domestic plants in the same field (Leviticus 19:19). The purity that emerges from separateness is God's command and desire from the first moments of creation onwards.

The creation of humans on day six also contains within it a vital commandment. Although they are basically terrestrial, humans are not limited to the dry land as their only physical zone. They have dominion over all the zones and all that is therein. They are created in God's image and, therefore, are to be designated as God's stewards for his creation. With this role comes awesome power and awesome responsibility. God demands perfect order at all times, and humans are in charge of maintaining that order. When they fail to maintain the separateness of opposites and unlike things, the ramifications are potentially cataclysmic. If they mix up different cultures, for example, they are running the risk of God's ruin being rained down upon them. They also run the risk of causing havoc in the natural world. A solar eclipse might be one sign of God's wrath: making it dark (night) when it should be light (day) is a warning sign that creation can be unmade if the human disorder becomes too great. Water flooding the dry land is a similar sign. When people mix opposites, God does likewise in punishment. If human disorder becomes too great, they run the risk of having God destroy creation altogether.

Further reading

The French anthropologist Claude Lévi-Strauss was the grand master of structuralism, although most of his books are written in language that is opaque to professional anthropologists let alone the average reader. The general anthology of Lévi-Strauss's earlier works Structural Anthropology (1963) contains some chapters that are more accessible than his later writing. For a secondary source that is a little clearer about structuralism read Edmund Leach's: *Culture and Communication: The Logic by which Symbols are Connected* (1976) and Claude Lévi-Strauss (1970). Structuralism has an extensive intellectual history. One of the most thorough investigations of the rise and fall of structuralism and allied theories in the academic community is *History of Structuralism* by François Dosse (1998).

Victor Turner introduced the concept of liminality into US and British anthropology in his analysis of rituals, especially rites of passage, by adopting

The creation formula

the earlier analysis of these rites by French anthropologist Arnold van Gennep. During a rite of passage, the person undergoing a transition from one life stage to another experiences a period of being liminal, or of being in-between both stages. Read either *The Ritual Process: Structure and Anti-Structure* (1969) or *The Forest of Symbols: Aspects of Ndembu Ritual* (1967). You could also read van Gennep's *Les Rites de Passage* (1909).

For a taste of how precise and detailed an investigation of the creation stories in Genesis can be, look at David Tsumura's *The Earth and the Waters in Genesis 1 and 2: A Linguistic Investigation* (1989). Tsumura does a careful cross-cultural analysis of creation narratives from various ancient Near Eastern cultures.

For the text of the Babylonian creation story and to see how it does and does not mesh with Genesis, you can read Alexander Heidel's *The Babylonian Genesis* (1942). A more recent translation plus related texts can be found in, James B. Pritchard ed. *Ancient Near Eastern Texts Relating to the Old Testament* (1969). See also Richard Clifford, *Creation Accounts in the Ancient Near East and in the Bible* (1994) and Wilfred G. Lambert, *Babylonian Creation Myths* (2013).

Many books explore timekeeping and calendars in various ancient cultures. One of my favourites is *The Seven Day Circle: The History and Meaning of the Week* by Eviatar Zerubavel (1985). You can also look at E.G. Richards, *Mapping Time: The Calendar and History* (1999) or Niels-Erik Andreasen's *The Old Testament Sabbath: A Tradition-historical Investigation* (1972).

5

Don't let your daughter marry an angel

※

The flood story is one of the most widely known tales from the Bible. In anticipation of a devastating flood, Noah leads specimens of all the animals on earth, two by two, into his ark. He has painstakingly constructed this ark with his own hands, according to God's plan, and in preparation for weathering the most perfect of all storms, one that would destroy every living thing outside his floating sanctuary. Two less well-known aspects of the flood story concern its moral cause and Noah's drunkenness after it was all over. This chapter provides a cultural interpretation of the cause of the flood based on what occurred before the heavens opened.

Prior to the flood, divine beings made a habit of coming down from heaven to earth to have sex with humans. After leaving the ark, when the waters had receded, and after thanking God for his salvation with a sacrificial ritual, Noah gets drunk on wine and passes out, in the process exposing his genitals to his younger son. While these tales that act as bookends for the flood narrative are scarcely known to the general public, they are vital to its interpretation as a whole and speak directly to issues that are of the utmost important to the Judean exiles. I pick up the issue of Noah and his dealings with wine in a later chapter (Chapter 9). Here I am concerned with the union of humans and heavenly beings.

The story of the flood is one of the longest narratives on a single topic in all of Genesis. Most of the tales in Genesis are short, crisp and to the point, with little in the way of details. The flood narrative occupies four chapters, 6 through 9, and is rich in historical and technical specifics, such as the precise material used to stop leaks in the ark, and the species of birds sent out to find dry land when the rains ceased.

In terms of interpretation, the story of the flood in Genesis is another great ideological battleground, probably only second after the creation account, for evangelical Christians, theologians and scholars of all stripes.

Many evangelicals are eager to prove that such a flood took place, and they have gone to extraordinary lengths to do so, such as asserting that there is, or was at one time, a literal canopy of water and ice more than a kilometre thick hovering over the earth that could descend and deluge all dry land (see, for example, Whitcomb and Morris 1961). From an anthropological perspective, the important issue is not whether the flood happened or not. What is important is what the story of the flood meant to the redactors of Genesis and their audience at the time.

Flood stories in literary perspective

The analysis of the biblical flood narrative prior to the late nineteenth century was rather one dimensional, because it was the only tale of its type that scholars knew. But as archaeology came of age as a profession and started uncovering ancient texts throughout the Near East, specialists in ancient Mesopotamian languages started translating a number of similar stories from across the region. The most famous and most complete flood narrative outside the Bible is included as a tale within a tale in the great Babylonian epic poem, Gilgamesh. (see George 2003).

By the early twentieth century, because of all of this new-found material, a heated scholarly battle had broken out between, mostly German, scholars who were convinced that many of the narratives in Genesis, especially the creation and the flood, were based on Mesopotamian (primarily Babylonian) originals, and those who vehemently opposed such an idea. To some extent the controversy, though muted, still continues.

I support the idea that the basic story of a massive flood that wiped out all of humanity, except for a loyal man and his family, came to the Judeans from somewhere in Mesopotamia. Two facts convince me. First, the stories from Mesopotamia and the biblical story match on too many details to be the products of independent invention. Second, a flood story is unlikely to have originated in the Judean hill country, or the wider territory of the Levant, where there is more dry wilderness than arable river land. In Mesopotamia, vast tracts of riverine and canal-side flatlands were subject to annual flooding, sometimes disastrously. While the archaeological record shows evidence of several catastrophic floods in ancient Mesopotamia, nothing remotely equivalent exists for Israel or Judah. When and how the flood story entered the Judean scriptural canon is impossible to determine. All of the Babylonian flood narratives predate the Exile, some of them by many centuries. What is most important for this chapter is why the flood story came into the Judean canon at all, as a tale about flooding would not resonate with shepherds from arid hill country. It would make more sense to Judean exiles living on rivers and canals in Babylon, so it is reasonable to imagine that they adopted the story at that time. There is much more to the issue, however. The crux of the matter lies not in the flood itself, but in its causes. The ultimate cause, according to Genesis, seems to have been the sexual encounters of divine beings with human women.

The Mesopotamian and biblical flood stories have a large number of narrative components in common, although general comparison is hampered by the fact that some of the tales are found only in fragments. The most complete narratives from Mesopotamia that pre-date, or are contemporary with, the Babylonian Exile are: Utnapishtim's story of the flood in the famous epic of Gilgamesh (found in a number of versions dating from the seventh century BCE); a Sumerian flood story from a tablet found at Nippur and dating to the time of the sixth Babylonian king, Hammurabi (c.1810–1750 BCE);[8] the Atra-hasis epic available now in four small fragments, two of which are from the first Babylonian dynasty (1894–1595 BCE), and two from the excavations of the library in Ninevah of the last Assyrian king, Ashurbanipal (reigned 669–627 BCE). A late version included in the history of Babylon written by the priest Berossus was published in Greek around 275 BCE, but is probably much older.

The tales cited above have the following elements in common:
- the high god decides to eradicate humanity in a flood;
- a hero is warned to take refuge from the flood;
- the hero is obedient and god-fearing;
- humanity is given a grace period before the flood begins;
- the hero builds an unusual vessel;
- the hero loads his kin and animals into the vessel;
- rains fall and rivers flood;
- all living things are destroyed except for the occupants of the vessel;
- the flood waters remain for a fixed period;
- the vessel comes to land on a mountain top;
- the hero sends out a series of birds to seek dry land;
- the occupants of the vessel emerge and sacrifice to the high god; and
- the high god grants a gift to the hero.

This list is virtually identical with the outline of the biblical flood narrative, indicating that in terms of its basics the Genesis story is not especially original, and was almost certainly copied from older Mesopotamian sources. What makes it unique and what makes it fascinating for our purposes, however, is that the specific reason for God bringing the flood in the Genesis story is

---

8   The dates for early Babylonian kings are all approximate and could be off by as much as a century.

markedly different from the reasons given in the other stories, and it is this aspect of the Genesis tale that fundamentally alters the interpretation of the whole narrative.

God and the Genesis flood

In many respects the flood story is an anomaly in the book of Genesis, because normally God is commanding people and animals to be fruitful and multiply. This message of increase is the watchword for the exiles: expanding rapidly in numbers is one key to their survival and a pillar of the 'Genesis option'. So why is there suddenly this tale of utter destruction of life running counter to this most basic and most common of commandments? There are three plausible, but distinct, answers to this question.

First, the flood tale may be a simple metaphor to comfort the exiles. They could imagine Noah boxed up in his ark as being symbolic of them boxed up in their exilic communities. Noah was surrounded by hostile waters as far as the eye could see; the exiles were surrounded by hostile cultures as far as the eye could see. Noah's only comfort was a window in the roof of the ark through which he could view God's creation in the heavens; likewise, the exiles could look up to the sun and stars to be reassured that God was still with them. Noah was utterly obedient to God and in the long run he survived and prospered. The exiles could look forward to the same heritage if they too were utterly obedient. If they lapsed in their obedience, they would be 'drowned' in the foreign cultures that surrounded them, just as the disobedient were drowned in the waters of the flood.

Second, the story of the flood could bring hope of better times to the exiles by emphasizing the fact that fate and fortune come in cycles. Time is both linear and cyclical. In the linear view, which sees time as starting at some distant point in the past and extending infinitely into the future in a linear fashion, the future is essentially unknowable and therefore scary. A linear conception of time leaves little sense that the bad things that happened in the past can be overcome in the future. It gives a sense of an accumulation of problems over time, a growing burden for people as they move forward. In this view, we can never revisit the past and we go forward into the future carrying all that is past with us. To a large extent, the Deuteronomic view of history, which the exiles had inherited, was linear. Their view of history did contain high points and low points, but they did not occur in cycles per se. That is, disaster could be overcome through right action, so that high and low points could balance each other out, but there was no inevitable cyclic return. Deuteronomic time marched forwards.

Cyclical time is quite the opposite of linear time. It offers hope for renewal each new cycle, whether it is a new day, week, month or year. In the cyclical frame, we can resolve to do things better this (new) time around. We also have a sense that with the end of the old cycle we have put the past behind us. Celebrations in Europe, Asia and the Americas associated with the New Year are classic examples of the power of cycles. Annually, revellers take stock of all the mistakes they have made in the previous year and make resolutions that they hope will redeem them, and give them a fresh start in the coming year. (see Eliade 1954)

The story of Noah and the flood is cast in the cyclical mode: it represents the end of one cycle and the beginning of a new one. Noah is characterized in Genesis genealogies as the first man born after the death of Adam. As I demonstrate more explicitly in Chapter 8, Genesis offers a consistent theme of the world undergoing periodic renewal, usually every seven or ten generations. Noah is the tenth generation after Adam, for example. The message is: no matter how bad things get for the faithful in the current cycle – even if the rest of the world is obliterated in a flood – they will survive and be renewed and revived by the beginning of a new cycle.

The importance of cycles is established at the very beginning of creation. God could have created everything all at once if he had wanted to – in one day or even a microsecond. But he chose to create the world over the course of a seven-day week that would ever after cycle around in a constant pattern of renewal. In fact, much of the creation story underscores the importance of cycles. The first day sets up the diurnal cycle of day and night; the fourth day sets the sun and moon in the sky to indicate months, seasons, and years. Everything is pointing to the value of cyclical time over linear time.

The third answer, however, is the most compelling because it directly concerns God's reasons for bringing the flood: his wrath over the wickedness of humanity. Most of the Mesopotamian stories give little reason for the fury of the high god that warrants wiping out all living creatures. Gilgamesh has a vague reference to sin. The Atra-hasis epic is more specific in stating that human overpopulation is the cause: there are so many humans on earth making so much noise that the high god cannot sleep. This notion could not possibly find a parallel in Genesis. God's favor in Genesis is shown via the fertility of his chosen people. He wants them to multiply freely. He frequently promises those whom he especially cherishes that their offspring will be more numerous than grains of sand on the seashore or stars in the sky. He would not send a flood to destroy humans because they are peopling the earth too much: quite the contrary. For God to undo so much of his beloved handiwork there has to be a monumental problem that needs to be corrected.

The immediate statement of God's distress and his desire to eradicate all living things is found in Genesis 6:5–7.

> 5. The LORD saw that the wickedness of humankind was great in the earth, and that every inclination of the thoughts of their hearts was only evil continually.
>
> 6. And the LORD was sorry that he had made humankind on the earth, and it grieved him to his heart.
>
> 7. So the LORD said, 'I will blot out from the earth the human beings I have created – people together with animals and creeping things and birds of the air, for I am sorry that I have made them.'

What is this evil that is so vile that humanity must be wiped out? Up until this point in the narrative flow of Genesis only two sins have been recorded. The first is the disobedience of Adam and Eve in the garden. Their punishment is severe but not completely calamitous. God does not eradicate them and then start again. Rather, he gives them the ability to procreate and explicitly commands them to reproduce and populate the earth. Second is Cain's murder of his brother Abel. This is a heinous crime on many levels, including the fact that it undermines God's desire to see the earth populated with humans. Yet Cain's punishment is merely exile, and he too takes a wife and has children. God even puts a mark on Cain's forehead to protect him. So, direct disobedience and murder bring forth punishment, but not absolute devastation, and the sinners live on to produce offspring. What could be worse than murder or disobedience to God? The answer lies in the passage in chapter 6 of Genesis that comes just before God's declaration of the impending flood.

Genesis 6:1–4 is a little-known biblical passage that is so telegraphically brief that it is extremely difficult to interpret:

> 6:1. When people began to multiply on the face of the ground, and daughters were born to them,
>
> 2. the sons of God saw that they were fair; and they took wives for themselves of all that they chose.
>
> 3. Then the LORD said, 'My spirit shall not abide in mortals forever, for they are flesh; their days shall be one hundred twenty years.'
>
> 4. The Nephilim were on the earth in those days – and also afterwards – when the sons of God went in to the daughters of humans, who bore children to them. These were the heroes that were of old, warriors of renown.

The original Hebrew is impossible to understand in places; the English translation makes the passage seem clearer than it really is. However, the overall gist of the tale seems to be straightforward enough, namely, heavenly beings came to earth and had children with human women. The phrase 'sons of God' does not necessarily mean the literal offspring of the deity, but can have a looser sense of divine beings. The Hebrew term 'son of …' carries the metaphoric meaning of something like, 'in the service of …' or 'in the tradition of …' Hence, the 'sons of the prophets' are men who act as prophets or have been trained by prophets, not the literal offspring of prophets. Although rare, some broad hints in the Hebrew Bible suggest a belief in a heavenly kingdom ruled by Yahweh and populated by divine beings of some sort (these 'sons of God'). The book of Job, for example, opens with a rudimentary description of 'heavenly beings' appearing before Yahweh as if at a kingly court (Job 1:6 and 2:1). Ezekiel, likewise, describes a celestial retinue of Yahweh's that he has seen in visions (Ezekiel 1) and the prophet Micaiah describes his vision of heaven in I Kings 22:19, 'Therefore hear the word of the LORD: I SAW THE LORD SITTING ON HIS THRONE WITH ALL THE MULTITUDES OF HEAVEN STANDING AROUND HIM ON HIS RIGHT AND ON HIS LEFT.'

The key verse is 6:2:

ויראו בני האלהים את בנות האדם כי טבת הנה ויקחו להם נשים מכל אשר בחרו

The sons of God saw that the daughters of Adam were sensually appealing, and they took as many of them as they wanted to copulate with.[9]

The passage in Genesis seems to be saying that members of Yahweh's court were attracted to earthly women and greedily took as many wives from them as they wanted. The Hebrew original is quite crude and gives the impression of wanton lust with raw unbridled copulation as the outcome. The result was a hybrid race of giants known as the Nephilim. They are described in Numbers 13:33 as being so large that regular humans appeared to be the size of grasshoppers beside them. Such a tale is strikingly similar to stories told by the Greeks and other ancient cultures. The legendary hero Hercules, for example, was the offspring of Zeus and a mortal woman. In the Greek tradition, though, there is no sense that the coupling of god and human is wrong. In the story of the Nephilim, by contrast, there is a sense of ambivalence. These giants

---

9 My translation is not word-for-word, but tries to capture the spirit of the passage. The sense of the original is that the 'sons of god' wantonly acted as they pleased without external rules or restraints. Such activity stands in strict contrast with the formal rules of marriage that the Judeans followed (see Chapter 6).

are described as 'warriors of renown' but Yahweh appears displeased with the unions that produced them and reduces the normal lifespan of humans as a penalty (Genesis 6:3).

I suspect that this story was once independent of the flood narrative and that the redactors of Genesis placed it immediately before the flood story to contextualize the flood itself. It tells specifically of the evil that has overtaken creation. This evil has incensed Yahweh to the point where he wants to destroy it all. Murder and disobedience are bad enough, but what has happened between heavenly males and human females threatens the roots of creation. Beings that should be separate – that should breed according to their own kinds – have become mixed up. Creation was a series of acts of separation, and any act that mixes up what should be separate undoes creation itself.

The story of the Nephilim is a great caution to the exiles. Judeans living in Babylon will have beautiful daughters. Powerful Babylonian leaders – princes, generals, rich merchants – will lust after them. If Judean fathers succumb to the temptation of marrying their daughters to these powerful men, or their sons, they stand to gain a lot and lose a lot. They and their families will gain prestige in the Babylonian community, and the sons of the mixed marriages may become rich and powerful in their own right. But they will speak the Babylonian language and act like Babylonians, and even though they may be bilingual and bicultural, their lineage will eventually turn its back on Judean culture.

The two worlds of the immigrant
The Judean exiles were likely similar to any immigrant population newly arrived in a large multicultural nation. The typical pattern for new adult immigrants is to cleave to their native culture, learning only as much of the local language in their new situation as is necessary to manage their affairs. The generation born to these immigrants in the new culture, however, tends to be torn. They are usually bilingual, speaking the native language of their parents within their homes, and the dominant language outside it. Their tendency is to idealize the nation to which their parents have travelled and to try to assimilate to it as much as possible, while at the same time downplaying their cultural and national origins. Growing up in Australia in the 1950s I had many school friends whose parents came from various parts of Europe. I knew them by names such as Pete or Tony or Stacy, but at home their parents called them Pyotr or Antonin or Anastasia. They habitually lived in two worlds (see, for example, Portes and Zhou 1993).

The third generation is often more fully integrated into the national culture than the second. Because their parents (second generation) are ambivalent about their origins, it is the norm for them not to teach their children the native language of their parents, and there is no necessity to speak the native language at home, because both parents and children are fluent in the dominant language. This process of assimilation into the majority culture is further accelerated if a child of immigrants marries someone from the dominant community. Over a short period of time, only two generations, the original immigrant culture is vastly diluted because of its interactions with the dominant culture.

The only certain way to avoid the assimilationist's fate is to avoid all meaningful contact with the dominant culture in a multicultural setting. For instance, a few subcultures in the contemporary United States of America have tried to maintain their integrity in this way, and it is a daily struggle to do so. In north-eastern USA, ultra-orthodox Jews and Old Order Amish are probably the best-known examples. They maintain distinctive language, dress and cultural habits that ensure their separation from the mainstream society. As such, their children are kept isolated from outsiders, and are, therefore, all but compelled to marry within their group (see Chapter 13).

The evil that brought the full weight of God's anger on the world was miscegenation: mixed marriages. When heavenly beings married mortals, they committed the worst of possible sins. Cain's murder of his brother was a bad thing to do, but his parents, and he, were capable of having more children within a well-defined and pure lineage to make up for the loss. When cultures and lineages get mixed up through intermarriage, though, their purity is lost. Creation was a series of acts of separation. When God separated light from darkness and sea from dry land he declared the results 'good'. He wanted opposites kept apart.

The story of the Nephilim must begin the flood narrative because it represents in a basic way the evil that so angers God. The particulars of the flood narrative in Genesis reveal that God's actions in reprisal for miscegenation come very close to undoing all the creative acts found in Genesis 1. What was once separate he mixes back into disorder, coming close to replicating the time of primeval chaos before creation. Here is the general description of the flood itself in Genesis 7:11–12 and 19–23.

> 11. In the six-hundredth year of Noah's life, in the second month, on the seventeenth day of the month, on that day all the fountains of the great deep burst forth, and the windows of the heavens were opened.

> 12. The rain fell on the earth for forty days and forty nights.

> ...

19. The waters swelled so mightily on the earth that all the high mountains under the whole heaven were covered;

20. the waters swelled above the mountains, covering them fifteen cubits deep.

21. And all flesh died that moved on the earth, birds, domestic animals, wild animals, all swarming creatures that swarm on the earth, and all human beings;

22. everything on dry land in whose nostrils was the breath of life died.

23. He blotted out every living thing that was on the face of the ground, human beings and animals and creeping things and birds of the air; they were blotted out from the earth.

Some acts of creation are left in place. Time keeps going and the sun and moon still mark the passage of time. But as the rains pelted down it would have been very dark and all the celestial bodies would have been hidden. So, the feeling of the time before creation when there was nothing except a dark watery abyss would have returned. The second part of the description is also explicit that the flood waters destroyed all living things, except for the contents of the ark. Nothing could survive outside the ark because the physical structure of the world created by the separation of opposites, and on which living creatures depended, had been destroyed. The separation of sea and dry land, effected on the third day of creation, was reversed. The tallest mountain was covered by fifteen cubits (perhaps around 22 feet) of water.

The description of the mechanism of the biblical flood is quite unlike that of the other Mesopotamian narratives. The Mesopotamian narratives describe a great inundation that the people of the region would have seen as catastrophic, yet natural. It rains a lot, and the rivers and canals overflow their banks and flood the land. People in the region saw that kind of thing all the time. Noah's flood involves rain too, but the description involves much more than just rain. The critical phrase is 'all the fountains of the great deep burst forth' along with 'the windows of the heavens were opened'. A simple paraphrase might be 'the waters below and the waters above were unleashed and allowed to meet and mix'. Days two and three of creation had been undone.

The echoes of the wording of the story of creation are evident and intentional: the creation and flood stories are symmetric opposites. The creation separates, the flood mixes. The flood ends one whole cycle of creation and begins another. After a period of cleansing there will be a new separation of sea and dry land, and a new Adam (Noah) to populate the new earth. The story contains an element of hope within it. The moral that it implies is that if you mix opposites you threaten the stability of the world. Not only will you die, but the world around you will be destroyed. So, if you are wondering about whether or not you should try to get ahead in the world by marrying your daughter to a Babylonian general, think twice, think three times, and then don't do it. The question remains: if she cannot marry a Babylonian, whom should she marry?

Further reading
For decades the authoritative comparative study of the ancient Mesopotamian flood narratives, including translations of all the main texts, was Alexander Heidel's *The Gilgamesh Epic and Old Testament Parallels* (1946). Heidel's discussion of the main elements of the various flood stories is old but remains insightful. Now the standard academic text is Andrew George's *The Babylonian Gilgamesh Epic* (2003). For other translations and analyses of some of the texts, see *Myths from Mesopotamia* by Stephanie Dalley (2000) and David Ferry, *Gilgamesh: A New Rendering in English Verse* (1993).

More general comparative works that look at the Mesopotamian flood story's meaning down to the present day include Norman Cohn's *Noah's Flood* (1996), Y.S. Chen's *The Primeval Flood Catastrophe* (2013), and Robert MacAndrew Best's *Noah's Ark and the Ziusudra Epic* (1999)

The classic work in anthropology on cyclical time is Mircea Eliade's *The Myth of the Eternal Return* (1954). He discusses how stories of cyclical creation and destruction are built into the fabric of culture worldwide, and how the ritual cycle supports and is supported by such narratives. More contemporary works on anthropology and time include, Alfred Gell, *The Anthropology of Time* (1992) and various articles in Wendy James and David Mills (eds), *The Qualities of Time* (2004).

To learn about the reasoning of evangelical Christians who argue that the earth is a few thousand years old and that a flood covering Mount Everest to a depth of twenty feet or more actually occurred, read *The Genesis Flood* by John C. Whitcomb and Henry Morris (1961). Morris coined the term 'creation science,' and founded an institute in California with the purpose of confirming the literal facts of the Genesis accounts of creation and the flood.

Modern geophysicists have periodically attempted to show that the Mesopotamian flood tales may have reflected an actual cataclysmic flood in the region. One such example is William Ryan and Walter Pitman, *Noah's Flood* (1998). Both evangelical and liberal Christian theologians find such inquiries irrelevant to the interpretation of the flood narrative.

The study of immigrants and assimilation has a rich history in anthropology. This book takes the approach that the exiles who redacted Genesis wished to avoid contact with outsiders in Babylon, and consequent assimilation, at all costs, whereas modern studies of immigrant dilemmas and their consequences have tended to begin with the assumption that assimilation is inevitable and have worked from there. Nonetheless, if you wish to pursue this topic you can start with the bibliographic essay 'Segmented assimilation revisited' by Waters *et al.* (2010). This article (online) links to a boatload of helpful resources. For anthropological research in particular, you might also consider *I'm Neither Here Nor There* (Zavella 2011) and *Flexible Citizenship* (Ong 1999).

6

Keeping it in the family

Some ancient pharaohs married their siblings; William the Conqueror infuriated the pope by marrying his fourth cousin, contrary to church law of the time. Rules governing sex and marriage vary widely from culture to culture. In some cultures first cousins are encouraged to marry; in others such marriages are unthinkable. In some, people may have more than one spouse at a time; others are rigidly monogamous. While some societies tolerate extra-marital sex; in others you can be stoned to death for straying from the marriage bed. It is not the place of anthropologists to make moral judgments about these various practices, but, instead, to document differences and ask why there are such different values and practices. This chapter, and much of the rest of the book, concerns rules about marriage and sex in the context of the Judean Exile. As the last chapter showed, marriage and sex are as important as language and ritual for cultural survival.

Commentators typically divide up Genesis into two unequal parts. The first, chapters 1 to 11, deals with the beginnings of the world and humanity, and is mostly made up of short narratives with simple moral lessons, plus some genealogies. The second, chapters 12 to 50, contains much longer stories, and the narrative vision shrinks from the entire world to just a few significant figures. The pivotal male players in the second part are usually called the patriarchs: Abraham, Isaac, Jacob and Joseph. Each, in his own way, is responsible for the development and maintenance of the nation of Israel. Once Abraham comes on the scene, the narrative interest shifts exclusively to his offspring, and the rest of the world is of concern only when it intersects with them. Abraham is expressly listed in the genealogies as ten generations from Shem, Noah's son and companion in the ark, so he represents the start of yet another era following the Flood. This chapter looks at the marriage and sexual practices that Abraham and his male line consider normative, and asks why that is. Anthropologists who study marriage patterns and sexual relationships consider three concepts as fundamental: incest, endogamy and exogamy.

Incest

Cross-culturally, incest is the practice of sexual intercourse between people who are perceived by local custom (or law) as too closely related for such behaviour (Wolf and Durham 2004). Because incest rules regulate sexuality and because one of the functions of marriage rules is also to regulate sexuality, it is a common mistake to think that incest rules are rules about marriage. Incest rules are much broader than that. They regulate the sexuality of partners whether or not they want to get married. There is no culture in which a closely related couple (by local standards) may have sexual intercourse freely, but it would be deemed incestuous for them to marry.

Contrary to a widely held belief in the Euro-American world, incest rules are neither absolute nor universal. Incest rules vary considerably from culture to culture, and sometimes within cultures. In the United States, for example, it is incestuous for first cousins to have sexual relations in some of the states, and not in others. Incest rules may also change over time within a culture as circumstances change. Incest rules concern what some kinship specialists call the 'perceived closeness' of the partners involved (Wolf and Durham 2004). Sometimes 'closeness' is defined in terms of biology ('blood relations') and sometimes not. Thus, in many cultures it is incestuous for men and women to have sex if they have been raised in the same household but are not biologically related. In some cultures it is incestuous to have sex with a person who shares a significant name with a sibling, even when there is no biological relationship between them whatsoever.

Sigmund Freud, in the opening essay in *Totem and Taboo* (1913), 'The horror of incest', argued that the formulation of incest rules was the beginning of human society. He claimed that incest rules were the foundation of all cultural rules. His line of reasoning was based on an imaginary prehistoric patriarchal family in which the father kept his daughters for his own sexual partners and so his jealous sons killed him. The sons then felt so guilty about what they had done that they vowed to seek sexual partners outside the family. While this model is too wildly speculative for modern scholars, Freud had an important insight. Although what counts as incest varies widely from culture to culture, all cultures have incest rules of some sort. Any universal set of rules must be extremely important.

Why are incest taboos so widespread? A number of hypotheses exist, each of which may hold a shred or more of truth, and none of which excludes the others. In the United States, the genetic argument is the most commonly circulated by the general public. In its popular form, this claims that incestuous sex produces birth defects in children born of such a union. Despite its popularity, the argument is weak when one looks at the evidence. In favour of the genetic argument, it is true that under special circumstances that are rarely found, inbreeding can have deleterious outcomes. For example, harmful genetic traits can become concentrated in small, closed or isolated populations if they practice long-term inbreeding. But many biological anthropologists agree that there are no predictable long-term negative consequences to inbreeding in large human populations. Furthermore, in the same way that harmful traits may be increased through close inbreeding, so may positive ones. (see, for example, Van Den Berghe 2010).

What is more significant as evidence against the genetic argument is the fact that incest rules do not apply to biological relatives only. Perceived closeness applies to partners who may or may not be related biologically. Among the Ju|'hoan (San bushmen of South Africa) it is considered incestuous for a man to marry a woman with the same name as his sister even though there is no biological relationship between them (Peters-Golden 2012:110). Likewise, the Ju|'hoan cannot marry a former affine. In some places, such as Kansas, incest laws apply to same-sex relationships, where there is no possibility of procreation. For all these reasons the genetic argument for a universal incest taboo is weak.

The family disruption theory is also a functional explanation for the incest taboo. By functional I mean that the theory assumes that the taboo exists because it has positive consequences for society. This theory argues that sexual relations between members of the same, or related, households can cause jealousies and rivalries that are destructive for the households involved. Therefore, such relations are taboo. Consider, for example, the mother-son incest rule, which, as far as I know, is universal and strongly held. Leviticus requires the death penalty for mother-son incest, and in Greek legend when Oedipus discovered that his sexual partner, Jocasta, was his mother he blinded himself and she committed suicide. Among the possible reasons for a mother-son incest taboo is the fact that sexual relations between a mother and her son would drive a wedge between the son and his father. The son being the weaker of the two males might then be at grave risk of harm from his father. Of course, Freud had much to say about this hypothesized pattern in his thoughts on the Oedipus complex. According to a more generalized family disruption theory, a society that allowed mother-son sexual relations would quickly see its sons marginalized or destroyed by jealous fathers, and would not thrive. It is possible to extend this argument to include other household members. Brother-sister sexual relations, for example, might set up excessive sibling rivalry among the other siblings.

One weakness of family disruption theory is that incest rules frequently extend well beyond people in the same household, or even in the same community. Current Catholic law, for example, prohibits sexual/marital relationships between third cousins without a special dispensation. Such taboos cannot possibly be linked to jealousy and household disruption. Most people do not even know who their third cousins are (or even how to identify them accurately genealogically). Furthermore, there are special conditions under which strong sexual bonds between family members provide benefits to the family. The pharaohs of ancient Egypt had sexual relations within the nuclear family – at least reputedly – as a way of stressing and maintaining their elite isolation. Such cases are rare and highly localized, however. While the case of the pharaohs is probably overblown in academic literature for the sake of sensationalism, persistent inbreeding within certain European royal lineages (notably the Habsburgs) is well documented.

The third possible explanation for incest taboos is favoured by anthropologists: cooperation theory (Leavitt 2013). This model stresses the fact that communities are stronger when they have multiple ties to other communities. If a community has no outside ties, it has no one else to call on in times of stress such as famine, drought, or warfare. There are many ways to forge links with other communities, such as trade relationships, but marriage bonds between members of different communities are arguably the strongest way to unite them. One way to promote marriage outside the community is to ban sexual relations, and hence marriage, within it (and that prohibition applies to both blood kin and non-blood kin).

Cooperation theory is highly situational, however. Anthropologists argue that incest rules are most likely to be extensive (ruling out close biological kin) in situations of risk, where having the widest possible group of related people to call upon in times of stress is critical to group survival (Schechner 1971; Wolf and Durham 2004:3). Conversely, in contexts where some groups have resources they wish to protect and not share with others, such as royal families, sex and marriage among close family relations are tolerated and sometimes promoted. Cleopatra married two of her brothers, at different times, and may or may not have had sex with them. Even if she did not have sex with them, it was perfectly legal for her to do so and she would not have been committing incest.

Thus, cooperation theory suggests that incest rules require a delicate balancing act between the need to keep resources within the family and the need to have outside allies to count on when necessary. Finding sexual/marital partners far afield increases the human resources you can call upon, but it also diffuses your resources over a wide area. While you can call on all of your kin by marriage in a crisis, they can also call on you when necessary.

If, however, you find your partners close to home, you consolidate and protect your resources. But you limit the socio-spatial range in which you can call on others in an emergency.

One of the strengths of cooperation theory is that it explains the wide range of incest taboos from culture to culture. The theory treats incest rules as a spectrum of possibilities and where you fall on this spectrum depends on a number of cultural circumstances. As suggested in previous chapters, the Judean exiles had to figure out where they wanted to be on this spectrum. They could open themselves up to the possibilities of relationships with the many ethnic groups in Babylon. They would thus expand their political and economic potential, but would pay the price of diluting their culture. Or, they could create relationships within their own group and maintain their cultural integrity at the expense of political and economic advancement and networking. The patriarchal narratives overwhelmingly support the latter course. To see how this strategy worked, we need to look at two more terms: exogamy and endogamy.

Exogamy and endogamy

Incest rules concern taboo sexual partners, and so are only partially concerned with rules about appropriate marriage partners. In most cultures there are rules or norms against marrying certain people, even though it would not be incestuous to have sexual relations with them. The rules that directly concern who is and who is not an acceptable marriage partner, for whatever reason, are called the rules of endogamy and exogamy. The root –gamy means 'marriage', and endo- and exo- mean, respectively, 'inside of' and 'outside of'. So, endogamy rules concern the group a person should marry inside of, and exogamy rules concern the group that a person should marry outside of. In some cultures these rules are rigidly codified into laws, in others they are norms. A norm is a principle that will not bring a legal penalty if transgressed, yet people within the culture feel compelled to follow it nonetheless. For example, there is no law against New Yorkers marrying their first cousins, but most find the idea objectionable. Genesis establishes the norms of exogamy and endogamy for the Judean exiles, some of which were also codified into laws.

Figure 4.1 helps clarify the principles associated with incest, exogamy and endogamy. At the centre of the diagram is a person labelled 'EGO', the generic anthropological term for the person who is the focus of the study. The concentric circles represent groups of people and how they relate to ego based on their perceived social distance. The innermost circle represents the closest. As the circles widen, the perceived closeness gets more and more distant. The innermost circle is that of incest. These are people with whom ego cannot have sex because they are too closely related (by cultural norms),

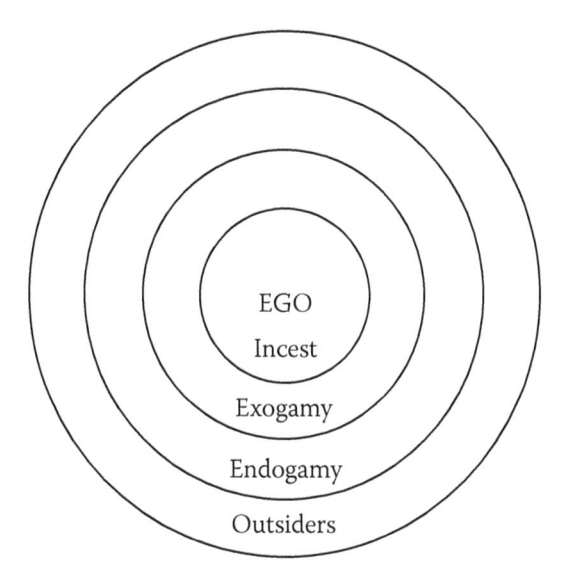

Figure 6.1 Marriage Rules and Perceived Distance.

and, therefore, too close to marry. Next is the exogamous group. This is the group of people ego should not marry because they are too closely related. Generally, the incest and exogamous groups are of similar size, but there can be a distinction. In most states in the USA it is not incestuous to marry your first cousin, but it is not a practice that most Americans approve of. Therefore, I would put first cousins in the USA in the exogamous group, but not in the incestuous group. The endogamous group is the group of people that ego should choose a partner from. Beyond that group are outsiders, people who are so far removed from ego that they are very unlikely marriage partners. There is a slew of cultural factors that might come into play with regard to this, such as age, ethnicity, national origin, race, religion and so forth.

All cultures have rules of exogamy and endogamy. Anthropologists have spent a great deal of time working out, through interviews and observation (see 'Further reading', below), how people in different cultures determine what relationships are incestuous versus exogamous, and which are endogamous. For Cleopatra, for example, the list of people in the incestuous and exogamous categories was extremely small, as was that of her endogamous circle, while the list of people it was unthinkable for her to marry (outsiders) was huge. This was because she and her lineal kin, the pharaohs, considered themselves to be gods, and, therefore, they could marry only other gods, that is, other members of their same lineage. All the mere mortals of the land, no matter how rich and powerful, were 'outsiders' (Ager 2005; Huebner 2007).

Endogamy and the Judean exiles

The case with the Judean exiles was not so different from that of Cleopatra's. Their biggest concern was that they not marry outside the Judean enclave. The borderline between the endogamous group and outsiders was clear cut and well established. Anyone not a Judean was an outsider. The stories of the patriarchs hammer home this lesson repeatedly. Endogamous marriage produces health, wealth and general prosperity. Anyone foolish enough to marry an outsider is doomed to a life of disaster.

The problem that all groups like the exiles face is that if you have a rigid code of endogamy that allows members of your ethnic group to marry each other and no one else, you may be faced with the difficulty of finding enough partners. One way to expand the pool of partners in the endogamous group is to shrink the incestuous and exogamous groups to the barest minimum. Among the Judean exiles only direct lineal kin were taboo as partners, and even this rule was broken sometimes when dire need arose. As far as I can tell, for the exiles the incestuous and exogamous groups are identical: if it was not incestuous to have relations with a person then he or she was fair game for marriage also. Full siblings were sexually taboo, but half siblings could marry provided they had different mothers (in anthropological terms, they are non-uterine siblings). Abraham and his wife Sarah were non-uterine siblings. Close-kin marriage, especially cousin marriage, including first-cousin marriage, appears to be the norm. We can look at the details in Genesis, starting with Abraham.

Abraham (who was called Abram before God gave him a new name), was the son of Terah who lived in Ur, an ancient city south of Babylon located near the mouths of the Tigris and Euphrates Rivers (see Figure 2.1 p. 24). Terah had three sons, Nahor, Haran and Abraham, by one wife, and a daughter Sarai (later named Sarah) by a second wife. Haran had a son, Lot, and two daughters, Milcah and Iscah, and then he died in Ur. Nahor married his brother Haran's daughter, Milcah, and Abraham married his half-sister, Sarai.

Some scholars question whether Abraham actually married his sister. They point to some episodes in Genesis in which he journeys to what he perceives as hostile country and is afraid the local ruler will find Sarai attractive and want to kill him if he thinks Abraham is her husband. So, he tells her to say he is her brother, which will make the local ruler want to protect Abraham. This statement is not so much a lie as a half-truth. In Genesis 20:12, when the local ruler uncovers his disingenuousness, Abraham says:

> 12. Besides, she is indeed my sister, the daughter of my father but not the daughter of my mother; and she became my wife.

Keeping it in the family

This statement is clear: she is, in English kinship terminology, a non-uterine half-sister. Such a marriage would not have been completely unusual, even though half-sibling marriage of any sort is forbidden under Mosaic Law (Leviticus 18:9). A curious story in 2 Samuel 13 supports the notion that non-uterine sibling marriage was acceptable under certain circumstances, although what these circumstances are is not explicit in the narrative. The story concerns king David's son Amnon by one wife, and his daughter Tamar by another wife. Amnon lusts after Tamar and foments a plan to get her close to him while he is in bed, by feigning sickness, so that he can rape her. When he gets aggressive, Tamar says (2 Samuel 13:12–13):

12. 'No, my brother, do not force me; for such a thing is not done in Israel; do not do anything so vile!

13. As for me, where could I carry my shame? And as for you, you would be as one of the scoundrels in Israel. Now therefore, I beg you, speak to the king; for he will not withhold me from you.'

The import of her entreaty is that it is the act of rape that is obscene and not the act of sex between half-siblings, although it is also arguable that the act of pre-marital consensual sex between half-siblings would have been shameful. Nevertheless, Tamar is saying that if Amnon goes to David and asks for her hand in marriage, he will grant it and there will be no shame. So, despite the letter of the law in Leviticus against it, two clear examples exist of half-sibling marriage being acceptable. The general rule for the Judean exiles to take from these stories was that it is better to marry a close relative than to go outside the community for a partner.

Terah sets off from Ur with all of his descendants and their families via the Euphrates river valley toward what was then called Canaan, peopled by groups scholars label Canaanites, but in what was to become the lands of Israel and Judah. Instead of entering Canaan, though, he sets up camp in Haran (also spelled Harran), which is just to the north of Canaan (Figure 2.1, p. 24). It is up to Abraham, accompanied by his nephew, Lot, to complete the journey south into what would become the Promised Land. It is likely that this journey was deeply symbolic for the exiles. Their ancestor Abraham came up out of Babylonia and was promised offspring so numerous they could not be counted, and a land for them to live in forever. The exiles no doubt wished to be able retrace Abraham's steps back to the home he was granted in perpetuity.

When Abraham and Lot arrive in Canaan they split, and go their separate ways. Lot ends up in the infamous town of Sodom which later is destroyed by God because of its people's sexual sins. Lot escapes the destruction of Sodom with his two daughters. His wife, whose origins and even name are unknown, is turned into a pillar of salt because, as she is leaving the city, she looks back on its destruction, against the express wishes of God. Lot and his daughters go to live in a mountain cave, where they believe they are the only survivors left on earth. His elder daughter hatches a plan with the younger to repopulate the world.

The daughters get Lot drunk. Then first the elder and then the younger daughter have sex with him. Both become pregnant and eventually give birth to sons who are the ancestors of Moab and Ammon, powerful neighbouring states to Israel. Because these states were the traditional enemies of Israel and Judah, some commentators suggest that this apparently incestuous set of unions produced cursed offspring (Sarna 2001). The text, however, says no such thing. Furthermore, Deuteronomy 2 characterizes Moab and Ammon as exceptionally strong, and indicates that God has endowed them with lands that are not to be coveted by the children of Israel. They are to be left in peace.

There is only slight indirect evidence that the daughters did anything wrong. The fact that they had to get Lot drunk is significant. Presumably he would not have had sex with his daughters otherwise. But the daughters are not condemned for tricking their father into incestuous acts. Apparently, therefore, in times of great crisis even father-daughter sexual relationships are acceptable. Genesis appears to say that the earliest ancestors faced the choice of having sex with a close relative such as a half-sister or daughter, finding a mate outside the clan of Terah, or not procreating at all and having the lineage die out. Sex with a close relative wins every time. The only penalty in the case of Lot is that his sons are illegitimate, not because the sex was incestuous, but because Lot was not legally married to his daughters. His descendants are not full members of Terah's lineage and are, therefore, unacceptable partners for legitimate heirs.

Abraham settles in Canaan and eventually has a son, Isaac, with his wife, whom God renames Sarah when she becomes pregnant. He and his household, which includes Sarah's Egyptian maid Hagar and her son with Abraham, Ishmael, are completely surrounded by Canaanite peoples. The question arises as to whom Isaac will marry. Here Abraham is clear (Genesis 24:2–4):

> 2. Abraham said to his servant, the oldest of his house, who had charge of all that he had, 'Put your hand under my thigh
>
> 3. and I will make you swear by the Lord, the God of heaven and earth, that you will not get a wife for my son from the daughters of the Canaanites, among whom I live,

4. but will go to my country and to my kindred and get a wife for my son Isaac.'

Isaac must also marry within Terah's clan but, with a generation gone by, he has more choices and, furthermore, he does not have a sister to marry. Abraham is forceful here. He makes his servant swear an oath packed with symbolism. Not only must he swear by Yahweh, he must also put his hand under Abraham's 'thigh'. Commentators agree that this expression means placing his hand on or near Abraham's genitals, the source of his procreative and masculine power (von Rad 1961; Sarna 2001). Anyone who breaks such an oath will be in big trouble. Abraham is not going to have a wife for his son from anyone other than a legitimate heiress of his lineage.

Abraham is a rich pastoralist with camels, cattle, sheep and goats. He sends his servant with ten camels and other gifts in search of a suitable bride. Gifts from the groom or groom's family to the bride's father and family, called bride wealth, is still the norm in many pastoralist cultures. Read Genesis 24 to get the full story of how the servant travels north to the land where Abraham's kin live and how he finds Rebekah, the perfect wife for Isaac. Briefly, the servant travels to the city of Nahor and when he arrives asks God for a sign concerning which of the young women coming to the city's well is suitable as a bride for Isaac. God indicates Rebekah to the servant, and he then showers her with gifts. She walks back home from the well laden with Abraham's gold: a large nose ring and two golden bracelets. She is the chosen one. The servant gives more gifts to her and her father. In return, she leaves her family, and journeys with the servant to Canaan to marry Isaac and have children.

The bride wealth ensures that Rebekah is completely severed from her birth family and cannot go back, because under those circumstances her father would have to return the gifts. Pastoralist fathers are reluctant to return bride-wealth gifts. They have sons whose marriages will require gifts and for whom they often use incoming bride wealth. A married daughter's bride wealth is likely to have been used for her brothers' marriages and widely dispersed.

Rebekah is related to Isaac in several ways. Following the male line, Abraham's brother, Nahor, had a son, Bethuel – Isaac's first cousin. Rebekah is Bethuel's daughter, so she is Isaac's first cousin once removed. In English kinship terminology a first cousin is any relative in your generation who shares a grandparent with you and is not your sibling. A second cousin is anyone who does not share a grandparent with you but who shares a great-grandparent. A third cousin is someone who shares only a great-great-grandparent, and so on. If the two people involved are in different generations, and so trace a different number of steps back to a common ancestor, the difference in the number of steps is referred to as degrees 'removed'.

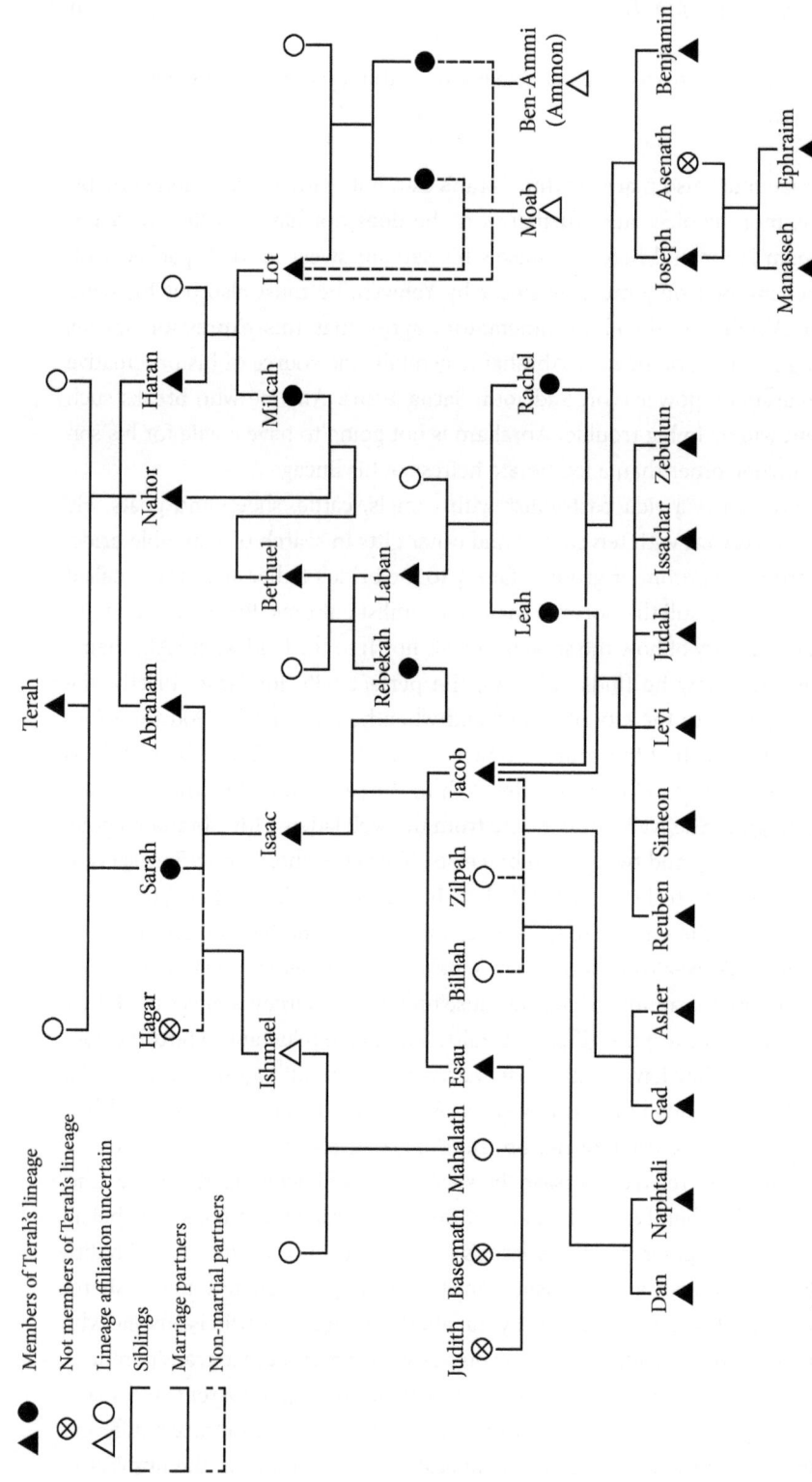

Figure 6.2 Terah's lineage.

Keeping it in the family

Isaac was Rebekah's first cousin once removed when traced through the male line. She was also his first cousin twice removed when traced through Bethuel's mother, Milkah. Either way, Isaac was related to Rebekah through both her father and her mother, and also through his father and his mother. They were quadruply related; technically they were 'double cousins'. And that's the whole point. This was a truly endogamous union, symbolizing the ideal for future generations.

Many (foreign) wives, many problems

Back in Canaan, Isaac and Rebekah have twin sons: Esau and Jacob. Although Esau is the elder and therefore likely to be favoured, he does just about everything wrong, including marrying the wrong women. He has three wives, which is not a problem in and of itself. Anthropologists apply the term polygamy to a marriage in which one person has multiple spouses, with gender undefined. Polygyny refers to a marriage of a man to more than one woman. A much less common form of plural marriage is polyandry, in which a woman is married to multiple men.

Polygyny has probably always been a common form of marriage worldwide. In contemporary societies where polygyny is allowed, however, most men are monogamous. Having multiple wives, especially when bride wealth is involved, is often a sign of a man's wealth. David and Solomon had enormous numbers of wives, symbolizing their wealth and power. Solomon is reputed to have had more than 700. While having that many wives does indeed indicate Solomon's overflowing riches, there is a problem. It was impossible for him to have hundreds of wives who were all legitimate descendants within Terah's lineage; many of them were outsiders. Having many 'foreign' wives eventually got Solomon into trouble. The Deuteronomists describe the problem in a nutshell (1 Kings 11:1–4):

> 1. King Solomon loved many foreign women along with the daughter of Pharaoh: Moabite, Ammonite, Edomite, Sidonian, and Hittite women,

> 2. from the nations concerning which the Lord had said to the Israelites, 'You shall not enter into marriage with them, neither shall they with you; for they will surely incline your heart to follow their gods'; Solomon clung to these in love.

> 3. Among his wives were seven hundred princesses and three hundred concubines; and his wives turned away his heart.

4. For when Solomon was old, his wives turned away his heart after other gods; and his heart was not true to the Lord his God, as was the heart of his father David.

The lesson is simply, marry foreigners and you are in danger of adopting their customs and thus diluting your own culture. The previous chapter outlined the perils of Judean women marrying foreigners. Here we see the mirror image that completes the rule of endogamy for men. Neither Judean women nor men should marry outsiders.

Esau also marries foreign women, and by so doing he and his line are removed from the patriarchal narrative. He becomes an irrelevance, even though he is the first-born. Jacob steals Esau's birthright in actions that have little to do with marriage, but Esau directly disobeys his father concerning whom to marry (Genesis 28). Isaac tells his sons not to marry Canaanite women; Jacob heeds the advice and Esau does not. The genealogies of Esau are slightly obscure when it comes to the identity of Esau's first two wives (Genesis 26 and 36), although there is no doubt that they are foreigners. Genesis 26 records that they are both Hittites. The Biblical table of nations (Genesis 10) places the Hittites (sons of Heth) in the direct line of Canaan, making them one of the explicitly forbidden nations for marriage partners for the descendants of Abraham.

The first mention of these Hittite wives comes directly before the narrative in which Jacob steals Esau's blessing from their father, Isaac. The implication is that, even though Jacob's actions are a trick, Esau has already proven unworthy to be the male heir because of his marriages. So, the trick is justified. But there is also condemnation from his parents:

34. When Esau was forty years old, he married Judith daughter of Beeri the Hittite, and Basemath daughter of Elon the Hittite;

35. and they made life bitter for Isaac and Rebekah (Genesis 26:34–5).

Rebekah's bitterness acts as a provocation for her subterfuge (discussed in the next chapter), through which she helps Jacob to appropriate Isaac's blessing from Esau. She complains about the Hittite wives (Genesis 27:46):

46. Then Rebekah said to Isaac, 'I am weary of my life because of the Hittite women. If Jacob marries one of the Hittite women such as these, one of the women of the land, what good will my life be to me?'

Keeping it in the family

Esau has done the unthinkable. If Jacob follows suit, the line of Terah will become worthless. Jacob must marry someone within the direct line of Terah to preserve the purity of the lineage. Esau eventually realizes his error and tries to do the right thing by marrying a descendant of Abraham. But he still gets it wrong.

> 6. Now Esau saw that Isaac had blessed Jacob and sent him away to Paddan-aram to take a wife from there, and that as he blessed him he charged him, 'You shall not marry one of the Canaanite women',
>
> 7. and that Jacob had obeyed his father and his mother and gone to Paddan-aram.
>
> 8. So when Esau saw that the Canaanite women did not please his father Isaac,
>
> 9. Esau went to Ishmael and took Mahalath daughter of Abraham's son Ishmael, and sister of Nebaioth, to be his wife in addition to the wives he had.

The problem is that Ishmael was Abraham's son by Hagar, Sarah's Egyptian maid. Ishmael and Hagar are eventually exiled on Sarah's command, so as to be certain that it is her son Isaac who is the inheritor of the direct lineage. Ishmael, by contrast, lives in the desert as an exile and eventually marries an Egyptian. So, his daughter, whom Esau marries, is as much a foreigner as any Canaanite.

Instead of sending a servant north to find a wife from his kin in Haran, Jacob flees there himself to escape Esau's anger over losing his paternal blessing. There he meets up with his mother's brother, Laban, and falls in love with his daughter, Rachel (his first cousin). Although Jacob is renowned as the master of trickery, this trait clearly runs in the family, because Laban outwits him in his efforts to marry Rachel. Jacob agrees to work for Laban for seven years as his gift for Rachel's hand. Anthropologists refer to this practice as brideservice, the labour version of bride wealth, in which a husband works for a specified time for the wife's family. On his wedding night, though, he finds himself in bed with Rachel's elder sister Leah, whom Laban has switched for Rachel. Laban is coy, but unrepentant. He tells Jacob that it is their custom to marry the eldest daughter first; so, if Jacob wants Rachel he has to marry Leah first. Jacob agrees and does another seven years of brideservice. He finally gets Rachel, his beloved.

With his two wives, and their maids as concubines, Jacob eventually has twelve sons. Leah is blessed because she has so many sons, but Rachel, who initially has none, is cursed. Rachel refers to herself as essentially 'dead' if she cannot bear children, echoing Sarah's sentiment about having foreigners as grandchildren (Genesis 30:1–8):

1. When Rachel saw that she bore Jacob no children, she envied her sister; and she said to Jacob, 'Give me children, or I shall die!'

2. Jacob became very angry with Rachel and said, 'Am I in the place of God, who has withheld from you the fruit of the womb?'

3. Then she said, 'Here is my maid Bilhah; go in to her, that she may bear upon my knees and that I too may have children through her.'

4. So she gave him her maid Bilhah as a wife; and Jacob went in to her.

5. And Bilhah conceived and bore Jacob a son.

6. Then Rachel said, 'God has judged me, and has also heard my voice and given me a son'; therefore she named him Dan.[10]

7. Rachel's maid Bilhah conceived again and bore Jacob a second son.

8. Then Rachel said, 'With mighty wrestlings I have wrestled[11] with my sister, and have prevailed'; so she named him Naphtali.

The text hints at a kind of socially acceptable surrogate motherhood. By placing one of the newborns on Rachel's knees (which may be a euphemism for genitals), she accepts the children as her own. Such a practice may have occurred widely in the ancient Near East, as a way of avoiding the shame of

---

10   Hebrew for 'judge'.
11   Hebrew for 'I have wrestled' is *niphtalti* which sounds like Naphtali.

infertility. 'Be fruitful and multiply' is an absolute command for the exiles. When Leah ceases bearing children, she emulates Rachel and gives Jacob her maid as a concubine. The text often uses the Hebrew terms for 'wife' and 'concubine' interchangeably. The main difference between a wife and a concubine is that, in the case of a concubine, the groom's family does not give bride wealth to, or perform brideservice for, the woman's family.

The question as to whether the children born of a concubine become members of the father's patrilineage or not rests on decisions made by the father's wife: a rare case of a woman's direct agency, discussed more fully later (Chapter 10). Sarah, troubled by her own childlessness, allows Abraham to have a son, Ishmael, by her maid/slave woman, but then actively rejects him as a legitimate member of the patriline (see Chapter 7 for details). In this case Abraham is torn, because Ishmael is his firstborn, but it is Sarah's decision, not Abraham's, that is decisive. In Rachel's, and later Leah's, case, the outcome is the complete reverse. Rachel, through a symbolic act that could well be imitative of childbirth, accepts her maid's sons as her own biological offspring, and, hence, they become legitimate members of Jacob's patriline. Her actual biological firstborn, Joseph, has much higher status in the lineage, but her maid's sons are full members of the lineage as well – and that decision is Rachel's.

Anthropologists usually use the terms 'pater' (male) and 'mater' (female) to label the socially acknowledged father and mother of a child, and the terms 'genitor' (male) and 'genitrix'[12] (female) to denote the biological parents. This distinction makes sense within the context of modern, Euro-American conceptions of human biology, but it is not as clear-cut as one might hope globally. Different cultures have different ideas concerning the way that sexual reproduction in humans works, so discussions of parentage can get murky. But for the purposes of discussing parentage and inheritance in Genesis, its biological concepts are in line with our own.

Genesis treats Jacob as both the pater and the genitor of all twelve of his sons, who grow up to be the heads of the twelve tribes of Israel. In terms of paternity, all twelve are nominally equal, with Reuben theoretically occupying a special place as the firstborn (although things get complicated later – pp. 139ff.). It is maternity that is the deciding factor in the overall ranking of the sons/tribes – not paternity. The tribes associated with Rachel are a good case in point. Two of Jacob's sons, Dan and Naphtali, are the biological offspring of Rachel's maid, Bilhah, and two, Joseph and Benjamin, are Rachel's own. In anthropological terms, Rachel is the mater of all four, but the genitrix of only Joseph and Benjamin, while Bilhah is the genitrix of Dan and Naphtali.

---

12   Also often spelled 'genetrix'.

Inasmuch as all four have Rachel as their mater, they are bonded to one another and expected to show loyalty to one another in times of conflict with other tribes, but when it comes to more local affairs, Dan should be more attached to Naphtali than to either Joseph (represented by the 'half tribes' of his sons, Ephraim and Manasseh) or Benjamin. Rachel, being both the mater and genitrix of Joseph and Benjamin gives the tribes descended from them especial prominence. Historically, Manasseh was the largest and most powerful of all the tribes of Israel. Because a 'lowly' slave girl is the genitrix of Dan and Naphtali, their tribes are of much less importance – though not entirely insignificant (see Figure 8.6, p. 127).

Don't covet our daughters

Genesis 34 provides a brief interlude in the Jacob narrative to show what one should do if Canaanites (foreigners) come seeking one of your daughters in marriage. The passage concerns Leah's daughter, Dinah. A Canaanite named Shechem lusts after her and rapes her. He apparently, however, has genuine affection for her. So, he asks his father to go to Jacob and request her hand in marriage. In the process he makes numerous offers, asking Jacob to set the size of the bride wealth as high as he wishes and also to spell out reparations for the rape. He suggests that Jacob's family and the Canaanites can live together in peace, and exchange daughters as brides. In the process they will also share lands and wealth. What he proposes is an immense bargain for the sons of Jacob.

Dinah's brothers feign interest, but set a difficult condition. They ask that the Canaanite men, including Shechem, all be circumcised on the grounds that this is an Israelite custom, and it would be unseemly for their women to sleep with the uncircumcised. Shechem is completely fooled and so hastens to get himself circumcised. His companions follow suit. While their wounds are healing, Dinah's brothers descend on the Canaanites in a fury, slaughter them all, and take their wealth. Such is the punishment for an outsider presuming to marry and have sex with a daughter of Israel.

Odd man out

The real problem case in this whole recital of marriages is Joseph, Rachel's eldest son, who eventually becomes the patriarch of two of the most powerful tribes of Israel: Ephraim and Manasseh. According to Genesis 41, Joseph marries a woman named Asenath, who is the daughter of an Egyptian priest and was given to him by the pharaoh himself. Thus, Joseph married into the cream of Egyptian society. Later commentators and apocryphal writers tried to soften this radical departure from the norms of endogamy by proposing that Asenath really did not look like an Egyptian, but resembled the wives of the former patriarchs, and that when betrothed to Joseph she immediately converted to his religion. This notion is reflected in the work *Joseph and Aseneth* from the first or second century CE (Charlesworth 1985).

Other sources from Jewish Midrash try to place Asenath as the daughter of Dinah (as a result of her rape by Shechem), who was adopted by the Egyptian priest after being forced out of Canaan. This interpretation may help out a little, in that Dinah would fall within Terah's lineage, but Shechem was a Canaanite. Because Shechem was a Canaanite, by inheritance through the male line, Asenath was a Canaanite as well. Asenath could be considered an Israelite only if matrilineal inheritance (in which property and identity pass through the female line) was acceptable among the patriarchs. It is impossible, however, that matrilineal kinship rules prevailed. If they had, there would have been no objection to Israelite women marrying foreigners as their sons would still be Israelite. Clearly, they were not.

Joseph remains a puzzle. He married a rich Egyptian woman and prospered. His sons became powerful too, and the tribes descended from them eventually occupied some of the most fertile land in Palestine. In this one case, exogamy was productive and unpunished.

Further reading

Kinship is a central topic within anthropology. Most specialized studies of kinship are detailed and technical. For further information in more readable form, you might try *Kinship and Gender* by Linda Stone (2006). A website maintained by Brian Schwimmer, of the University of Manitoba provides information about kinship and marriage in tutorial form and ties it to Genesis: www.umanitoba.ca/faculties/arts/anthropology/tutor/kinmenu.html (accessed 29 September 2022). This site will provide more than enough detail on the specifics of kinship for the novice.

Incest is a complex and contested issue. Sigmund Freud's *Totem and Taboo* (1950) offers an old-fashioned and discredited psychoanalytic stance. Freud was not an anthropologist and had no qualms about being ethnocentric when it came to discussing so-called primitive cultures. Anthropological theory has come a long way since his time. A modern survey can be found in Wolf and Durham's *Inbreeding, Incest, and the Incest Taboo* (2004). The opening sections of Joseph Shepher's *Incest* (1983) and *The Red Lamp of Incest* by Robin Fox (1980) also provide helpful surveys, although both are dated and should be read critically. Gregory Leavitt's article, 'Sociobiological Explanations of Incest Avoidance' (1990), discusses claims concerning genetics and incest in human populations from a Darwinian (or sociobiological) viewpoint.

7

Be fruitful and multiply

People who know Genesis only from the short quotations they hear in temple or church are often surprised to discover how much of it is concerned with sex. It permeates the entire book in quite direct language. But this does not mean that Genesis is in any sense prurient or pornographic. All the discussion of approved and forbidden sexual and marital practices is completely pragmatic and directed toward the survival of the Judean people. This chapter looks at the emphasis the patriarchal narratives in Genesis place on fertility and reproduction. This discussion connects to male infant circumcision and bride wealth.

Fertility and God's grace
In the cultural world of Genesis, fertility is a gift from God. When a woman bears children, especially sons, it is through God's gift. When a woman cannot conceive, God has withheld his gift from her for some reason. The man is never at fault. The husband of a wife who cannot conceive is entitled to seek another wife or a concubine so that he may have children. In fact, a good wife who cannot conceive will supply her husband with another sexual partner so that she can have offspring in her stead. As we have seen, the wives of Abraham and Jacob did just that very successfully.

The story of Abraham is of special note because of the circumstances of the birth of his two elder sons. He (called Abram at the time) and his wife Sarai are first introduced in a short genealogical passage at the end of Genesis 11:

> 29. Abram and Nahor took wives; the name of Abram's wife was Sarai, and the name of Nahor's wife was Milcah. She was the daughter of Haran the father of Milcah and Iscah.
>
> 30. Now Sarai was barren; she had no child.

Descriptions of people and their actions are exceptionally rare in the genealogies, which are usually just straight lists of offspring. The mention of daughters and wives is especially uncommon. But here, Sarai is not only mentioned, her infertility is expressly noted. She is a marked woman. The initial scenario plays out in exactly the same way as Rachel's dealings with Jacob (Genesis 16:1–3):

> 1. Now Sarai, Abram's wife, bore him no children. She had an Egyptian slave girl whose name was Hagar,
>
> 2. and Sarai said to Abram, 'You see that the Lord has prevented me from bearing children; go in to my slave girl; it may be that I shall obtain children by her.' And Abram listened to the voice of Sarai.
>
> 3. So, after Abram had lived for ten years in the land of Canaan, Sarai, Abram's wife, took Hagar the Egyptian, her slave girl, and gave her to her husband Abram as a wife.

As with Rachel's maid, Hagar is only a surrogate, and her children will technically be Sarai's. If Sarai accepts Hagar's firstborn as her own, he is the legitimate offspring of Abram and Sarai. The fact that Hagar is an Egyptian is not a problem, because Hagar is not officially acknowledged as the boy's mother. Genetics and biology are irrelevant. If Abram had been married to Hagar, it would have been a different story. Her offspring would then have been her own, and they would have been considered part Egyptian. Abram could then be accused of watering down his heritage and running the risk of assimilating to another culture. But Hagar was merely a household servant, and her reproductivity was yet another service she was expected to offer Sarai, her mistress.

Things start to get uncomfortably complicated when Hagar oversteps the bounds of her role. Instead of acting as Sarai's servant and surrogate, Hagar starts lording it over Sarai (Genesis 16:4–6):

> 4. He [Abram] went in to Hagar, and she conceived; and when she saw that she had conceived, she looked with contempt on her mistress.

5. Then Sarai said to Abram, 'May the wrong done to me be on you! I gave my slave girl to your embrace, and when she saw that she had conceived, she looked on me with contempt. May the Lord judge between you and me!'

6. But Abram said to Sarai, 'Your slave girl is in your power; do to her as you please.' Then Sarai dealt harshly with her, and she ran away from her.

Eventually Hagar returns to Abram's household and bears Ishmael, who grows up to become the ancestor of the Ishmaelites, a nomadic pastoralist culture. The antagonism between Hagar and Sarai continues though, and when Sarai gives birth to Isaac, Sarai drives Hagar and Ishmael out of the household and into exile in the desert, where she expects them to die. Unlike Rachel, Sarai never accepts maternity of her surrogate son born by another women. Therefore, Ishmael is not a full member of the lineage, and so Sarai must make sure Abram exiles him to prevent him from trying to claim the place of the legitimate heir, Isaac (see Chapter 10).

Sarai's infertility is a painful lesson to all childless women. Genesis makes it clear, repeatedly, that an infertile woman has no prestige. The status of women was determined almost exclusively by their ability to bear children, especially sons. Sarai is furious because a foreign slave girl ends up with more status than she. Both she and Rachel claim that being childless is the cultural equivalent of being dead. They are non-existent in the household. In many pastoralist societies, where fertility (of people and of cattle) is the highest value, a woman's infertility may be grounds for divorce. Divorce requires return of the bride wealth from her family to the groom and his family and is an extremely serious matter.

People who live in a culture with a cash economy might view the process of a man and his family transferring goods to a bride's father or family, and receiving the bride in return, as an exploitative act and degrading to women (men essentially buying brides). Anthropologists often take a more nuanced view of bride wealth in terms of how patrilineages work and the reproductive value of women (see e.g. Borgerhoff Mulder 1995; Ensminger and Knight 1997). In anthropological terms, the major players of Genesis were men who lived in a culture that was *patrilineal* (inheritance follows the male line only) and *patrilocal* (married couples live with the families of the groom). Patrilineality is a unilineal (one-line) system of inheritance that contrasts to the view of Western biology, which says that everyone has two parents, who each play a vital role in bringing us into the world. Patrilineal kinship says that only the male line counts: status, wealth, power and identity are determined by the male line, from father to grandfather to great-grandfather and so on back. Mothers and their mothers are of no consequence, and the maternal line involves no property or rights, nor expectations and obligations.

To effect a shift from having two parents of importance to only one requires several acts that are more than token symbols. One is patrilocal residence. Patrilocal residence requires that a bride move from her father's family to live with her husband and his patrilineage. In the cases of Isaac's and Jacob's wives, the physical distance between their families of birth and their new marriage families is considerable. They are geographically cut off from their birth families, and they have to adjust to their new ones. They are, according to the rules of patrilineal identity, never fully members of their husband's family. Only by bearing sons for their husband's lineage do they gain status. Their sons are full members of the patrilineage, and thereby their mothers gain position as well. Leah and Hagar crow about their sons because, with them, they have solidified their places in the patrilineage. Rachel and Sarai are sonless and are, in consequence, powerless.

The second important issue is bride wealth, which compensates a father for the loss of his daughter's labour and her procreative power: it purchases rights in a woman's abilities. Bride wealth also buys the bride's father's rights to the children that the bride bears. Subsequently, the father's patrilineage has complete claim on the children, and the mother's lineage has none. If the wife should leave the marriage for some reason, and thus her husband's patrilineage, she cannot take her children with her because they do not belong to her. Hagar and Ishmael prove this point. When Sarah banishes them, both can leave because Ishmael is not part of Abraham's patrilineage. He did not pay bride wealth for Hagar, and Sarai did not adopted Ishmael. So Ishmael was not enfolded into the lineage of Abraham, and he could be released without harm to either Abraham or the lineage.

The case of Abraham and Sarai is also important with respect to understanding lineage and bride wealth. Hagar was a complete outsider to Terah's line. Even so, she and her son could have been brought into Abraham's patrilineage by payment and by consent of the lineage members. Sarai, on the other hand, was already a full member of the lineage because she and Abraham had the same father. Therefore, her children would not have any ties to another lineage, because there was no separate maternal lineage for them to belong to. Their maternal line was also their paternal line. Abraham's kin could not have paid bride wealth for Sarai, because Abraham and Sarai were siblings: Abraham's father would have had to pay the bride wealth to himself.

The fact that Abram and Sarai are siblings means that they cannot divorce without tearing the family apart – another aspect of the family-disruption theory of incest. Sex and marriage with biologically close kin may set up rivalries and jealousies when things are going well, but divorce of these close kin would be even more problematic, setting siblings and parents against one another. Abraham and Sarai, therefore, have to just hope for the best in regard to her infertility. Like many other couples with fertility problems, Abraham and Sarai were eventually successful. Sarai was supposedly ninety years old when she conceived Isaac! The underlying message is that one should never give up on a woman's reproductive capacity, and, hence, infertility is never an ironclad reason for divorce. Thus, biologically close kin marriages are stabilized, and family disruption via divorce proceedings is avoided.

Covenants, reproduction and male circumcision
The supreme value of having a legitimate male heir to continue one's lineage is given ritual and symbolic power by two covenants between God and Abraham. The first, described in Genesis 15, is difficult to understand. The second, from Genesis 17, concerns the institution of male infant circumcision. Both lean heavily on the concept of separation that is so important throughout Genesis. In chapter 15, God comes to Abraham and promises that he will have offspring beyond number (Genesis 15:5):

> 5. He brought him outside and said, 'Look towards heaven and count the stars, if you are able to count them.' Then he said to him, 'So shall your descendants be.'

After this promise comes the following scene (Genesis 15:7–11):

> 7. Then he said to him, 'I am the Lord who brought you from Ur of the Chaldeans, to give you this land to possess.'
>
> 8. But he said, 'O Lord God, how am I to know that I shall possess it?'
>
> 9. He said to him, 'Bring me a heifer three years old, a female goat three years old, a ram three years old, a turtle-dove, and a young pigeon.'
>
> 10. He brought him all these and cut them in two, laying each half over against the other; but he did not cut the birds in two.
>
> 11. And when birds of prey came down on the carcasses, Abram drove them away.

Intimations of an ancient magical rite are embedded in this passage. In ancient Mesopotamia, land grants to vassals by overlords were accompanied by just such a ritual in which the overlord and the vassal walked between the halves of split animals as the sign of a solemn oath sealed in blood (Ellickson and Thorland 1995). Reference to a similar ritual covenant appears in Jeremiah 34:18–20:

> 18. And those who transgressed my covenant and did not keep the terms of the covenant that they made before me, I will make like the calf when they cut it in two and passed between its parts:

> 19. the officials of Judah, the officials of Jerusalem, the eunuchs, the priests, and all the people of the land who passed between the parts of the calf

> 20. shall be handed over to their enemies and to those who seek their lives. Their corpses shall become food for the birds of the air and the wild animals of the earth.

Here Jeremiah is prophesying what will happen should such a covenant be broken, in this case the Babylonian Exile. The offenders are slain and left for carrion. Presumably Abram drives off the birds from the carcasses as a sign that he will not break the covenant.

In verse 10 the imagery is compelling. While most commentators shy away from the literal meaning of the passage, Robert Alter's translation provides a version that is closer to the Hebrew than most:

> 10. And he took all of these and clove them through the middle, and each set his part opposite the other…

That is, Abraham took the animals and split them in two. Then he took one side and Yahweh took the other, each taking the corresponding halves of the cloven animals and laying them out in two symmetrical files with an aisle down the middle. The blatant anthropomorphism, with Yahweh acting like a human, is too theologically problematic for most translators, but it helps explain the passage. The God who created the world by separating opposites is using the same symbolism of separation to establish his bond with Abraham. The aisle in the middle is the boundary between the world of God and the world of mortals. This aisle also prefigures the boundary that must remain between Abraham's kin and other peoples of the world. Having separated the animal halves, the covenant is further affirmed by one final act from Yahweh (Genesis 15:17):

17. When the sun had gone down and it was dark, a smoking fire-pot and a flaming torch passed between these pieces.

While the language of this passage is obscure, my interpretation is that at night Yahweh, in the form of smoke and flame, passed down the central aisle and validated the process.

The covenant act that establishes male circumcision in Genesis 17 is a much clearer act of separation and separate identity for Abraham and his offspring. It begins with yet another promise that Abraham's progeny will be boundless (Genesis 17:2–6):

2. And I will make my covenant between me and you, and will make you exceedingly numerous.'

3. Then Abram fell on his face; and God said to him,

4. 'As for me, this is my covenant with you: You shall be the ancestor of a multitude of nations.

5. No longer shall your name be Abram, but your name shall be Abraham; for I have made you the ancestor of a multitude of nations.

6. I will make you exceedingly fruitful; and I will make nations of you, and kings shall come from you.

The name change seals Abram's destiny. The etymology of the two names is, however, controversial. Both contain the initial Hebrew root *ab*, meaning 'father' or 'ancestor', which is found in a large number of Hebrew names: Abner (father of light), Abimelech (father of the king), Abimael (father of fatness), Abishag (father of error), Absalom (father of peace) and so forth. Commentators normally accept fairly straightforward meanings such as 'father of greatness' for Abram and 'father of nations' for Abraham. The two are quite closely related, in any case, but the etymologies are more based in folklore, as evidenced in the Genesis text, than in scientific linguistics. The main point is that Abraham's fatherhood as a progenitor is his key trait, established by God and enshrined in a name. He is to be the father of multitudes, and that is his chief claim to fame.

God seals the bargain by asking Abraham to circumcise himself and all the male members of his household. While many cultures use permanent physical marks to indicate ethnic and gender identity, this particular brand of body marking is special for several reasons. First, the permanent mark is on the penis. Many ethnic identity markers are placed, even more visibly, on the face, arms, legs or chest. Male circumcision is generally not visible in everyday public life, but it cannot be disguised during sexual intercourse. The female partner will certainly know whether the man she is in bed with is a descendant of Abraham or not.

Ritual male circumcision is common in cultures around the world from Africa to Asia and Oceania. To the best of my knowledge, though, in all non-Western cultures in which ritual male circumcision is practised, it is a rite of passage conducted either when a boy is a young child or around the time of puberty. In the case of the Judeans, God commands Abraham to circumcise the male members of his household, but then adds (Genesis 17:12–14):

> 12. Throughout your generations every male among you shall be circumcised when he is eight days old, including the slave born in your house and the one bought with your money from any foreigner who is not of your offspring.
>
> 13. Both the slave born in your house and the one bought with your money must be circumcised. So shall my covenant be in your flesh an everlasting covenant.
>
> 14. Any uncircumcised male who is not circumcised in the flesh of his foreskin shall be cut off from his people; he has broken my covenant.'

The Bible conveys the sense that infant (within a few days of birth) male circumcision was a highly distinctive Judaic practice in the ancient world. It is thus almost certain that infant male circumcision separated out the Judean exiles from all other peoples in Babylonia. Today, the circumcision of newborns is not a ritual practice outside the Abrahamic faiths – although it is a common medical procedure which entails no ritual obligations (Gollaher 2001).

God makes it crystal clear in this passage, using the language of separation, that any male who is not circumcised will be cut off from Abraham's people. Parentage is not sufficient to be a member of the culture. More than the right bloodline, a male must bear the permanent, ineradicable, outward mark of ethnic origin. Abraham's people are completely separate from others.

Producing an heir, no matter what

Any man who ignores the commandment to keep separate from other people gets forcibly separated from the chosen lineage. In Leviticus 20 the clear implication of many of the commandments concerning marriage and sexual behaviour is that doing the wrong thing means being 'cut off' because of your sins: either you will die or be childless, or both. 'Cut off' means that your lineage ends with you.

A counter position exists though. Just because a man has died childless does not mean that his lineage will end. Under the right circumstances he can be dead and yet still produce heirs. This seeming paradox reminds us once again that kinship is more concerned with cultural rules than with biological facts. To see this paradox in play, consider the tale of Judah and his sons found in Genesis 38. The story begins in a most inauspicious way with Judah marrying outside his patrilineage (Genesis 38:1–5):

> 1. It happened at that time that Judah went down from his brothers and settled near a certain Adullamite whose name was Hirah.
>
> 2. There Judah saw the daughter of a certain Canaanite whose name was Shua; he married her and went in to her.
>
> 3. She conceived and bore a son; and he named him Er.
>
> 4. Again she conceived and bore a son whom she named Onan.
>
> 5. Yet again she bore a son, and she named him Shelah.

Judah is not supposed to marry a Canaanite, and so the story is likely to end unhappily. The story continues as follows (Genesis 38:6–9):

> 6. Judah took a wife for Er his firstborn; her name was Tamar.
>
> 7. But Er, Judah's firstborn, was wicked in the sight of the Lord, and the Lord put him to death.
>
> 8. Then Judah said to Onan, 'Go in to your brother's wife and perform the duty of a brother-in-law to her; raise up offspring for your brother.'
>
> 9. But since Onan knew that the offspring would not be his, he spilled his semen on the ground whenever he went in to his brother's wife, so that he would not give offspring to his brother.

To some extent, the precise nature of Er's wickedness is not important because the story is really about what happens after he dies. There is, however, a direct implication that none of this would have happened if Judah's wife were from acceptable stock. So Er is out of the picture and his younger brother has an obligation that anthropologists call *levirate* marriage, that is, the legal duty of a younger brother to marry his elder brother's widow.

Tamar, the wife, has not done anything wrong. The fact that she has no children is not her fault at all. Therefore, she cannot reasonably be sent back to her father's lineage, and Judah cannot reasonably reclaim her bride wealth. So, he has to keep her and make the best of it. After all, at this point Judah's lineage is as much in jeopardy as Er's. If Er has no sons, Judah's patrilineage is threatened as well. The compromise position of levirate marriage requires Judah to transfer Tamar to her dead husband's brother, Onan, so that she can conceive children by him. Even though the offspring of such a union are biologically Onan's, they are socially the offspring of the dead brother whose line is thereby continued. That is, in anthropological language, while Onan would be the genitor, Er would be the pater. Judah commands Onan to take Tamar as much for his own sake as for Er's. If Er has no sons, not only will his lineage die, Judah's will die also.

Onan objects. While the text says nothing about Onan's marital state, it seems reasonably certain that he does not have a wife of his own. It appears that Onan had no objection to having a sexual partner and did go 'in to his brother's wife' – that is, he had some form of sexual interaction with her, though it is impossible to know the details. The English word 'onanism' is a synonym for masturbation, but this is a modern Christian interpretation based on a misunderstanding of the text. Most Biblical commentators agree that Onan was not masturbating when he visited Tamar: he was practicing coitus interruptus. It does not matter, however, what Onan did with Tamar. His sin was refusing to get her pregnant no matter the precise method.

Onan's sin and complications for Judah

Onan's sin has multiple facets. First, his act of birth control denies heirs to his father, Judah, as Onan has no wife of his own. Thus, he is a threat to the continuance of Judah's patrilineage. Second, he is denying Tamar her rightful place in the household, as a woman who has no children is socially dead and has no status. The childless Tamar is a non-person who needs Onan's seed to bring her to life within the lineage. Third, Onan is cutting off his brother, Er, from the lineage. If Er has no sons, he has no place in history.

Onan is being greedy and selfish. Presumably, he would not have minded the situation if Judah had also found him a wife of his own. If he had had his own wife in addition to Tamar, he could father sons with Tamar to continue Er's line, and father sons by his other wife to start his own lineage. Onan's chief complaint was that if he has sons with Tamar then they will not be counted as his, they will be Er's. Therefore he, Onan, will fail to have a lineage of his own and have no place in history. Financial greed may also play a part here, in that if Onan's seed begets a son who is counted socially as Er's offspring, Judah's wealth will, through the rules of patrilineal inheritance, pass to that son and not to Onan. If Er has no sons, the patrimony must pass to Onan.

God does not approve of such selfishness. Procreation for the continuance of the lineage comes first, and personal interests are a distant second. Hence (Genesis 38:10-11):

> 10. What he [Onan] did was displeasing in the sight of the Lord, and he put him to death also.

> 11. Then Judah said to his daughter-in-law Tamar, 'Remain a widow in your father's house until my son Shelah grows up' – for he feared that he too would die, like his brothers. So Tamar went to live in her father's house.

Judah's hopes for a healthy lineage are in trouble. He has only one son left, Shelah, and he's a youth. Judah should have kept Tamar as a widow in his household until Shelah had grown up and taken her (Tamar) as his wife according to the levirate. As long as Tamar is childless it is the responsibility of her husband's brothers to get her pregnant.

Judah has to partner Shelah and Tamar, but he is terrified that if something goes wrong he will lose his last surviving son. What if in haste, for example, he couples them when Shelah is still too young to sire children? Will God kill him and leave Judah without sons? He does not want to risk it. So, he sends Tamar back to her father, which would be shameful for her because she has no status there. It is understood that the arrangement is meant to be temporary. Tamar ultimately belongs in Judah's household, and will return as soon as Shelah has grown up.

Further complications for Judah

Time passes and Judah's wife dies. Judah, therefore, has one surviving son and no chance for more. While he might have thought of coupling Tamar and Shelah, instead he observes the usual mourning period and goes off to a place called Timnah to meet his sheep shearers. Shearing time was traditionally a period of high fun and games. Judah wants to party and act irresponsibly. Tamar gets wind of his plans and sets about to waylay him, tricking Judah into fulfilling his responsibilities to her. She has been dressed as a widow in her father's house, but she sheds these clothes and dresses like a prostitute, with her face veiled so that she will not be recognized. She waits along the way to Timnah to spring a trap for the party boy, Judah, as he travels by.

Judah sees Tamar and, thinking she is a prostitute, wants to have sex with her as part of his holiday revels. She demands a young kid from his herd as a fee. Admitting that he does not have one with him, he leaves his signature cylinder (a seal used for putting his personal mark to official documents) and his staff as a surety until he can send along the promised kid and reclaim his possessions. After their brief sexual encounter, Judah goes on his way and Tamar dresses again in her widow's clothes and returns to her father. Later, Judah sends a kid through his friend to the spot where he met Tamar. There is no prostitute there, and no one in the vicinity knows anything about the woman. So, Judah resolves to forget the issue rather than pursue it and look like a fool to all his friends. While he has lost his seal and staff, he is at least satisfied that he tried to do the right thing and pay for the prostitute's services.

Three months later Judah hears that Tamar is pregnant. He is outraged. He has not done the right thing by her by giving her as a wife to Shelah, but she is still a member of his household and his responsibility. Her procreative power still belongs to him. She appears to have committed adultery and, therefore, has endangered Judah's lineage. The normal judicial penalty for adultery is death for both parties involved. Judah demands that Tamar be burned for her sins. In response, she sends the signature cylinder and staff to Judah with word that it was the owner of these items who got her pregnant.

Judah is abjectly apologetic. He acknowledges that he was in the wrong for not coupling her with Shelah to have children, and that her actions forced the issue of getting her pregnant in a blameless way. The narrative does not in any way suggest that Tamar has done anything wrong. She needed to mate with someone in Judah's patrilineage, and did so. She is the righteous heroine. In fact, she is pregnant with twins, and one of them is the ancestor of the royal line of King David and his mighty dynasty. There is no sense that the children are illegitimate or disadvantaged in any way.

In fact, Tamar did Judah an enormous favour. We know nothing about her lineage, but the silence of the text on the matter suggests approval. In other situations, when members of Terah's line marry or have children with Canaanites and other forbidden foreigners, the text mentions it. The text also notes that when Judah married a Canaanite woman, he produced sons that were wayward, wicked, selfish and greedy. When he slept with Tamar, he produced sons who were strong and righteous. Tamar's agency was exceptionally powerful in producing a healthy lineage for Judah.

Could it be that Tamar was an acceptable partner for Judah, producing good sons in consequence, as opposed to his Canaanite wife, who was unacceptable and therefore, produced wicked sons? Regardless of the rights and wrongs of the liaison, the text makes it clear that Judah and Tamar never had sex again. Once she had given birth, the obligations of the levirate were satisfied.

The law with respect to avoiding one's obligations under levirate marriage rules was explicit and severe. Here is the pertinent section from Deuteronomy 25:5–10:

> 5. When brothers reside together, and one of them dies and has no son, the wife of the deceased shall not be married outside the family to a stranger. Her husband's brother shall go in to her, taking her in marriage, and performing the duty of a husband's brother to her,
>
> 6. and the firstborn whom she bears shall succeed to the name of the deceased brother, so that his name may not be blotted out of Israel.
>
> 7. But if the man has no desire to marry his brother's widow, then his brother's widow shall go up to the elders at the gate and say, 'My husband's brother refuses to perpetuate his brother's name in Israel; he will not perform the duty of a husband's brother to me.'
>
> 8. Then the elders of his town shall summon him and speak to him. If he persists, saying, 'I have no desire to marry her',
>
> 9. then his brother's wife shall go up to him in the presence of the elders, pull his sandal off his foot, spit in his face, and declare, 'This is what is done to the man who does not build up his brother's house.'
>
> 10. Throughout Israel his family shall be known as 'the house of him whose sandal was pulled off.'

Procreate or be eternally shamed. The law is merciless when it comes to dealing with actions that threaten the fertility (e.g. Deuteronomy 25:11–12). Likewise, people who are fertile should keep reproducing until the day they die. There is no benefit to Judean culture in having prosperous, well-to-do people remain unmarried, even if they are old. If they are still capable of having children, then they should be having children. Abraham, for example, loved his wife Sarah very much, and when she died he made elaborate plans to bury her in such a way that his love for her was manifest. Then he found another wife, Keturah, and had six sons by her (Genesis 25:1–2). His main patriline was secure through Isaac, but there was still every good reason to want to keep producing sons. The commandment to be fruitful and multiply extends to the day you die.

Further reading

For anthropological perspectives on fertility and reproduction, see chapters in Susan Greenhalgh ed., *Situating Fertility* (1995); Faye Ginsburg and Rayna Rapp eds, *Conceiving the New World Order* (1995) and Soraya Tremayne ed., *Managing Reproductive Life* (2001).

The classic article on the levirate in South Asia is Kashyap P. Chattopadhyay's 'Levirate and kinship in India' (1922). A more up-to-date examination of levirate practices cross-culturally, especially in the ancient Near East, can be found in Jack Goody's *The Oriental, The Ancient and The Primitive* (1990).

For an overview of bride wealth and other economic aspects of marriage practices see Jack Goody and Stanley J. Tambiah's *Bridewealth and Dowry* (1974). There is also a cogent and nuanced analysis in David Graeber's *Debt: The First 5,000 Years* (2011:131ff.).

For polygyny worldwide, see Douglas R. White, 'Rethinking polygyny: co-wives, codes, and cultural systems' (1988) and John Dalton and Tin Cheuk Leung, 'Why is polygyny more prevalent in western Africa? An African slave trade perspective' (2014).

A non-technical work that looks at aspects of medical and ritual male circumcision is David Gollaher's *Circumcision* (2001).

8

What's my line?

The genealogies provide the framework for the entire narrative structure of Genesis. Without them, Genesis would be a series of loosely connected stories with numerous gaps. If we continue my analogy of Genesis as a patchwork quilt (Chapter 1), the genealogies are the threads that stitch all the scraps together, and they provide the borders, backing and other materials that transform the pieces from individual units into a single integrated whole. No matter what metaphor you use, the genealogies are vital to the coherence of the work as a whole.

When reading the genealogies in Genesis, and elsewhere in the Bible, it is easy to think of them as tedious, pointless and not worth your time, but to the redactors of Genesis, and many of its readers, they were profoundly compelling: they told a vital story in much the same way that some modern readers are riveted by a detective story. When you know how to read them, the genealogies in Genesis reveal how the authors conceived of social structure in general, and kinship more particularly. Before looking at individual genealogies and their specific members, we can look at the pattern of the genealogies as a whole and make some important points about ancient Hebrew social structure. Two technical areas we need to explore are unilineal descent and segmentary lineages. Both govern the way genealogies are recounted in Genesis and are fundamental to the cultures of ancient Judah and Israel.

The patrilineages that I mentioned in Chapter 7 are a type of unilineal descent, in which children gain their status and position in their societies from one parent only: either the mother or the father. All males in a particular patrilineage can trace a single line of descent, through males only, back to the founder of the lineage. Most of the genealogies in Genesis are straight patrilineal lines of descent of this sort. Here is an example, part of the genealogy of Cain from Genesis 4:17–18:

17. Cain knew his wife, and she conceived and bore Enoch; and he built a city, and named it Enoch after his son Enoch.

18. To Enoch was born Irad; and Irad was the father of Mehujael, and Mehujael the father of Methushael, and Methushael the father of Lamech.

A single line of males connects father/son relationships from Cain down through Enoch, Irad, Mehujael, and Methushael to Lamech. No women are mentioned, because they are not an essential part of the patrilineage. This genealogy is also notable because it excludes younger brothers or younger sons. Only eldest sons can represent the central spine of the patrilineage. Brothers or younger sons have status only because they are related to this spine, which is why the levirate was so important in Mosaic law. As noted in the last chapter, Er, Judah's eldest son, had to have a son of his own, otherwise the spine of the lineage would have been broken. This principle of only the eldest son inheriting property and position from his father is known as primogeniture, and it is the prevailing descent rule in the Genesis genealogies.

When I drew Figure 6.2 (p. 92) I was following the conventions of modern anthropology and not the kinship norms of the ancient Judeans. The diagram would not have made much sense to the authors of Genesis because it shows more links and connections than an ancient Judean audience cared about. Anthropologists call such groupings of people on a diagram, related in multiple ways, a kindred, a specialized form of kinship chart in which multiple lines of descent and relationship are all displayed together. The authors of Genesis were concerned only with single lines of descent through males, and not with these complicated tangles of multiple relationships mapped in kindreds. That is why it was perfectly convenient for them to relate them in lines of text (or speech).

To understand the difference between a modern kindred-based approach to descent and a unilineal one, we can explore in more detail how the Judeans would have traced Jacob's relationship to his wives. Modern Euro-Americans would most likely look at Figure 6.2 and declare that Leah and Rachel are Jacob's first cousins (they are Jacob's mother's brother's daughters). The people who lived at the time that Genesis was redacted would have known that Jacob and his wives were first cousins through the female line, but they probably would have preferred to trace his relationship to them through patrilineal descent lines. Figure 8.1 shows how Leah and Rachel are related to Jacob using patrilineal descent only.

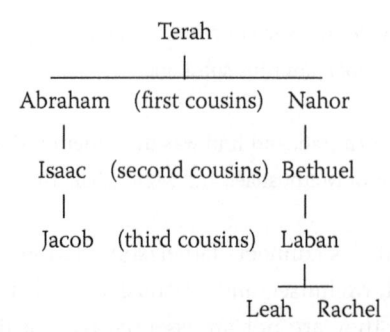

```
                        Terah
              ┌───────────┴───────────┐
          Abraham   (first cousins)  Nahor
             │                         │
           Isaac   (second cousins) Bethuel
             │                         │
           Jacob   (third cousins)   Laban
                                       │
                                  ┌────┴────┐
                                 Leah    Rachel
```

Figure 8.1 Jacob's patrilineal relationship to his wives.

Jacob's father was Isaac, Isaac's father was Abraham, and Abraham's father was Terah. Terah was also the father of Nahor, who was the father of Bethuel, who was the father of Laban, who was the father of Leah and Rachel. Following the male lines of descent only, Leah and Rachel are Jacob's third cousins once removed.

Patrilineage, male identity, and property in ancient Israel

For the ancient Israelite man, lineage represented his identity in a complex way. As he recited the lineage, the ancestor at its head of would represent the most basic aspects of his self-identity. Then, the various links in the patriline would represent additions to that ancestral base. Take a man from the tribe of Reuben as an example. He is patrilineally descended from Reuben, the founder of the Reubenite tribe. Reuben's father was Jacob, the ancestor of the twelve tribes of Israel. Jacob's father was Isaac, and Isaac's father was Abraham. The genealogies in Genesis trace Abraham all the way back to Adam, and they also show all the branches from the line. But we can stop at Abraham for now because a Reubenite of the time would probably have stopped there: Abraham represents his most basic identity as a member of a distinct ethnicity. If he traced his ancestry all the way back to Adam, he would be saying that he is a brother to all the peoples of the world. For the members of the tribes of Israel, it was more important to identify themselves as descendants of Abraham than as citizens of the world, because they were concerned with separating themselves from the rest of the world and maintaining their distinctiveness.

By reciting his lineage, a Reubenite of the time would be making statements about himself. Abraham was scrupulously obedient to Yahweh, to the point of being willing to sacrifice his son on command, therefore I, as his descendant am loyal to Yahweh. He was circumcised; I am circumcised. Isaac's personality is not all that clear because there are few stories about him. Nonetheless, he seems to have been honest and generous; so I am honest and generous. Jacob was noted for his craftiness and cunning, and so am I. As the father of the nation of Israel, he also provides me with my national identity. I am an Israelite. Finally, I am descended from Reuben, Jacob's eldest son and founder of the tribe of Reuben. He was noted for his judgment and mercy when his brothers tried to kill their youngest brother Joseph. Reuben gives me my tribal identity, as a member of the senior branch of Israel, and empowers me with a strong sense of justice and mercy. I acquire all these qualities through my patriline by a process of accretion.

The patriline was also the avenue for inheritance of property. Eldest sons inherited wealth, land and titles from their fathers, who had inherited them from their fathers and so on: thus, the importance of the eldest son having a son to continue the line. What happens if the eldest son has only daughters? The law says that while a daughter can be an heiress, the property passes from her to her husband and then down through her husband's patriline. This situation has the potential to create long-term problems of property inheritance for the heiress's patrilineage and violates the Genesis rule of separateness and boundedness. Numbers 36:1–4 illustrates the problem using the case of Zelophehad of the tribe of Manasseh, who has daughters but no sons:

> 1. The heads of the ancestral houses of the clans of the descendants of Gilead son of Machir son of Manasseh, of the Josephite clans, came forward and spoke in the presence of Moses and the leaders, the heads of the ancestral houses of the Israelites;

> 2. they said, 'The Lord commanded my lord to give the land for inheritance by lot to the Israelites; and my lord was commanded by the Lord to give the inheritance of our brother Zelophehad to his daughters.

> 3. But if they are married into another Israelite tribe, then their inheritance will be taken from the inheritance of our ancestors and added to the inheritance of the tribe into which they marry; so it will be taken away from the allotted portion of our inheritance.

> 4. And when the jubilee of the Israelites comes, then their inheritance will be added to the inheritance of the tribe into which they have married; and their inheritance will be taken from the inheritance of our ancestral tribe.'

The problem of having no sons starts within the tribe of Manasseh. While it is something that an individual tribe member has to cope with, it has the potential to affect other tribes of Israel. If the predicament had rested inside the tribe of Manasseh the petitioners would have solved it by going to the heads of Manasseh. But because the issue may involve other tribes, they have to go further up the patriline to Moses, who stands as the representative of Jacob, ancestor of all the tribes, for a judgment. Note that the text begins with a recitation of the credentials of the leaders in the form a genealogy. This act validates who they are very specifically, and identifies them as suitable men to be bringing the case.

The problem they are worried about is that Zelophehad has only daughters. What especially concerns the leaders of the tribe of Manasseh is that each of the tribes of Israel occupied areas of Canaan that had been established as their ancestral lands for all time. With the exception of Levi, the tribes had bounded zones in which they lived and owned property. The boundaries of these lands are clearly documented in the book of Numbers. The tribe of Judah, for example, occupied the hill country around Jerusalem. If an heiress from the tribe of Judah married a man from Simeon, the land she stood to inherit would pass to her husband and then to her eldest son. Therefore, what was once a part of Judah would subsequently belong to Simeon. Over time, the boundaries of the tribal lands would become confused, with members of one tribe living on lands that once belonged to another. Remember that God reacts violently when things that are supposed to be separate become mixed. There can be no mixing up of the tribes and their patrimony. Here is the judgment of Moses (Numbers 36:5–9):

> 5. Then Moses commanded the Israelites according to the word of the Lord, saying, 'The descendants of the tribe of Joseph are right in what they are saying.
>
> 6. This is what the Lord commands concerning the daughters of Zelophehad, 'Let them marry whom they think best; only it must be into a clan of their father's tribe that they are married,
>
> 7. so that no inheritance of the Israelites shall be transferred from one tribe to another; for all Israelites shall retain the inheritance of their ancestral tribes.
>
> 8. Every daughter who possesses an inheritance in any tribe of the Israelites shall marry one from the clan of her father's tribe, so that all Israelites may continue to possess their ancestral inheritance.
>
> 9. No inheritance shall be transferred from one tribe to another; for each of the tribes of the Israelites shall retain its own inheritance.

Moses rules that if a daughter is an heiress she must marry within her father's patrilineage. The land she inherits may leave her family or even her clan when she marries, but because of this special rule of patrilineal endogamy, it always stays within the tribe. That way order prevails. Endogamy is, again, the prime method for maintaining social and economic order in the face of potential chaos. Proper rules of kinship and marriage are the keys to social ordering. The Judean exiles were expected to follow these classic rules as yet another reinforcement of their separate nature. In exile, strong patrilineage endogamy played a crucial role in maintaining ethnic identity.

How to read a genealogy

While single male lines of descent are vital to all the Genesis genealogies, there is more to the picture than that. The genealogies in Genesis also have points where the lineages split into separate segments. Here is the continuation of Cain's lineage from Genesis 4:19–22:

> 19. Lamech took two wives; the name of one was Adah, and the name of the other Zillah.
>
> 20. Adah bore Jabal; he was the ancestor of those who live in tents and have livestock.
>
> 21. His brother's name was Jubal; he was the ancestor of all those who play the lyre and pipe.
>
> 22. Zillah bore Tubal-cain, who made all kinds of bronze and iron tools. The sister of Tubal-cain was Naamah.

Many commentators argue that Lamech's polygyny was sinful, but that is not really why his two wives are mentioned here.[13] Polygyny is routine in the detailed narratives of Genesis and is acceptable in Mosaic law. Lamech's two wives are identified because three of his sons are listed – as opposed to the usual citation of the eldest only – and the sons are not all from the same

---

13 Rabbinical scholars, from ancient times, have made much of the fact that Lamech is the first polyginist in Genesis with various negative interpretations: e.g. Jerusalem Talmud (*Yevamot* 6:5, 7c), Midrash (*Tanhuma*, Genesis 11) and Aggadah (*Gen. Rabbah* 23). The general tenor is that as humans developed after Adam, their values weakened (leading to the Flood). Evangelical Christian commentators often follow the moralizing of Victorians such as Charles Ellicott (1897): 'Lamech took unto him two wives. – Whether polygamy began with Lamech is uncertain, but it is in keeping with the insolent character of the man.' (2019: sect. 'Genesis 4:19-22'). Contrariwise, both Jewish and Christian commentaries also note that there is nothing in Mosaic Law making polygyny illegal.

mother. The two mothers have to be listed to show that Jabal and Jubal are full brothers from the senior branch of the lineage, and Tubal-cain is their half-brother from the junior branch. The identification of three brothers, instead of just the eldest, is what anthropologists call a point of segmentation (e.g. Evans-Pritchard 1940:147; Fortes and Evans-Pritchard 1940:296), a splitting of a lineage into multiple branches. (See Figure 8.2 for Cain's complete lineage.) In this case, the point of segmentation leads eventually to each of the three new lineages pursuing three different occupations.

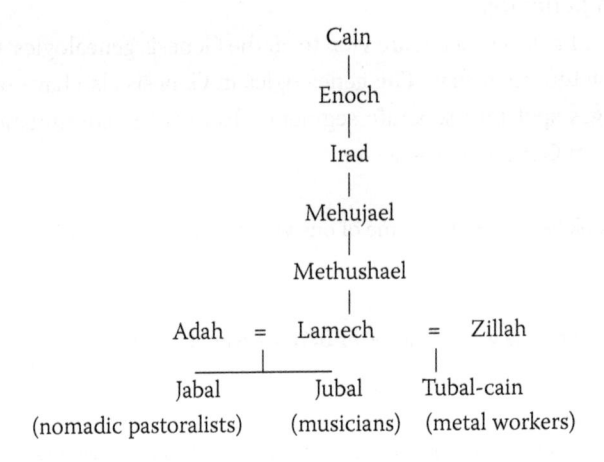

```
                            Cain
                             |
                            Enoch
                             |
                            Irad
                             |
                          Mehujael
                             |
                         Methushael
                             |
         Adah    =       Lamech    =    Zillah
         _____|_____                     |
         Jabal         Jubal           Tubal-cain
   (nomadic pastoralists)  (musicians)  (metal workers)
```

Figure 8.2 Cain's patrilineage.

Here are four guiding questions to ask when looking at a Biblical lineage of this sort.

Question 1: who is at the head of the lineage?

The person at the head of any lineage establishes the essential characteristics of everyone within it. Cain is the head of this lineage, so he gives his name and his identity to his descendants. In English we could call the people descended from Cain the Cainites, although their Biblical name is more usually transliterated as Kenites (or sometimes Kainites). Cain killed his brother Abel and was outcast as a consequence. God condemned him for his barbarous act, yet marked him with a special sign on his forehead to protect him. Genesis does not explain why Cain is under God's protection, but down through the ages the Kenites bore this mark, just as the descendants of Abraham bore the mark of circumcision. They were not to be harmed, and, indeed, the Bible indicates that the Kenites were loyal friends of the Israelites. Even though they were nomadic wanderers – because of their legacy from Cain – they were sophisticated in various arts, such as music and metallurgy, and had a great deal to teach the Israelites about them.

What's my line?

Question 2: how many generations are included in the lineage?
The entire lineage contains seven generations. Seven is a typical round number in Hebrew lineages and so Cain's lineage is satisfyingly complete. Seven and ten, and their multiples, are the standards for numbers of generations in lineages throughout the Bible.

Question 3: where is narrative included and why?
Cain's lineage recitation has narrative in two places only. At the beginning it records that Cain built the first city and named it after his eldest son, Enoch. This account links the building of cities to an outlaw, and so we can expect nothing good to come out of city life. His later descendants are nomads, though, and they are spoken of in much better terms. These descendants represent the beginning of specialization and the division of labour, and they have skills in crafts that everyone can use. The narrative at the end of the lineage recitation mentions the nature of these arts (coupled with a brief mention of Lamech's polygyny).

Question 4: where does the lineage segment and why?
Importantly, Cain's lineage splits, or segments, at the seventh generation. Up until that point it is a straight line with no side branches noted. The patrilineage recorded immediately after Cain's in Genesis 5 has a similar pattern.

```
                    Adam
                     |
                    Seth
                     |
                   Enosh
                     |
                   Kenan
                     |
                  Mahalalel
                     |
                    Jared
                     |
                   Enoch
                     |
                 Methuselah
                     |
                   Lamech
                     |
                    Noah
                     |
        Ham        Shem       Japheth
     (Africans)  (Asians)   (Europeans)
```

Figure 8.3   Adam's patrilineage.

Adam's lineage is ten generations deep before it segments into three parts. Some commentators (e.g. Doedens 2012; Murdoch 1994) describe this lineage as the Sethite lineage, but that is clearly a misnomer. It is headed by Adam in the text and therefore represents the main branch of the lineage from Adam to the Flood. This genealogy is of the Adamites. Noah is the tenth generation from Adam and that is a vitally important piece of information. Ten, like seven, represents a significant cycle in the life of a lineage. Noah is the new Adam – he is not the new Seth. Up until Noah all we see is the main trunk of the patrilineage, but after Noah it, like Cain's lineage, segments into three parts. There is no point in worrying about younger brothers before Noah's time because everyone, except Noah's lineage, gets wiped out in the Flood. After Noah's era his sons repopulate the earth, occupying three distinct territories. Roughly speaking, Ham becomes the ancestor of all the peoples of Africa, Shem is the father of people in the Near East and Asia, and Japheth is the lineal ancestor of Europeans.

Genesis 11 provides another lineage, following Shem's branch only (Figure 8.4).

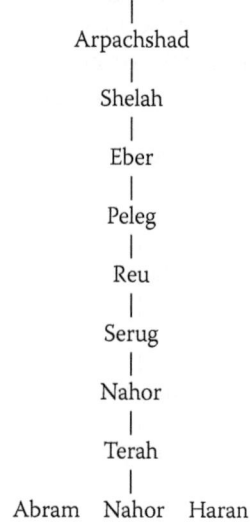

```
              Shem
               |
           Arpachshad
               |
             Shelah
               |
              Eber
               |
              Peleg
               |
              Reu
               |
              Serug
               |
              Nahor
               |
              Terah
               |
     Abram   Nahor   Haran
```

Figure 8.4 Shem's patrilineage.

It too is ten generations deep and then segments into three after Terah. If you keep reciting lineages ten generations at a time, you'll find that after the fiftieth generation (five sets of ten), you get to King Josiah of Judah, who began the renaissance of Judaic culture and whose three heirs were ultimately responsible for the Babylonian Exile. Ten generations complete a cycle, leading to a new covenant with God. Lineages are as much about cyclic time as they are about descent and inheritance.

What's my line?

The two main points of segmentation at the end of the Adamite and Shemite genealogies reveal what these lineages are all about. At the very broadest level, Noah is the common ancestor of all the peoples of the world. The broad division of those peoples into three continents, or regions as the ancients would have perceived them, is yet one more form of divinely ordained separation. As long as each one stays within its own region and procreates with its own lineal kin, peace reigns in the world. When one group starts migrating out or mixing with others, disaster follows.

Segmentary lineages and international affairs

Chapter 10 of Genesis employs segmentary lineages as a form of classification of all the known peoples of the world, something that is, as far as I know, unique in ancient literature. It is also an attempt to understand how and why different peoples act towards one another the way that they do. The following discussion of Ham's descendants provides a flavour of the whole narrative (Genesis 10:6–8, 13–18):

> 6. The descendants of Ham: Cush, Egypt, Put, and Canaan.
>
> 7. The descendants of Cush: Seba, Havilah, Sabtah, Raamah, and Sabteca. The descendants of Raamah: Sheba and Dedan.
>
> 8. Cush became the father of Nimrod; he was the first on earth to become a mighty warrior...
>
> 13. Egypt became the father of Ludim, Anamim, Lehabim, Naphtuhim,
>
> 14. Pathrusim, Casluhim, and Caphtorim, from which the Philistines come.
>
> 15. Canaan became the father of Sidon his firstborn, and Heth,
>
> 16. and the Jebusites, the Amorites, the Girgashites,
>
> 17. the Hivites, the Arkites, the Sinites,
>
> 18. the Arvadites, the Zemarites, and the Hamathites. Afterwards the families of the Canaanites spread abroad.

To understand the deeper cultural meanings and implications of this section, it is necessary to move on from unilineal descent and start talking about segmentary lineages. Ham is the ancestor of all the peoples in this segmented system. So, we refer to the descendant branches as Hamites when we are thinking of them as a whole. Ham's branch can be called a maximal lineage because it is one of three segments that divide off from the common trunk represented by Noah and his patriline. The Hamites embrace all the peoples of Africa. The lineage then splits into four segments – Cush, Egypt, Put and Canaan. These nationalities or ethnic groupings are all 'brother' cultures. That the Canaanites were under the domination of Egypt for a considerable period makes sense using this lineage classification scheme, because Egypt is the elder brother of Canaan. Elder brothers have power over their younger siblings; Egypt has power over Canaan.

These four branches are the major lineages of Ham. Each of these in turn branches into minor lineages. Sometimes the Bible, in English translation, refers to these minor lineages as tribes. Canaan's major lineage, for example, is divided up into minor lineages that are a classic list of all the Canaanite peoples who were in the land of Canaan when Abraham first journeyed there from Haran: Jebusites, Amorites, Girgashites, Hivites, Arkites, Sinites, Arvadites, Zemarites and Hamathites (Figure 8.5).

As members of Ham's lineage, the descendants of Canaan should have lived somewhere in Africa, but had migrated out to take over the region of the Levant (Figure 2.1, p. 24). Because they did not belong in the region ancestrally, it was, therefore, legitimate for the tribes of Israel to throw them out. As descendants of Shem the Israelites perceived themselves as the rightful heirs of this land, using a segmentary lineage system on which to base claims of land ownership and inheritance.

A deeper argument, based on my earlier discussion of the Levant as a profoundly liminal zone, is that the region has always been complexly contested historically. Because it sits on the intersection of Europe, Asia and Africa, it could be argued that the Levant belongs to everyone and no one. Or you could argue that its liminal nature makes it a land that will see multiple incursions from all sides, but is only truly governable and inhabitable by God's chosen people. All other peoples are there on sufferance. It rightfully belongs only to the sons of Israel (and ultimately of Abraham).

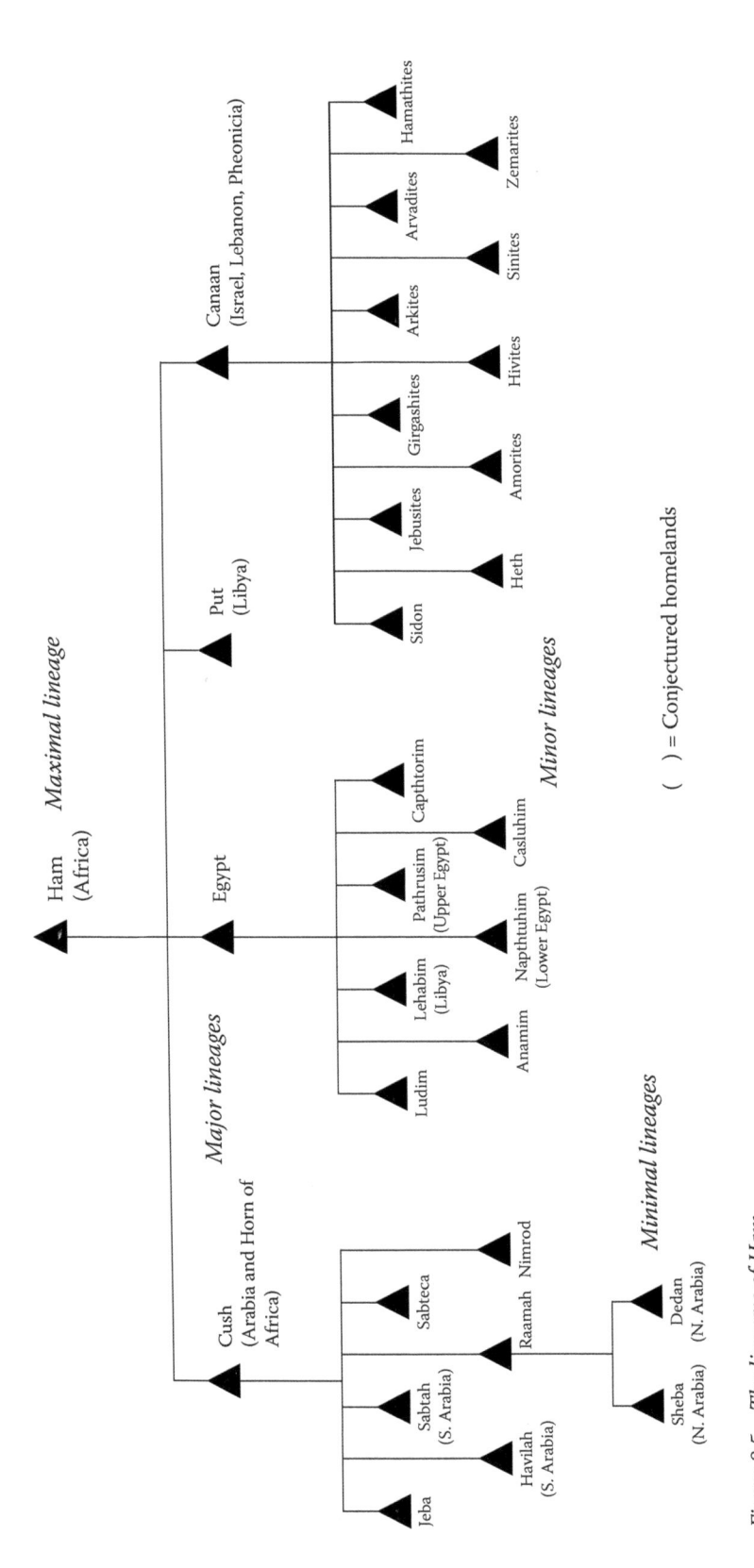

Figure 8.5 The lineages of Ham.

Jacob's sons and land tenure

According to Genesis 29 and 30 Jacob had twelve sons by his two wives and two concubines. The order of their births, who their mothers were and other circumstances of kinship ordered and controlled the land claims of the twelve tribes of Israel descended from these men. Examination of the kinship narrative provides further insight into the use of segmentary lineages by the ancient Judeans to validate land rights.

Jacob's elder wife Leah bore four sons: Reuben, Simeon, Levi and Judah. They were born before Jacob had any other sons by other women and so their descendants would have had seniority over the other tribes (and note that Judah is one of the four). Rachel could not bear children and so gave Jacob her maid, Bilhah, as a concubine. She bore two sons in Rachel's name, Dan and Naphtali. Leah's maid Zilpah next bore Jacob two sons in her name, Gad and Asher. Then Leah gave birth to Issachar and Zebulun. Finally, Rachel had her own son, Joseph. Much later she had a second son, Benjamin. All of these men, with the exception of Joseph, became the ancestral heads of tribes of Israel – Reubenites, Levites, Simeonites etc. Joseph had two sons, Manasseh and Ephraim, and they became the ancestors of what were called 'half tribes' because they had half shares in the patrimony of Joseph. If Joseph had headed a tribe of Joseph it would have been a full tribe. Because his portion was shared between twin sons, however, they each headed half a tribe (Figure 8.6).

This recitation suggests that some of these tribes would be more closely related than others, and that their fortunes might differ. Figure 8.6 shows where these tribes supposedly settled in the period of the monarchies of Israel and Judah, although much of it is conjectural, or based on unreliable sources (e.g. *Joshua* 13:1–22:34). It can be used for only highly generalized analysis. The senior sons of Leah – Reuben, Simeon and Judah – lived in large adjacent areas in the south (with the fourth son, Levi, not occupying any territory because his descendants performed religious and other duties in Jerusalem and throughout Israel). Manasseh and Ephraim as sons of the most favoured son of the beloved wife, Rachel, had the largest and wealthiest lands. The tribes born of Rachel's maid, Dan and Naphtali, had smaller regions adjacent to them. If Dan was to feud with Naphtali they would have to slug it out alone because they were full brother tribes, and brothers are on their own in disputes. But if the tribe of Dan were fighting with their neighbour Ephraim, they could expect Naphtali to help them, and Ephraim would call on support from Manasseh. If Judah had a quarrel with Dan, then they would call on Simeon and Reuben to help, and would be opposed by Naphtali, Ephraim and Manasseh on Dan's side. If Moab attacked any of the tribes of Israel, all twelve would unite to defend themselves from the outsider. The Moabites are descended from Abraham's nephew Lot, and so are cousins to the brother tribes of Israel.

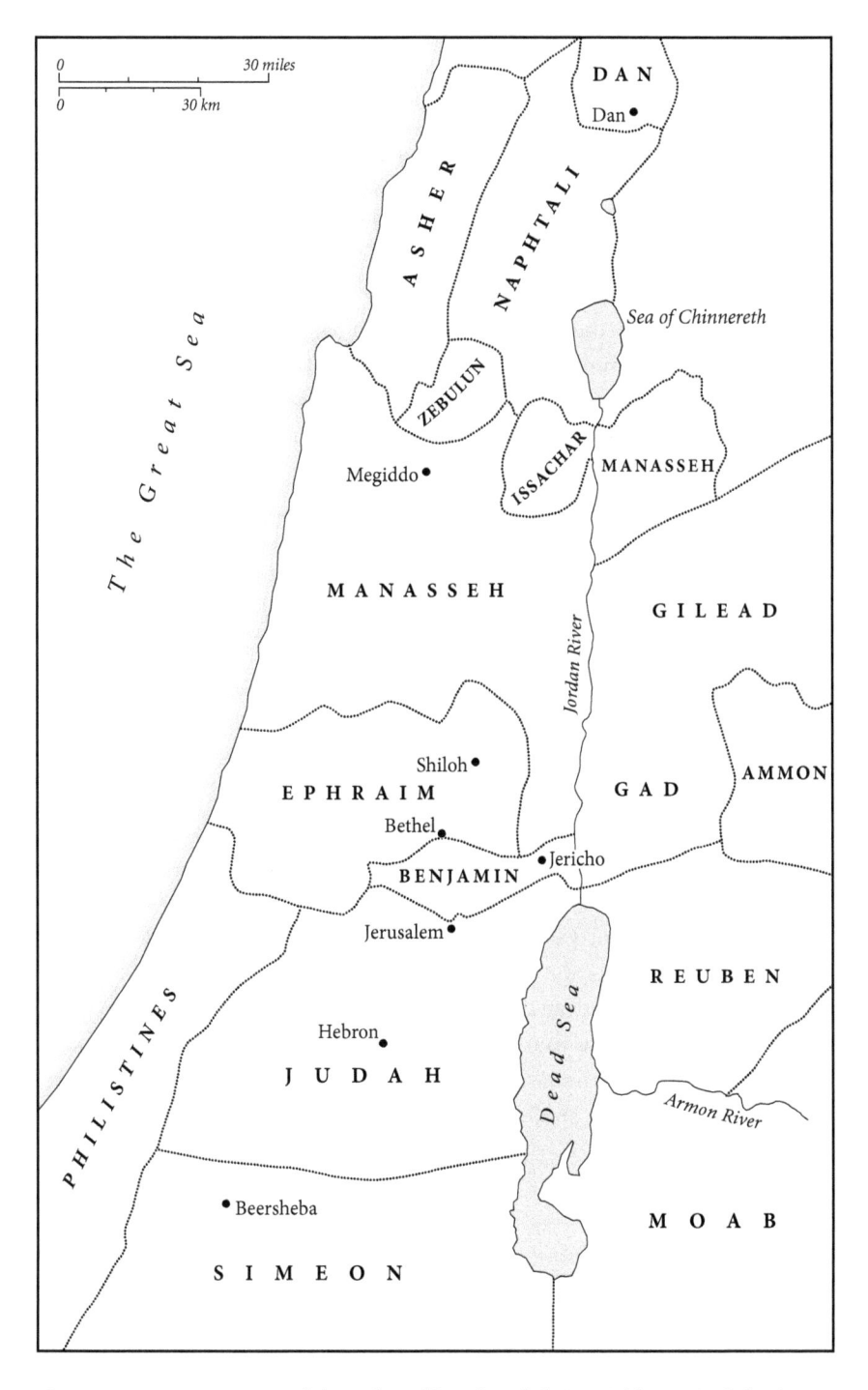

Figure 8.6 Home regions of the tribes of Israel and their neighbours in Palestine.

The segmentary lineages of Genesis, thus, are a form of classification of tribal and ethnic groups using kinship as the basic metaphor. Unilineal descent systems answer the question 'who am I?' and segmentary systems answer the question 'who are you?' Put them together and they allow people to classify all possible relationships with others, and provide rules for interactional behaviour. The Judean genealogists (probably the temple priests) devised a classification system that embraced the entire known world. Imagine running into a Maori from New Zealand or a Nuer from southern Sudan and being able to identify clearly their ethnic and regional background, trace their lineal histories and find common kinship links with them, even if remote. That is exactly what the Genesis genealogies allowed the Judeans in exile to do.

The Genesis genealogies classify all the peoples of the earth and indicate where they should be located and how they should behave. Implicit in the genealogies is condemnation of gigantic multicultural empires, especially Babylon, which deliberately displaced whole peoples from their ancestral lands. The people of Judah did not belong in Babylon, they belonged in Judah. Their primary, God-given task was to get back there. Meanwhile, it was supremely important that they maintain the genealogical records scrupulously so that they preserve their sense of lineal identity, and therefore know where to dwell when they returned. Not only did the tribes have large ancestral lands, so did the smaller lineal groups such as clans and families. The genealogies inscribed the view that everyone has a place, and there is a place for everyone.

The priests kept the broader tribal records, but individual clan and family heads also had to maintain their own records. How well these were kept is testified to by the fact that 600 years later the gospel writers, Luke and Matthew, had sufficient genealogical records to document the patrilineage of Jesus, a descendant of the Davidic line. Luke traces the lineage all the way back to Adam. For the Judeans, such knowledge was a vital component of their cultural survival kit. Lose your genealogy and you become nobody. You have no identity, you have no home to go back to, no property on which to support yourself, and you will be swallowed up in the great multicultural maw of the urban empire.

Further reading

British social anthropologist E.E. Evans-Pritchard first popularized the idea of segmentary lineage systems based on his research in Sudan. His main works on this subject are *The Nuer* (1940) and *Kinship and Marriage among the Nuer* (1951). As a model for understanding contemporary kinship systems, it is not favoured much these days, and for a more contemporary assessment and critique of classic theory on segmentary lineage systems you can look at Ladislav Holy, *Anthropological Perspectives on Kinship* (1996) or the lengthy references outlined in the comprehensively exploratory article by Radim Tobolka, 'Gellner and Geertz in Morocco: a segmentary debate' (2003).

Many sane and crackpot views of the genealogies in Genesis exist. For a good, sane overview see Marshall D. Johnson, *The Purpose of the Biblical Genealogies* (1969).

For a fascinating look at how the Judeans mapped their world genealogies on to the physical landscape, read Philip S. Alexander. 'Early Jewish geography' (1992).

9

The last shall be first

The technical term for the inheritance principal by which the eldest son inherits his father's entire fortune is patrilineal primogeniture (that is, male line/first born). It is the norm in the Genesis genealogies, and for good reason. Consider the example of the patrilineal inheritance of a kingship, where winner takes all. For obvious reasons you cannot keep dividing kingdoms among multiple sons. After a few generations each 'king' would be ruling a small farm. Therefore, having one heir take everything is functional. But, it is theoretically possible to have someone other than the eldest inherit everything. This situation, while hypothetically feasible, creates its own problems. If, for example, the inheritance principle were patrilineal ultimogeniture, in which the youngest son inherits the throne, the eldest son would likely be jealous and might do something unpleasant, such as kill his younger brothers. In general, the eldest son is probably the strongest and most experienced, and therefore not only a possibly dangerous person but, more importantly, someone logically most worthy to assume the mantle of power.

Even though primogeniture was the prevailing inheritance rule in the Genesis genealogies, last-born sons sometimes acquired the kingship in the monarchies of Israel and Judah according to the Biblical record. We must not necessarily take these narratives at face value, but even if they are fiction, they embody important principles for the historians who enshrined them (mostly the Deuteronomists). These cases usually occurred during times of political instability, when, as in the case of David, his elder sons had fought and killed each other – another nasty side effect of eldest takes all. Sometimes, imperial overlords placed younger sons on the thrones in nations they controlled. Being young and inexperienced, the imperial masters could control them better than their elder brothers. In the minds of the Biblical writers, inheritance by younger sons was a sign of political weakness. One salient question remains: if patrilineal primogeniture was the norm in ancient Israel/Judah, as attested by the genealogies throughout Genesis, and a sign of political strength and stability, why is it the case that in every single patriarchal narrative in Genesis, after Abraham, it is the younger/est son who inherits the patrimony?

Primogeniture has long been, and still is, the normative inheritance model among pastoralists worldwide. The Genesis patriarchs were pastoralists (their economy depended to a large extent on the products of domesticated herd animals), but unlike some of the outcast groups mentioned earlier, such as the Kenites and Ishmaelites, they were not normally nomadic (pastoralists who move from place to place with their herds). They usually kept their flocks and herds in fixed pastures within their ancestral lands.

The wealth of the Genesis patriarchs was in camels, cattle, sheep and goats. The Biblical tales of the riches of these men frequently enumerate the numbers of animals that they owned. The substantial herds described in Genesis would have taken time and effort to build up and maintain. That level of investment means that it was not efficient to divide a herd on the death of the patriarch, and so the eldest-takes-all aspect of their primogeniture makes rational economic sense. The Nuer, cattle herders of Sudan, have a saying that when the eldest son dies, the younger son 'weeps with one eye and counts the cattle with the other'. (*The Nuer* [film], Breidenbach and Harris 1971).

Normally within Genesis, primogeniture is the rule among the patriarchs. But, in the narrative sections that cover the lineal descendants of Terah, primogeniture is constantly overruled. While it is quite obviously still the cultural norm of the land in general, the younger/est sons of Abraham, Isaac, Jacob, Joseph and Judah all inherit in preference to the eldest. This chapter considers why this reversal happened and what lessons it held for the Exiles.

The term 'primogeniture' is derived from 'primo-' meaning 'first' and 'geniture' meaning 'born'; whereas 'ultimogeniture' comes from 'ultimo-' meaning 'last'. Ultimogeniture is relatively rare cross-culturally. To be successful, ultimogeniture requires several conditions, the most important of which is long life-expectancy rates. The youngest child needs to be adult and experienced by the time he (in the case of patrilineal ultimogeniture) takes over. If fathers routinely die in middle age leaving an heir who is still a child, ultimogeniture is dysfunctional. Ultimogeniture is also more likely to succeed in rich families, allowing elder siblings to take a portion early, while their fathers are still alive, to set themselves up on their own, without having to wait for their fathers to die to inherit. Allowing elder sons a portion of the inheritance, rather than completely excluding them, also helps maintain the system.

The typical conditions for ultimogeniture generally include the following: people have to live well into old age so that their youngest child who will inherit is an adult when the parents die; there has to be enough family property or other options for all offspring to do well for themselves; a rationale for the eldest leaving home at an early age while the youngest stays at home; a norm of the youngest taking care of parents; and an expectation that the youngest receives the inheritance to compensate for service to the elderly.

When the last inherits

In wealthy families in medieval Scandinavia the youngest son typically inherited the ancestral manor house and lands. This practice was based on the condition that there were enough estates to share out among the elder sons while the parents were still living, so that the only son still living at home at the time of the father's death would be the youngest. He got the manor as a reward for taking care of his ageing parents while the elder sons were off away from home seeking their fortunes (Sawyer and Sawyer 1993).

A related type of inheritance pattern with the same basic rationale was widespread in south-west Japan, especially Kyushu, prior to the 1890s, but was abolished when the Meiji reforms were enacted. Under this system the inheritance was shared among all the sons. The youngest, however, received a bonus of double shares for staying at home to take care of the ageing parents (Wall, Hareven and Ehmer 2001:343–4).

Ultimogeniture can also be matrilineal, or bilineal (following either the male or female line), as in some parts of South-east Asia. The underlying reasons are the same as for the patrilineal example, namely, that the youngest daughter gains a greater share of the inheritance, often including the family residence, because she stays at home to care for her ageing parents (Potter 1977).

The Biblical patriarchs lived to a ripe old age, but none of the other conditions I have discussed obtain in the Genesis accounts. Therefore, I do not believe that the stories of ultimogeniture among the patriarchs reflect an ancient Judaic tradition of inheritance by the youngest. Anthropologically speaking, it is unlikely in the extreme for classic pastoralists to do such a thing. Nor can dynastic succession have occurred in this way. Admittedly, Solomon was David's youngest son and was the one who inherited the crowns of the united monarchies, but this occurrence was considered to be highly unusual by Deuteronomic historians, who went to great lengths to explain how and why it happened (2 Samuel 11 – 1 Kings 2). Otherwise, the kingships of Israel and Judah were almost always inherited by the eldest son.

When the younger sons Isaac, Jacob and Joseph became the inheritors from their fathers, it was because primogeniture failed. The redactors of Genesis emphasized this fact to grab the reader's attention. They wanted to make it clear that ultimogeniture was the rare exception meant to symbolize something very important to Israel and Judah and, especially, to the Judeans in exile. Examining the narratives in detail, starting with Terah and his sons, helps up to get to the bottom of this seeming anomaly.

Ultimogeniture, purity and territory

While the sibling status of Abraham is not absolutely clear, the genealogies suggest that he was Terah's eldest son. Two separate genealogies for Terah appear in Genesis 11, one right after the other. Both list Terah's sons in the same order with Abram first:

> 26. When Terah had lived for seventy years, he became the father of Abram, Nahor and Haran.

> 27. Now these are the descendants of Terah. Terah was the father of Abram, Nahor and Haran;

In the Biblical genealogies, sons are conventionally listed in birth order. So, it is likely that Abram was the first-born son. The youngest son by this calculation, Haran, died in Ur before Terah moved away, leaving Nahor as the younger of the two remaining sons. Terah moved up the Euphrates to the city of Haran and settled there, while Abram continued on into Canaan, where he established himself. Nahor stayed behind in Haran with his father. The eldest son striking out on his own while the younger stays behind to care for an ageing parent has echoes with the cross-cultural examples cited earlier, but other than that, no signs of ultimogeniture as a norm appear. Abram (later named Abraham), Terah's eldest son, will receive the full inherited magnificence of God's blessing that has descended through the patrilineal line. The text follows him and not Nahor. Abraham inherits the Promised Land as his patrimony and it is supposed to remain in his line forever. Oddly, though, for the next three or four generations, it is the younger son who gets the lion's share of land, herds and valuables.

One fact that is crucial to understanding the underlying symbolism of ultimogeniture at this time is that the Promised Land was not empty when Abraham got there. Quite the opposite: it was teeming with Canaanite tribes. Yet this land was to be God's gift to Abraham. Somehow, therefore, the ownership by the Canaanites had to be voided. Narratives of lineage and genealogy provide a way for Abraham and his heirs to contest the Canaanites' claim. Genesis has to show that the longstanding inhabitants of Canaan, the Canaanites (symbolically the elder brother), had forfeited their claim to the land, and that the newcomers, the Israelites (symbolically the younger brother), were better suited to inherit it.

As shown in Chapter 8 of this book, Genesis 10 provides an implied genealogical case against Canaanite ownership based on patterns of land inheritance by Noah's sons. Canaan was Ham's son, and as such his offspring belong in Africa, not Asia, which is Shem's share. But this is not the best of arguments. The ancient Judeans did not define the continents the way modern geographers do, and the location of Canaan in ancient geography is not clear. Canaan is more like the place where all these regions meet (see Figure 2.1). Its ultimate ownership by the tribes of Israel was meant, in part, to be testament to how pivotal the land and its owners were in geopolitical history, then and now.

The more definitive claim that Israel would and should supersede Canaan comes from the immediate aftermath of the Flood recorded at the tail end of Genesis 9:

> 20. Noah, a man of the soil, was the first to plant a vineyard.
>
> 21. He drank some of the wine and became drunk, and he lay uncovered in his tent.
>
> 22. And Ham, the father of Canaan, saw the nakedness of his father, and told his two brothers outside.
>
> 23. Then Shem and Japheth took a garment, laid it on both their shoulders, and walked backwards and covered the nakedness of their father; their faces were turned away, and they did not see their father's nakedness.
>
> 24. When Noah awoke from his wine and knew what his youngest son had done to him,
>
> 25. he said, 'Cursed be Canaan; lowest of slaves shall he be to his brothers.'
>
> 26. He also said, 'Blessed by the Lord my God be Shem; and let Canaan be his slave.
>
> 27. May God make space for Japheth, and let him live in the tents of Shem; and let Canaan be his slave.'

Like many such terse tales in Genesis, this one is not quite clear in meaning, although the general drift is apparent. The Flood has wiped the slate clean so that humanity can begin again. Unfortunately, as the new cycle begins, things quickly deteriorate. Noah's drunkenness is not especially to be applauded, but it is not the issue that is being addressed directly here. The main problems are, as ever, sex and kinship.

Scholars are divided about the exact nature of Ham's offence (Cohen 1974; Pleins 2004). The debate centres on exactly how to interpret the statement that Ham 'saw the nakedness of his father'. The simplest reading is the straightforward one: he walked into the tent and saw his father's genitals. This act in itself might be forgivable as it was an accident. But Ham failed to cover up his father, and instead blabbed about the incident to his brothers. They had more sense than Ham, and did what Ham failed to do, in what reads like an almost comical act of modesty on their part. So, Ham stands accused of lacking filial piety and respect, and of gross sexual indecency. Many cultural historians of the Near East argue that these grounds were sufficiently shameful for Ham to be cursed (Goldenberg 2003).

Other commentators have been more daring (Goldenberg 2003; Levenson 2004). They suggest that, because the general expression 'to uncover the nakedness of' is a common euphemism for sexual acts in Mosaic law, Ham used his father's drunken incapacity to have sex with him. I find this conclusion a bit far-fetched, not least because I cannot see any obvious reason why Ham would have a particular desire, sexual or otherwise, to have sex with his inebriated father. I am, however, inclined to think that Ham's seeing his father's genitals was close to committing a sexual act with him in the minds of the ancient Judeans. Voyeurism is a form of sexuality.

Because Ham committed a lewd act, of whatever degree, and was condemned for it, his lineage would bear the curse down through the generations. Canaan, in fact, bears almost the full brunt of it, and the text, both here and in the narrative immediately preceding, is quick to point out that Ham is Canaan's father. Canaan will be heir to all manner of sexual lewdness and perversion (as in Sodom and Gomorrah), and in consequence will lose title to its lands. Leviticus is explicit on this point. Heading the section of the law on forbidden sexual practices is the following (Leviticus 18:1–3):

> 1. The Lord spoke to Moses, saying:
>
> 2. Speak to the people of Israel and say to them: I am the Lord your God.
>
> 3. You shall not do as they do in the land of Egypt, where you lived, and you shall not do as they do in the land of Canaan, to which I am bringing you. You shall not follow their statutes.

The first ordinances are to the point (Leviticus 18:6–7):

6. None of you shall approach anyone near of kin to uncover nakedness: I am the Lord.

7. You shall not uncover the nakedness of your father...

The consequences of contravening these laws are dire (Leviticus 18:24–30):

24. Do not defile yourselves in any of these ways, for by all these practices the nations I am casting out before you have defiled themselves.

25. Thus the land became defiled; and I punished it for its iniquity, and the land vomited out its inhabitants.

26. But you shall keep my statutes and my ordinances and commit none of these abominations, either the citizen or the alien who resides among you

27. (for the inhabitants of the land, who were before you, committed all of these abominations, and the land became defiled);

28. otherwise the land will vomit you out for defiling it, as it vomited out the nation that was before you.

29. For whoever commits any of these abominations shall be cut off from their people.

30. So keep my charge not to commit any of these abominations that were done before you, and not to defile yourselves by them: I am the Lord your God.

According to this narrative, the Canaanites might well have once been the rightful owners of the land, but they forfeited that right because of their inappropriate sexual behaviour. Inheritance of land is neither absolute nor permanent: it depends on right behaviour. The Canaanites were like an eldest son who takes his patrimony and squanders it. They lost their rights. Abraham, in contrast, was pure, righteous and obedient. He was rather like the junior brother in this situation, that is, he did not come by ownership of Canaan by right of inheritance, it became his by default, because the legitimate heir did not deserve it.

Ultimogeniture in Genesis is a signal that the eldest son was not worthy of his inheritance for some reason. One of the many lessons that the Exiles could take from this is that the Canaanites lost their land because they contravened laws concerning marriage and reproduction. The Exiles were under punishment for their sins, mostly having to do with loss of ethnic purity, through failing to keep separate from other cultures. If they wanted their land back, they must scrupulously follow all the laws associated with sexuality and kinship in order to return to a culturally pure state.

These ideas provide the context for taking another look at Abraham's sons. His eldest was Ishmael, and Ishmael's younger (half) brother was Isaac. Ishmael's conception, and later circumstances, were all wrong. His mother, Hagar, was not married to Abraham but was Sarah's maid, serving as a concubine. Hagar was an Egyptian: she was outside Terah's lineage, which was bad enough, and she was not even within the maximal lineage of Shem. Worst of all, she was a descendant of the cursed Ham. She was not a suitable concubine in any sense, so she (and Ishmael) could not possibly be the progenitor of the Israelite line that would succeed Canaan. To compound the problem, Hagar finds a wife for the adult Ishmael from Egypt (Genesis 21:21), so in all respects he failed as the eldest son.

Isaac, the younger son, is the appropriate heir to inherit from Abraham. His mother, father and wife are all from the patriline of Terah. He has neither married a Canaanite nor some other foreigner, but has been true to his lineal obligations. As a blessing he has twin sons, who turn out to be almost exact opposites of each other.

The sibling rivalry of Isaac's sons

Isaac's elder son was Esau. He was a man of nature: hairy, ruddy, impulsive. He loved to hunt and to be out in the wild by himself. He was his father's favourite. The younger was Jacob, a man of culture. He was smooth skinned, smart and prefered the communal life. He was a herder rather than a hunter. He was the favourite of his mother. From the circumstances of their birth, Esau should have inherited his father's patrimony. Two problems prevented him from doing so. First, he was indifferent to his place in the family and does not value his inheritance. Second, Jacob was clever and usurped Esau's place by cunning. Being intelligent and willing to use guile to get what you need are both symbolically important to the exiles. The scene in which Esau carelessly renounces his birthright says it all (Genesis 25:29–34):

> 29. Once when Jacob was cooking a stew, Esau came in from the field, and he was famished.

> 30. Esau said to Jacob, 'Let me eat some of that red stuff, for I am famished!' (Therefore he was called Edom.)

31. Jacob said, 'First sell me your birthright.'

32. Esau said, 'I am about to die; of what use is a birthright to me?'

33. Jacob said, 'Swear to me first.' So he swore to him, and sold his birthright to Jacob.

34. Then Jacob gave Esau bread and lentil stew, and he ate and drank, and rose and went his way. Thus Esau despised his birthright.

The last sentence is especially compelling because open moral commentary is rare in Genesis. The message is clear: your birthright is sacred and if you treat it as worthless you become worthless yourself. Esau was a man of passion and of immediacy. His birthright was valuable, but only in some distant future; whereas he was hungry *now*. Jacob, on the other hand, understood the value of a long-term investment and was willing to put aside immediate needs for a secure future. Jacob was the man the exiles need to model their behaviour after, not Esau. The exiles were lonely, poor, isolated and destitute. They could have prostituted themselves before the Babylonians for immediate short-term gains; however, in the long run they would have lost their birthright. Judah and Jerusalem would have been lost to them. Getting Judah back required long-term planning and patience. What is more, Jacob was their ancestor. He was the one whose blood ran in their veins.

Perhaps an even more compelling message, and one more directly connected to ultimogeniture, is that the eldest is rich and powerful by right, but he can lose his power to the youngest if they are clever and patient. Implicit in this story is the fact that Jacob had everything meticulously planned. He knew well his brother's passions and appetites, and his impetuousness and lack of forethought. He laid a trap for Esau, who fell into it without a murmur. It behoves the exiles to be as clever and as patient as Jacob.

Another significant piece to this story is a play on words in the Hebrew in connection with the words for 'red' and 'Esau'. When Esau first sees the 'red stuff', he thinks it is some extravagant meaty concoction. He confuses the 'red' (visually and linguistically) with blood. But the stew is only red lentils, a cheap and easy dish to make. Jacob did not have to invest much at all in his ruse; he did not even have to kill an animal to get the birthright. Better to be poor and clever (Judean) than rich and stupid (Babylonian).

Jacob's ability to outwit the strong while in a weak position becomes his hallmark. Read Genesis 30 and 31 for examples of his dealings with his father-in-law, Laban, who was pretty subtle in his own right. My favourite tussle between the two concerns Jacob's efforts to get his wages from Laban. Jacob tells Laban that he will accept as payment for many years of devoted service the sheep and goats in his flock that have unusually distinct markings. Laban agreed. But he was greedy. He immediately removed all sheep and goats with these markings from his flocks and hid them with his sons, so that in the coming years he would have to give up few, if any, animals. Jacob saw the bad-faith plot and was not in the least fazed. He embarked on a highly specialized form of selective breeding to guarantee that practically all the animals in the herds in his keeping had the distinct markings. He ended up with an enormous flock to take home with him at the end of his service to Laban.

Reuben loses his place to Joseph

You will remember that Jacob married Laban's daughters, Leah and Rachel, favouring Rachel over Leah. His first-born was Leah's son Reuben. Rachel's son, Joseph, was younger. Benjamin was born to Rachel much later, when Jacob was an old man. Joseph was the youngest son of Jacob's household when he was sold into slavery. He was also Jacob's favourite, to such an extent that his brothers were violently jealous and wanted to kill him. As is well known, Joseph had a special coat (Genesis 37:3). It was made for him as a mark of his father's great love for him and of his high esteem within the family, in large part because he was Rachel's son (and Jacob's youngest son by his youngest wife). The Hebrew in the passage is unfortunately obscure, so it is not clear what kind of coat it was. Nonetheless, it is evident that the wearing of the coat symbolized his father's deep affection.

Despite Jacob's overwhelming love for Joseph, Deuteronomic law is clear that Reuben, the eldest, should not be denied his rights according to primogeniture (Deuteronomy 21:15–16):

> 15. If a man has two wives, one of them loved and the other disliked, and if both the loved and the disliked have borne him sons, the first-born being the son of the one who is disliked,

> 16. then on the day when he wills his possessions to his sons, he is not permitted to treat the son of the loved as the first-born in preference to the son of the disliked, who is the first-born.

Despite Jacob's preferences for Joseph, Reuben as the first-born son must be the heir. Just as with Esau and Jacob, however, Reuben has the capacity to lose his birthright through foolish actions. A small, almost throwaway line shows that Reuben is, indeed, careless of his birthright and that someone else more worthy should inherit his place (Genesis 35:22):

> 22. While Israel [Jacob] lived in that land, Reuben went and lay with Bilhah his father's concubine; and Israel heard of it.

The text provides no further comment, and Jacob takes no action at the time. Nonetheless, an ancient audience would understand Reuben's intent perfectly well: he was attempting to emasculate his father. While it may have been usual in the ancient Near East for a son to inherit his father's wives on his death, as a sign the son had assumed his father's potency, this act was strictly outlawed in Judah. In Mosaic law sleeping with one's father's wives and concubines is forbidden and is serious enough to incur the death penalty (Leviticus 18:8 and 20:11; Deuteronomy 27:20). Despite the gravity of the law there are numerous examples of sons violating it in the Hebrew Bible, and its meaning is clear. A conquering king typically took possession of the vanquished king's wives and concubines as a symbol of his mastery. Sexual and political power are synonymous. When David replaced Saul as the king of Israel and Judah he took Saul's wives (2 Samuel 12:7–8). In an ironic twist of fate, when David's son Absalom rebelled against him, he publicly made a show of having sex with the concubines that David had left behind when he fled Jerusalem (2 Samuel 16:22). In David's advanced old age he took a young virgin, Abishag the Shunammite, as a concubine, though the text emphasizes that he was not able to have sex with her (1 Kings 1:1–4). This fact emboldened his son Adonijah to attempt to usurp the throne. His usurpation is symbolized by his desire to take Abishag as his wife, which Solomon considers treasonable and so has him put to death (1 Kings 2:13–25).

Reuben's sexual encounter with Bilhah, therefore, is an attempt to replace Jacob as the head of the lineage before he is dead. At the time of this treacherous act Jacob is silent. But when Jacob is dying and pronouncing his blessings on his sons, this is what he has to say to Reuben (Genesis 49:3–4):

> 3. 'Reuben, you are my first-born, my might and the first fruits of my vigour, excelling in rank and excelling in power.

> 4. Unstable as water, you shall no longer excel because you went up on to your father's bed; then you defiled it – you went up on to my couch!

Reuben's impetuous and selfish sexual act cost him his birthright. Incestuous relations with one's father's wives and concubines destroy the power lines of the patrilineage. They breach the necessary authority of fathers over sons. Such acts will eventually bring down families, clans, tribes and cultures. They cannot be tolerated.

Joseph's jealous brothers sold him into slavery in Egypt, but he was neither vindictive nor vengeful. Abused and mistreated, he bides his time, eventually using his wits and skills as a dream interpreter to rise to a position of great prestige and influence in the pharaoh's court. As such he was able to help his family when famine struck the Near East region, leaving them in great peril. He does everything in his power to keep his family together no matter what wrongs they have done to him. So, he became the blessed son in place of Reuben. Joseph's blessing from Jacob was powerful, and the tribes of his two sons, Manasseh and Ephraim, grow larger and richer than all the others stemming from Jacob.

Joseph's sons and ultimogeniture

Even Manasseh and Ephraim have a strange experience with ultimogeniture. To begin with, Jacob, on his deathbed, adopts them as his own sons (Genesis 48:1–5):

> 1. After this Joseph was told, 'Your father is ill.' So he took with him his two sons Manasseh and Ephraim.
>
> 2. When Jacob was told, 'Your son Joseph has come to you,' he summoned his strength and sat up in bed.
>
> 3. And Jacob said to Joseph, 'God Almighty appeared to me at Luz in the land of Canaan, and he blessed me,
>
> 4. and said to me, 'I am going to make you fruitful and increase your numbers; I will make of you a company of peoples, and will give this land to your offspring after you for a perpetual holding.'
>
> 5. Therefore your two sons, who were born to you in the land of Egypt before I came to you in Egypt, are now mine; Ephraim and Manasseh shall be mine, just as Reuben and Simeon are.

Jacob is claiming Joseph's sons as his own because he perceives that they are of a mighty stock, and he needs them to counter the more frail and fractious nature of his other sons. The family structure has become problematic, though, because now Jacob has fourteen sons, yet there should be only twelve tribes of Israel. While Joseph becomes the nominal inheritor from Jacob, his sons reap the reward and not him. There is no tribe of Joseph. That cuts the number down to thirteen. Jacob's son Levi heads a tribe that has no land. The Levites served ritual and political functions for all of Israel, and lived in cities where they were supported by a tithe from the other tribes. When the land of Canaan is finally distributed after the Exodus, therefore, there are twelve tribal claimants, all nominally 'sons' of Jacob.

The ancient authors had little problem in adjusting kinship to fit historical circumstances, and this was certainly the case with Jacob's blessing of Joseph's sons (Genesis 48:8–22):

8. When Israel saw Joseph's sons, he said, 'Who are these?'

9. Joseph said to his father, 'They are my sons, whom God has given me here.' And he said, 'Bring them to me, please, that I may bless them.'

10. Now the eyes of Israel were dim with age, and he could not see well. So Joseph brought them near him; and he kissed them and embraced them.

11. Israel said to Joseph, 'I did not expect to see your face; and here God has let me see your children also.'

12. Then Joseph removed them from his father's knees, and he bowed himself with his face to the earth.

13. Joseph took them both, Ephraim in his right hand towards Israel's left, and Manasseh in his left hand towards Israel's right, and brought them near him.

14. But Israel stretched out his right hand and laid it on the head of Ephraim, who was the younger, and his left hand on the head of Manasseh, crossing his hands, for Manasseh was the first-born.

15. He blessed Joseph, and said, 'The God before whom my ancestors Abraham and Isaac walked, the God who has been my shepherd all my life to this day,

16. the angel who has redeemed me from all harm, bless the boys; and in them let my name be perpetuated, and the name of my ancestors Abraham and Isaac; and let them grow into a multitude on the earth.'

17. When Joseph saw that his father laid his right hand on the head of Ephraim, it displeased him; so he took his father's hand, to remove it from Ephraim's head to Manasseh's head.

18. Joseph said to his father, 'Not so, my father! Since this one is the first-born, put your right hand on his head.'

19. But his father refused, and said, 'I know, my son, I know; he also shall become a people, and he also shall be great. Nevertheless, his younger brother shall be greater than he, and his offspring shall become a multitude of nations.'

20. So he blessed them that day, saying, 'By you Israel will invoke blessings, saying,

"God make you like Ephraim and like Manasseh."' So he put Ephraim ahead of Manasseh.

21. Then Israel said to Joseph, 'I am about to die, but God will be with you and will bring you again to the land of your ancestors.

22. I now give to you one portion more than to your brothers, the portion that I took from the hand of the Amorites with my sword and with my bow.'

The last two verses confirm all that has gone before. By making Joseph's sons his own sons by adoption, Jacob has bestowed two portions of his inheritance on Joseph and only one on all the rest of his sons. This was one of the ways stated in the law that a father could indicate the priority of a certain son when there was a large legacy to be shared, and conforms with the principles of ultimogeniture mentioned earlier in this chapter. Joseph is formally acknowledged as the leading son even though he is low in the birth order. Subsequently, for what seem like entirely arbitrary reasons, Jacob blesses the younger Ephraim before the elder Manasseh.

Joseph is careful to place his sons on Jacob's knees so that the elder one is on his right knee and the younger is on his left. When Jacob stretches out his hands to bless the two boys the elder will get the right hand (the dominant hand), and the younger the left hand. But Jacob crosses his hands when he makes the blessing. When Joseph tries to switch them back, Jacob will not allow it. What could this possibly be all about? To answer this question, we have to remember the purpose of these kinship stories.

The redactors of Genesis in exile were trying to fit many narrative pieces together to create a satisfying pattern. Among other things, they had a long tale about Jacob's son, Joseph, which was of paramount importance because it helped explain how the tribes of Israel ended up in slavery in Egypt (crucial to the exodus story that was central to Judean identity). The Joseph narratives are longer, more sequential and more coherent than those of any of the other patriarchs and cannot be excluded. Yet despite the fact that Joseph is pivotal in Israelite history, there is no tribe of Joseph. Why? Why were there two very strong (half) tribes called Manasseh and Ephraim, even though they were not Jacob's sons? Why was Ephraim richer and more powerful than Manasseh? Kinship narratives help provide the answers.

In the case of Ephraim and Manasseh my suspicion is that at one time Manasseh was the stronger, more dominant tribe. For reasons unknown at this juncture, however, Ephraim overtook Manasseh. Some rationale had to be inserted into the primordial history to explain how the junior tribe could become more powerful than the senior. Hence, we have the hand-crossing business at the time of blessing.

The rivalry of Tamar's twins

One last case of ultimogeniture in Genesis is tucked at the end of the story of Onan and Judah. Tamar becomes pregnant with twins who struggle in their birth, much like Esau and Jacob (Genesis 38:2730):

> 27. When the time of her delivery came, there were twins in her womb.
>
> 28. While she was in labour, one put out a hand; and the midwife took and bound on his hand a crimson thread, saying, 'This one came out first.'
>
> 29. But just then he drew back his hand, and out came his brother; and she said, 'What a breach you have made for yourself!' Therefore he was named Perez.
>
> 30. Afterwards his brother came out with the crimson thread on his hand; and he was named Zerah.

Both boys became ancestors of clans within the tribe of Judah. The Perezites gained pre-eminence when their lineage produced David, the youngest son in his family.

This evocation of David, famous for his contest with Goliath when he was just a lad (1 Samuel 17), leads to two general points about the underlying meaning of ultimogeniture for the exiles in Babylon. First, no matter what the odds, the youngest and weakest can be successful against the powerful. Second, even those who are powerful by right can lose their power by ill-conceived actions, while those who have nothing can succeed to power by well-thought-out actions. Judah can, thus, succeed in Babylon by following the examples of Jacob and Joseph.

The cases of ultimogeniture in Genesis suggest that the youngest sons succeeded precisely because of their weak position in terms of inheritance. With no guarantee of property they could not be complacent. Instead, they honed their skills in their chosen professions and sharpened their wits, while the eldest sons sat on their laurels and got fat and lazy. The last and the little may conquer through effort and righteousness. Babylon looked like an unconquerable giant in relation to Judah. Goliath was toppled by a stone from a sling wielded by a shepherd boy.

Further reading
The classic ethnography on the problems of patrilineal primogeniture in cultures with limited resources and long lifespans is Conrad Arensberg's *The Irish Countryman* (1937). When the book was re-issued in 1968 Arensberg noted that changing patterns of migration since the original publication had changed patterns of inheritance. Articles in John O'Brien's collection, *The Vanishing Irish* (1953), address issues of migration and marriage in Ireland in the early to mid-twentieth century. More recent works include Timothy Guinnane's *The Vanishing Irish* (1997) and Nancy Scheper-Hughes' *Saints, Scholars, and Schizophrenics* (2001), in which she argues that ultimogeniture was normative in some rural regions.

For an ethnography about a kinship system built around female ultimogeniture, read Sulamith Heins Potter, *Family Life in a Northern Thai Villlage* (1977).

The drunkenness of Noah has fascinated scholars, poets and painters alike. The last main panel of Michelangelo's Sistine chapel ceiling depicts Noah in a slumped state of inebriation, quite a contrast to the more commonly celebrated images. For a specialized, though controversial, analysis of the sexual overtones of the passage, take a look at a rather strange book, *The Drunkenness of Noah* by H. Hirsch Cohen (1974). As a counterbalance to Cohen's interpretation, see David J. Pleins (2004), 'When myths go wrong: deconstructing the drunkenness of Noah'.

10

Matriarchs, Mother Eve and gender

It is clear from textual history as well as literary analysis that Genesis as a complete book was crafted by men for the consumption of men and that the book has an overtly patriarchal tenor and substance – duly noted by feminist scholars (Shectman 2022; West 1981). Women are not typically the featured characters, but when they are, they are usually portrayed as auxiliary to the men in their lives. They are spoken of as 'the wife of...' or 'the mother of...' and more often than not are unnamed and without real importance. In many of the genealogies you get something like:

> The days of Adam after he became the father of Seth were eight hundred years; and he had other sons and daughters.
>
> (Genesis 5:4)

The 'other sons and daughters' are usually not relevant to the narrative thread, because its typical focus is on patrilineal primogeniture (bearing in mind the glaring exceptions associated with segmentary lineages and ultimogeniture analysed in previous chapters). Whatever the kinship particulars are, the lineages follow the male line exclusively, and the immediate male forebears of the twelve tribes of Israel – Abraham, Isaac, and Jacob – are known collectively as the Patriarchs and their era is known as the Patriarchal Age. Not much room for nuance there. Nonetheless, feminist readings of the text are possible, and a few prominent ones are highlighted at the end of the chapter.

When exploring gender roles (and gendered language) in Genesis there is a great danger of being either ethnocentric or chronocentric, or both. We can legitimately infer some of the character of men and women in our period (the Babylonian Exile), as well as their bases of power, from the text itself, but this exercise has profound limits. This current book has the task of examining the book of Genesis in the context of the Babylonian Exile only, not in the more general context of Judean culture both before and after the Exile. Therefore, my quest concerns what the redactors of Genesis expected its readers (and listeners) to take from the text as pertains to their situation in exile. Women had a highly specific role to play.

First and foremost, women bear children and their duty was to be 'fruitful and multiply'. They were also expected to be guardians of the ethnic purity of the Judean people. Procreation is their solemn responsibility. Seeing the women of Genesis in this light only, gives an exceedingly narrow vision. It happens to be a prominent feature simply because procreation is a major component of the 'Genesis option' (see p. 16). Yet, it is clear from the narratives in Genesis that women had much wider functions, even within an overtly patriarchal political structure, and, with care, it is possible to tease these out.

Power struggles

How power actually plays out in a culture, as opposed to how it is represented, is a complex issue. The task is not unlike differentiating between what people say they do, or think they should do, and what they actually do. Bearing this limitation in mind, the tales of Genesis offer us some clues.

The social psychologists John R.P. French and Bertram Raven (1959) came up with a schema, influential in the social sciences, of five bases of power in society. It has its weaknesses, but it remains a useful starting point. The five bases are:

- Positional power is held by individuals by virtue of their publicly acknowledged status within a social system. Within Genesis, positional power is held by men: heads of household, heads of lineages, national leaders etc. Such is the essence of patriarchy. But it is a major error to assume that positional power is all there is. It can easily be countered by other forms of power.
- Referent power is used by individuals to influence others by virtue of their interpersonal skills. In this regard, the women of Genesis quite often outshine the men, who sometimes lacked such ability and had to be guided back to the right path. Guile and subterfuge are forms of referent power, used frequently by the women of Genesis in their goal of ensuring that the men in their orbit do not use the other forms of power at their disposal to fall into error. The classic example of the use of referent power by a woman is Tamar's dealings with Judah to become pregnant (Genesis 38).
- Reward power is exerted by people who can distribute things of material value (as perceived by a culture). The strength of this power is directly related to the perceived value of the rewards on offer. This sphere is controlled principally by the men of Genesis, who have reserves of pastoral

- animals, gold and land at their disposal. Sometimes women can gain access to things of power typically owned by men and use them as bargaining chips, as in the case of Rachel stealing her father's household gods as a way of ensuring her safe escape with Jacob (Genesis 31).
- Expert power is possessed by people with valued skills and information, who can use them to control situations. The men and women of Genesis share expert power equally inasmuch as both are privy to the will of Yahweh. But even though the men and women have equal knowledge, the men sometimes have to be corrected by the women, as in the case of Rebekah steering Isaac away from granting his patrimony to their eldest son, Esau, in favour of Jacob, Yahweh's chosen heir (see pp. 137ff.).
- Coercive power relies on punishments, or the threat of them, for its effectiveness. It can involve actual physical harm, or the denial of desired rewards. When it comes to raw physical strength, men have the upper hand, but punishments can come in many forms including the withholding of favours. For example, Potiphar's wife has Joseph thrown in prison (via her husband) when she gets offended because he will not have sex with her (Genesis 39).

Were men the true power brokers in the Exilic community? It's hard to be definitive, because Genesis deals in shades of grey. It is probably more accurate to say that men had a great deal of power in public, but women often balanced that power with their own, exercised outside of the public eye.

Women of the Forest by Yolanda and Robert Murphy (2004) provides an invaluable corrective to the common assumption that the people who wear the symbols of power are the ones with actual power (that is, the ability to make decisions of communal importance and to carry them out successfully). The Mundurucú of Brazil, whom the Murphys studied, split their time annually between their home villages, where they grew their subsistence crops in the rainy season, and the rubber-tree groves on the river banks in the dry season, when they collected rubber latex for commercial sale.

When they moved their residences from village to rubber groves and back again was a complex matter that was overtly in the hands of the men, who held all the public positions of power. This was seemingly confirmed by observation of the men meeting to hash out the details of their annual migrations. Without the benefit of intensive fieldwork among the Mundurucú, it would be natural to assume that the men were the sole decision makers, and that the women followed their lead. Not so. Behind the public posturing of the men was a great deal of private negotiation between men and women. The women generally had a much more comprehensive understanding of the environmental conditions and the practical details of seasonal migration than the men; yet the men, for reasons of personal pride, had to keep up appearances. This is a case of the women's expert and referential power being used to influence the positional power of the men, and provides an excellent cross-cultural comparison with which to interpret the actions of the women of Genesis.

Feminine qualities

Genesis does not provide us with a comprehensive view of gender roles in the Exilic (or Judean) community, because its remit is much too limited. We do get glimpses, nonetheless. One point that is evident is that the division of labour is not as clear-cut as one might expect, nor as one-dimensional. On the few occasions where domestic tasks are mentioned, women are in the forefront – but not always. Abraham instructs Sarah to make fine wheat cakes for his visitors at Mamre (Genesis 18:6–7), and Rebekah makes a special savoury goat stew for Isaac as part of her plan to elevate Jacob's status (Genesis 27:8–9). But in the parallel tale of Lot greeting his visitors in Sodom, the text implies that it was Lot himself who prepared the (inferior) bread, his wife is not mentioned at all (Genesis 19:3); and when Jacob persuades Esau to sell his birthright for a bowl of lentil stew, it is Jacob himself who boiled the lentils (Genesis 25:29). Likewise, we tend to think of boys and young men as the prime shepherds and herdsmen, yet Rachel is clearly the one in charge of her father's flocks when Jacob arrives (Genesis 29 6–10).

Genesis makes no bones about the fact that the most desirable feature of a woman is her physical beauty, whereas a man's attractiveness resides more in his strength and manly skill. The text expressly states that Sarah, Rebekah and Rachel are beautiful women. In the cases of both Sarah and Rebekah, in parallel doublets recounting their journeys through foreign lands during times of famine (Genesis 20:1–10 and 26:6–11), their husbands, Abraham and Jacob, float the deception that their wives are actually their sisters, because the women are so blindingly beautiful and sexually appealing that the foreigners, if they think they are married couples, will kill the husbands in order to have sex with the women. Conversely, Leah, Rachel's sister, is euphemistically described as having 'tender' (רכות) eyes, wording which rabbinical scholars have puzzled over for centuries. Whatever the exact meaning, Leah is never described as attractive and it is made abundantly clear that Jacob does not love her. Fortunately, Yahweh is even-handed about such matters and rewards Leah with multiple sons (and a significant daughter), whereas Rachel is infertile for most of her life – as is also the case with Sarah.

Insofar as men's physical features are mentioned at all, it is almost always in the context of their masculine accomplishments.[14] When Jacob first meets Rachel at the well, she cannot water her flocks because the well is covered with a stone that the few shepherds who are assembled there at midday are unable to lift (because there are too few of them) and must wait for the rest of the men to gather at sunset to move it. When Rachel approaches, Jacob moves the stone by himself without hesitation. (Genesis 29:7–10). Esau is described as red and hairy (i.e. wild and uncouth), but he is noted for his skill as a hunter.

Women do have a part to play in the land claims of the Israelites, but it is indirect. Genesis (23:1–20) recounts the death of Sarah and Abraham's purchase of a burial site for her – which later also becomes his burial location, as well as that of Isaac, Rebekah and Jacob (and was known later, to this day, as the Cave of Machpelah – the second holiest site in Judaism after the Temple Mount). Sarah dies, at age 127, in Kiryat Arba near Hebron in the land of Canaan. Through a complicated transaction, Abraham buys a piece of land with a cave near Hebron from Ephron the Hittite in which to bury her, the first land owned by the Israelites in Canaan according to the biblical narrative. Abraham is at pains to buy the land outright for full market price, so that it will belong to him and his heirs in perpetuity. Rachel is recorded as dying giving birth to her second son, Benjamin, and her tomb is traditionally located near Bethlehem on the road from Bethel (Genesis 35:19–20), although within Judaic tradition the site is disputed. Nonetheless, the Bethlehem site is sacred to this day.

Without question, the most common quality of the women as represented in Genesis is deceitfulness, although this ostensibly negative characteristic is always excused because it serves a higher purpose, and is a main attribute of a woman's active agency (see below). Jealousy is also prominent, particularly when it comes to fertility. Sarah's jealousy of Hagar giving birth to Abraham's first-born leads to bitter conflict, matched in turn by Hagar's jealousy over Abraham's devotion to Sarah rather than her. The rivalry between the sisters Leah and Rachel over their respective procreative abilities is classic and, in fact, sororal polygyny (multiple sisters married to one man), although common at one time in many cultures worldwide (Inuit, Lakota, Chiricahua, Western Mono) and apparently serving to strengthen interfamilial bonds, is expressly banned in Mosaic Law (Leviticus 18:18), presumably because of the rivalry involved. Co-wives who are unrelated biologically can be expected to harbour jealousies against one another, as evidenced in numerous popular narratives (e.g. *Wives and Concubines*, *Raise the Red Lantern*), but siblings are a different matter. On the one hand, sisters can indulge in their own rivalries

---

14 Joseph is an exception (see p. 98).

between one another, making life uncomfortable for those around them; but on the other hand, they can also present a united front in opposition to their husband if need be, making his life a challenge.

Deceitfulness and sibling rivalry or jealousy are neither the exclusive domains nor hallmarks of women. The deceitfulness of Rebekah and Rachel (see Chapter 6) is matched by that of their kinsman, Laban, His deception, however, is spawned out of greed and self-interest rather than the nobler causes of the women. As mentioned, both Abraham and Isaac pass off their wives as their sisters when they are forced to travel in foreign lands because of famine – for their own safety more than for the safety of the women. The women are actually at considerable risk of being raped until the subterfuge is revealed, but that danger is not the stated concern of the men.

The sibling rivalries between Ishmael and Isaac, Esau and Jacob, and Joseph and his brothers, over their respective patrimonies are the central factors that drive the patriarchal narratives along. In the androcentric worldview presented in Genesis it is acceptable for men to be competitive. Male competition is the driving force and, one way or another, it is usually a woman who resolves the disputes of men. It would not be fair to characterize the women of Genesis as peacemakers. But they are capable of resolving disputes through various types of agency.

Agency

A superficial reading of Genesis can leave one with the impression that the women in the book lack agency, but this view is mistaken – perhaps engendered by the overwhelming prominence of men in the tales. The case of Tamar, Judah's daughter-in-law, already noted (pp. 110–12), is a clear counterpoint. Judah has made a great many mistakes in his life, beginning with marrying a Canaanite woman, outside the Israelite line. Given that Judah was the head of the patriline that became the central tribe of the nation of Judah, his fortunes would have been of vital importance to the exiles who were Judeans. He was central to their ancestry. Yet his whole life was spent making one mistake after another, threatening the very existence of the house of Judah. It was only Tamar's forethought, careful planning and flawless execution that saved the day for Judah and his patriline. He was useless. Lot's daughters are a similar case. Lot is manifestly a self-centred, greedy pig, who was willing to let his daughters be gang-raped by the men of Sodom to protect the angels he is hosting (Genesis 19:8). Yet when Sodom and Gomorrah are wiped off the face of the earth, and Lot and his daughters are huddled in isolation in a cave, the women are the ones who hatch a plot to restore order to the world. Lot, like Judah, is useless. Continuing in this same vein, it is worth highlighting the agency of women in Genesis through select case studies that are only tangentially mentioned in other chapters, starting with Eve.

Eve

If we set aside the long-standing theological interpretations of Eve for the time being (Pagels 1989 gives a good summary), we see that her character is quite complex. At the outset she is both temporally and physically secondary to the man – created as his helper:

> 18. Then the Lord God said, 'It is not good that the man should be alone; I will make him a helper fit for him.'
>
> 19. So out of the ground the Lord God formed every beast of the field and every bird of the air, and brought them to the man to see what he would call them; and whatever the man called every living creature, that was its name.
>
> 20. The man gave names to all cattle, and to the birds of the air, and to every beast of the field; but for the man there was not found a helper fit for him.
>
> 21. So the Lord God caused a deep sleep to fall upon the man, and while he slept took one of his ribs and closed up its place with flesh;
>
> 22. and the rib which the Lord God had taken from the man he made into a woman and brought her to the man.
>
> 23. Then the man said,
>   'This at last is bone of my bones
>   and flesh of my flesh;
>   she shall be called Woman, [אשה, *ishsha*)]
>   because she was taken out of Man.' [איש, *ish*]
>
> 24. Therefore a man leaves his father and his mother and cleaves to his wife, and they become one flesh.

Thus, the animals were not sufficient as helpers for the man, so Yahweh has to devise a new plan. There is an old apocryphal story that is current in some Jewish circles that God originally created a wife for Adam called Lilith, by forming her from the soil in the same way that Adam was created, but this situation was doomed. This passage is taken from the *Alphabet of Ben Sirach* (dated anywhere from the eighth to tenth centuries CE):

> While God created Adam, who was alone, He said, 'It is not good for man to be alone.' (Genesis 2:18). He also created a woman, from the earth, as He had created Adam himself, and called her Lilith. Adam and Lilith immediately began to fight. She said, 'I will not lie below,' and he said, 'I will not lie beneath you, but only on top. For you are fit only to be in the bottom position, while I am to be the superior one.' Lilith responded, 'We are equal to each other inasmuch as we were both created from the earth.' But they would not listen to one another. When Lilith saw this, she pronounced the Ineffable Name and flew away into the air.
> (jewishchristianlit.com//Topics/Lilith/alphabet.html, accessed 15 May 2023)

The tenor of this late fable is that Adam's first wife was no good because she wanted to be his equal, or perhaps even be his superior, and that outcome was not going to work. Eve, by this logic, was a better second choice. But, at the outset in the Genesis tale, the subordination of Eve to Adam, and her creation as a 'helper' only vaguely implies a secondary nature, and there is not yet a complete sense of inequality of power. That comes later. For the time being they are 'one flesh'. Verse 24 is cryptic, and subject to no end of speculative interpretations concerning Judaic marriage practices that seem anachronistic. In Genesis, men do not typically leave their parents on marriage: women do. They are patrilineal and patrilocal.

What follows in Genesis 3:6–7 is supremely important:

> 6. So when the woman saw that the tree was good for food, and that it was a delight to the eyes, and that the tree was to be desired to make one wise, she took of its fruit and ate; and she also gave some to her husband, and he ate.

The serpent pushed Eve in this direction, but it was up to her to act upon it – or not. She chooses the former. She wants to be wise. She eats the fruit first, and then gives it to Adam to eat. She is the one with the curiosity and agency, not Adam. Yet he is the one who gets the blame, which seems unfair. Biblical tradition, both Judaic and Christian, identifies Adam as the first sinner, and the genealogies in both the Hebrew and Greek bibles are forever searching for the 'New Adam' to rectify the original sin of the first Adam. Why isn't Eve the villain?

Furthermore, Eve is not only the first sinner, she is also the mother of history. Without her, nothing of any consequence would ever have happened. God created time and space but after that there was not much to do but eat and sleep and tend the garden – for eternity – and there is no telling how long the couple lived in the garden before Eve picked the fruit. We could also infer that the serpent picked Eve to beguile rather than Adam because she had a curious mind and an adventurous spirit (or maybe the exiles defined women as inherently unruly). Either way, she set history in motion and Adam simply followed along for the ride.

As a theological, not anthropological, counterpoint to this account of Eve, the patriarchate would probably argue that it was Adam's job to keep Eve in line, as he was the boss. When she ate the forbidden fruit, it should have been his job to correct her, not to go along with her sin. Therefore, by patriarchal thinking, he was as much to blame, if not more so, for the crime because he should have been able to keep her under control in the first place. This may well have been the line adopted by Judean priests in exile. That is, women have to be controlled by men because they are naturally undisciplined. Women are perceived as inherently dangerous because they like to colour outside the lines. Dangerous people are potentially powerful. Therefore, Eve's curse from God after eating the fruit is significant: 'he shall rule over you' (Genesis 3:16).

Hagar
Given that Hagar, Sarah's maid/slave, was a (despised) Egyptian foreigner and that both she and her son were banished from Israel, her place in the Genesis history is quite remarkable. The exact reason why Sarah had a specifically Egyptian servant, and how that came about, is not made clear, but there is an underlying sense that Egypt and Egyptians are not to be trusted (a warning of many things to come). All of the patriarchal narratives from Abraham onwards head inexorably in the direction of the voluntary migration of the entire Israelite nation into Egypt, because of famine in the Levant, and there was a foreshadowing of this journey by Abraham and Sarah (when they might possibly have acquired Hagar). There are also multiple trips to Egypt by Joseph's brothers in times of famine, until eventually they obtain land and settle there, beginning a long sojourn that starts with voluntary migration and ends in slavery, the situation which sets up the necessary conditions for the ethnically defining ritual of the Passover and the exodus from Egypt (itself a prefigurement of the Babylonian Exile – and its hoped-for end). Hagar's position is a reversal of the later fortunes of Abraham's descendants, inasmuch as in this narrative she is the slave and he is the rich overlord.

We first come in contact with Hagar in relation to Sarah's childlessness in Genesis 16:1. As indicated in previous chapters, the practice of using a childless woman's maid/slave as a surrogate mother to bear children on her behalf was an acceptable custom, so long as the two women accepted the fact that any child born to the maid became the legal offspring of the childless woman. In this case, things go wrong immediately because Hagar, as soon as she knows that she is pregnant, scoffs at Sarah's infertility and, implicitly refuses to concede to the terms of the surrogacy. This act, in turn, angers Sarah who treats Hagar harshly. Because of her rough treatment, Hagar escapes into the wilderness to a place identified as Shur, which may be along a route between Canaan and Egypt.

Here Hagar encounters an angel of Yahweh, who tells her that she will bear a son and his name will be Ishmael. He will be a wild man, hounded on all sides, but he will survive and his patriline will grow as mightily as Abraham's own and rival it. The language of this passage parallels that of Yahweh's promise to Abraham concerning his progeny, though extraordinarily this time the promise is made directly to a woman. To fulfil the promise, however, Hagar must return to Abraham's household and tolerate the abuse dished out by Sarah. Subsequently she returns of her own volition, despite what lies ahead, and gives birth to Ishmael in Abraham's household in order to give her son his destined start in life.

All seems well until Sarah gives birth to Isaac, setting up a potentially fatal conflict between the brothers (or their mothers). Both were predicted to engender mighty nations that would struggle endlessly with one another. The fortunes of the boys hinge on the fortitude of their mothers, with Sarah having the upper hand by virtue of her status as Abraham's wife and a member of his lineage (a non-uterine sister). When Isaac was weaned, Sarah demanded that Abraham send Hagar and Ishmael away so that her son would have no rivals, and Abraham very reluctantly complied with her wishes even though Ishmael was his first-born. (Genesis 21:8–21)

Abraham packs them off into the wilderness (desert) of Beersheba with a modicum of bread and water – seemingly a death sentence. At the very least, Abraham will not see them ever again. When the water has been exhausted, Hagar gives up hope and lies down to die at some distance from Ishmael, so that she will not have to witness his death. An angel, however, reveals a well to her at that moment, and they are saved. From then on, they make their home in the wilderness of Paran (in Exodus, this is mentioned as one of the areas the Israelites wandered after escaping Egypt – and where they encounter the Ishmaelites). Ishmael grows up to be a mighty hunter, and it is Hagar who finds an Egyptian wife for him – typically the father's role. Ishmael's destiny as the father of a mighty nation rests in the agency of his mother, not his father (Genesis 16 and 21).

Rebekah

Unlike Abraham, Jacob and Joseph, who have long and detailed histories in Genesis exploring the depths of their personalities, Isaac is an incomplete character within the text, with very little complexity. He exists only as the young son of Abraham, serving as a test of his father's faith; or as the ageing father of Esau and Jacob who gives his inheritance away to his younger, and not his elder, son. Rebekah, by comparison, is given a well-rounded personality and is not simply represented as Isaac's wife. Throughout her story she is described not only as attractive but also as a woman with a mind of her own who makes life decisions of her own choosing. It makes much more sense to speak of Isaac as 'Rebekah's husband' than vice versa. She is the key player.

We become aware of Rebekah's independence of spirit right from her first encounter with Abraham's servant who has journeyed to Paddan-aram/Harran to seek a bride for Isaac. In pastoral communities it is the fathers of the bride and groom, plus their kinsmen and retainers, who conduct the business of betrothal, not the couple themselves. Pastoral courtship rituals are not the equivalent of modern romance (see, for example, Evans-Pritchard 1951). Indeed, Rebekah's active role in the negotiations is something of an anomaly, suggesting to me that the urban, priestly redactors of Genesis were not especially familiar with the practices of pastoral cultures. Why would they be?

Here is the salient moment after the men have had their discussions and ogled all the camels and gold they are set to receive should Rebekah marry Isaac (Genesis 24:58–9):

58. And they called Rebekah, and said to her, 'Will you go with this man?' She said, 'I will go.'

59. So they sent away Rebekah, their sister and her nurse, and Abraham's servant and his men.

To be fair, this scene is not completely out of character for cultures that practice arranged marriages. It is not uncommon for the woman to have the right to refuse a particular man, although in this case she has not even met Isaac. All she knows is that his family is rich and lives so far away from her ancestral home that she will be cut off from them in perpetuity. Nonetheless, she does not hesitate to agree to the marriage. It is her choice to make, as is made abundantly clear in other places in the narrative, and Rebekah makes a bold decision. As a side note, I should point out that Abraham does not consider getting a bride for Isaac until after Sarah has died, and that one of his purposes is to replace Isaac's mother as a comfort (Genesis 24:67b). Rebekah is not exactly what he bargained for.

As time passes, the division and rivalry between the couple's two sons, Esau and Jacob, could not be more obvious, and the split also divides Isaac and Rebekah. Esau is the shaggy and impulsive hunter of the fields, and Jacob is the well-groomed, urbane, literate sophisticate. Esau is referred to as 'Isaac's son' whereas Jacob is called 'Rebekah's son', indicating their favourites (Genesis 25:19–34). It would not be fair to characterize Jacob as effeminate given his capacity to wrestle with an angel all night and nearly win (Genesis 32:22–32) and his ability to lift a stone covering a well on his own that is so big that it normally took a whole gang of shepherds to move. Jacob fits many of the stereotypes of a manly man, but in his battle with Esau it is reasonable to argue that the women's team won.

Jacob most decidedly follows in Rebekah's footsteps and not Isaac's. Isaac is something of a plodder, but Rebekah is shrewd and calculating, and Jacob inherits much of her skill – especially in his dealings with her brother Laban, who is also a tricky character. At this juncture it is apparent that traits are now passing through the matriline, and this fact is vital because Jacob is the father of the twelve tribes of Israel. His defining qualities, which are to become the defining qualities of a nation, are inherited from a woman.

Rachel

It is not correct to think of Rachel as a clone of Rebekah, her father's sister, but she does come from the same stock. Her father, Laban, is as devious as her aunt. Jacob's journey up to Paddan-aram is not the twin of Abraham's servant's journey there in search of a wife for Isaac, and therefore does not break the pastoral pattern of betrothal laid out in the previous section. Jacob's motives are entirely different. He does not have marriage in mind when he travels north; rather, he is escaping the murderous wrath of Esau, who is in a rage over his stolen birthright, and he needs a place far away from home to sojourn until Esau's temper abates. His mother's home is an ideal hiding place, and the chance meeting with Rachel at the well is a happy accident (Genesis 29). From then on, Jacob is repeatedly swindled by Laban until he finds a way to escape with the aid of Rachel's trickery.

Rachel's place within Laban's household is complicated by her sister Leah's marriage to Jacob seven years before her own marriage to him, and her lack of children. She manages to find a solution, nonetheless, similar to Sarah's use of her maid as a surrogate, but with more success for the patriline due to her better planning (see p. 126). Her agency is patent from the outset. Rachel, as well as Sarah, Rebekah and Leah, are all mindful guardians of the lineage despite their various difficulties. Their roles are crucial to the success of the men who are centre stage.

There is one further, rather cryptic, episode that highlights Rachel's watchful care over Jacob and his family. Because Jacob had to work a total of fourteen years for Laban in Harran to secure his marriages to Leah and Rachel, and then yet more years because Laban keeps cheating him out of his wages, making it impossible for him to return to Canaan – thus, jeopardizing the lineal covenant with Yahweh, beginning with Abraham, to be the father of a mighty nation – Rachel takes part in a complex scheme to enrich Jacob and to facilitate his departure and return to Canaan. The full story can be found in Genesis chapters 30 and 31.

It is apparently the birth of Joseph, Rachel's oldest son and destined to be a critical force in Israel's history, that triggers Jacob's desire to leave Paddan-aram and return to his father, Isaac, in Canaan. But Laban is not willing to let Jacob and his offspring go, thereby dishonouring the pastoral traditions of patrilineality and patrilocality. Laban has no legitimate claim over his daughters and their children, and is being selfish in retaining them – unlike his father, Bethuel, who easily consented to Rebekah's journey to Canaan to marry Isaac. In consequence, Jacob waits until Laban is away shearing and then takes the opportunity to sneak away with his wives and family, and, presumably as a kind of insurance, Rachel steals Laban's household gods (Genesis 31:19). The meaning of this act is not entirely clear but these gods (*terafim*) are usually thought to be analogous to figurines found in cultures throughout the ancient world (and still found in many parts of Asia) that were protective spirits of the household. Laban may fear Yahweh, but he is not a monotheist. Rachel appears to be securing Jacob's safety from Laban by taking his gods. Without them, Laban's power is reduced.

Laban returns home after three days and is furious to find Jacob gone. He sets out in hot pursuit, and after seven days catches up with the refugees, accusing Jacob of stealing his gods. Jacob knows nothing about the theft and invites Laban to search all the tents for them, offering to kill whoever has stolen them (perhaps foreshadowing Rachel's premature death at the birth of her second son). Rachel's secret plot and deviousness continues (Genesis 31:33–5):

> 33. So Laban went into Jacob's tent, and into Leah's tent, and into the tent of the two maidservants, but he did not find them. And he went out of Leah's tent, and entered Rachel's.
>
> 34. Now Rachel had taken the household gods and put them in the camel's saddle, and sat upon them. Laban felt all about the tent, but did not find them.
>
> 35. And she said to her father, 'Let not my lord be angry that I cannot rise before you, for the way of women is upon me.' So he searched, but did not find the household gods.

The Mosaic law forbidding the touching of women when they are menstruating was not in effect at this point, but cultural decency would still apply, and there would be no easy way for Laban to determine whether she was lying or not. Her scheme was successful, and in the end Laban and Jacob were reconciled, with Jacob continuing on his journey (still in possession of Laban's household gods). Chalk another success up to a woman.

Potiphar's wife

The tale of Potiphar's wife marks a significant turning point for Joseph's life in slavery in Egypt. Up to this point, Joseph has been a respected member of Potiphar's household, but his fortunes quickly change when Potiphar's wife has eyes for him. Uncharacteristically for Genesis, Joseph is described as an attractive man using the Hebrew word יפה, *yapheh*, for him twice (Genesis 39:6): once to describe his bodily physique and a second time for his facial features. This is the same word that Genesis uses to describe Sarah when she and Abraham are journeying among Egyptians and he is afraid that she will be lusted after by the men of the region, and to describe Rachel when she first appears at the well in Harran (Genesis 12:14 and 29:17).

Potiphar's wife is presented as the archetype of the foreign temptress – a snare for anyone of high position living in exile. Her sexuality is dangerous and to be avoided at all costs. By extension, attractive Babylonian woman are to be shunned by the exiles, no matter how sexually appealing there are. Stick with Judean women. The complete episode (Genesis 39) is revelatory in both dialog and action. At this stage Joseph is in a great position. Though he has been sold into slavery in Egypt by his brothers, he has landed a high position with Potiphar who is a well-placed courtier in the Pharaoh's inner circle. Potiphar's wife (unnamed) lusts after the handsome slave and is blunt with him – two words of command in Hebrew with no prelude – hard to capture in translation without being crude, but tantamount to 'sleep with me'. By contrast, Joseph is extraordinarily polite and drawn out in his reply, refusing the offer/command. Yet Potiphar's wife presses her point.

Joseph is caught in a delicate situation. Succumbing to Potiphar's wife's command could bring with it favours for Joseph. If she were to be discreet about the affair, all parties might get what they wanted. But Joseph is honourable and does not wish to be seduced. When Potiphar's wife presses on with her seduction by taking hold of Joseph's garment and repeating her blunt command, he wriggles out of it and escapes, leaving the garment in her hands. Consequently, Potiphar's wife, scorned in sex, uses the garment to frame Joseph with her husband, and he sends him to Pharaoh's prison as punishment where he languishes until fate steps in to free him and restore him to grace, and an even more exalted rank within the Egyptian court.

As noted already (pp. 98–9), Joseph's story is an oddity within the Genesis corpus, because after this incident and his consequent fall and then rise back to power, he marries an Egyptian woman and has two sons, whose descendants eventually become the rich backbone of Israel. Joseph's life history speaks less to the ills of marrying foreigners, and more to the necessity of avoiding married women (foreign or not). For this lesson, Potiphar's wife is a nameless, one-dimensional caricature of the foreign seductress who stands in stark contrast to the Judean women of Genesis, who are multi-dimensional agents, not just sexual partners and son factories, and who are vital to the success of the nation of Israel at its inception.

Wrapping up

On the whole, we have to accept the fact that Genesis does not give us an adequate picture of women in the ancient Near East, either in the purported patriarchal period or during the Exile. At best it gives us a glimpse of what educated men thought a woman's place in society should be – subservient, obedient housekeepers and childbearers. It is, therefore, a surprise when women are portrayed as complex characters with a will of their own, as the foregoing catalogue indicates. Their primary, clearly stated, function is to be pretty and have babies, yet, time and again, the women of Genesis break that mould.

To the extent that Genesis is pieced together out of oral narratives that had had a venerable and cherished history by the time of the Exile, the tales of the women described therein reflect deeply held values. The sexual misdeeds of the kings and queens of Israel and Judah, including David and his sons (Absalom, Amnon and Adonijah), Solomon and Jezebel, and their disastrous consequences, would have been well known to the Exiles via the Deuteronomic histories. The women of Genesis represent a powerful counterpoint to these tales. Women like Sarah, Rebekah and Rachel were necessary for the ascendancy of Israel, and are necessary again in a time of exile.

Further reading

Feminist perspectives on patriarchy and women in the Bible (Hebrew and Greek) proliferate these days, but there is not much attention paid specifically to the women of Genesis. I recommend these general texts for a theoretical overview: Athalya Brenner, *The Israelite Woman* (1985); Adela Yarbro Collins (ed.), *Feminist Perspectives on Biblical Scholarship* (1985); Tikva Frymer-Kensky. *Reading the Women of the Bible* (2002); Esther Fuchs, *Sexual Politics in the Biblical Narrative* (2000); Rosalyn Lachs, *Women and Judaism* (1980); and Rosemary Radford Ruether (ed.) *Religion and Sexism* (1974).

You can find a more targeted analysis of the matriarchs of Genesis in Sharon Jeansonne's *The Women of Genesis* (1990), but a certain care must be taken in reading this work because the author is not particularly familiar with ethnographic analysis and frequently misinterprets cultural values. Susan

Niditch's *Underdogs and Tricksters* (1987) concentrates heavily on Genesis and does contain some portions devoted to Sarah and Rebekah's subterfuges while sojourners outside Canaan. *Women and Exilic Identity in the Hebrew Bible*, edited by Katherine E. Southwood and Martien Halvorson-Taylor (2017), reviews feminist scholarship concerning Biblical texts of the Exile in general although there is scant attention paid to Genesis in particular.

The specific place in Israelite/Judean society, especially as it relates to childbirth, of the slave-girl, often euphemized in translation as 'maid' or 'maidservant', is a much-debated issue. 'Female slave vs female slave: אמה and שפחה in the Hebrew Bible' by Edward J. Bridge (2012) provides a thorough review of the debate, providing references to numerous commentators and their various interpretations.

11

Towering arrogance

❦

The story of the Tower of Babel in Genesis 11 is the last tale in the book to present Yahweh's universal judgment on the entire world. In some ways it echoes the themes of the flood narrative. Humans have acted wickedly, and so God condemns them all. In the case of the Tower of Babel, however, God's sentence on the sinners is not as severe as that of the flood. For their arrogance in attempting to build a tower that will allow humans to climb to heaven, God punishes their hubris by condemning them to speak different languages. Subsequently, they cannot understand one another and therefore they cannot work together.

The tale of the Tower of Babel is not long, so I present it here in its entirety (Genesis 11:1–9):

1. Now the whole earth had one language and the same words.

2. And as they migrated from the east, they came upon a plain in the land of Shinar and settled there.

3. And they said to one another, 'Come, let us make bricks, and burn them thoroughly.' And they had brick for stone, and bitumen for mortar.

4. Then they said, 'Come, let us build ourselves a city, and a tower with its top in the heavens, and let us make a name for ourselves; otherwise we shall be scattered abroad upon the face of the whole earth.'

5. The Lord came down to see the city and the tower, which mortals had built.

6. And the Lord said, 'Look, they are one people, and they have all one language; and this is only the beginning of what they will do; nothing that they propose to do will now be impossible for them.

7. Come, let us go down, and confuse their language there, so that they will not understand one another's speech.'

8. So the Lord scattered them abroad from there over the face of all the earth, and they left off building the city.

9. Therefore it was called Babel, because there the Lord confused the language of all the earth; and from there the Lord scattered them abroad over the face of all the earth.

Look at the last verse first to understand what the biblical authors saw as the immediate moral of the tale. Anyone familiar with the Bible as a whole is accustomed to the name Babel, so the translator uses it here in preference to other possibilities. The word 'Babel' is a direct transliteration of the Hebrew text. What this transliteration misses, however, is that 'Babel' is the common Hebrew name for Babylon. This story is not about some fictional, fabled, primordial city. It is about the real life, flesh and blood, bricks and mortar Babylon that the exiles were stuck in, or near. If the name were not enough, the location in the plain of Shinar is a dead giveaway: Shinar is a synonym for Babylonia.[15] I suspect that this story was written by the Judean priests during the Exile. This story is about why Babylon is such an evil place and why contact with it will do you nothing but harm.

The tale, better renamed 'The Tower of Babylon', is, I believe, a Judean attempt to write their own story of the origin of the city of Babylon to counter the indigenous Babylonian narratives of which the locals were so proud. The Babylonian creation story is called the *Enûma Elish* and exists in a number of forms and copies. Its exact date of composition is disputed and could be anywhere from the eighteenth to the twelfth century BCE. Most scholars prefer later dates in this span (e.g. Lambert 2013; Talon 2005). According to the *Enûma Elish*, Babylon was founded in honour of the great god Marduk after he had defeated Tiamat, a deity symbolic of primordial watery chaos. Here is a small portion from that narrative:

---

15 See www.jewishencyclopedia.com/articles/13582-shinar (accessed 7 November 2023).

47. The Anunnaki opened their mouths
48. And addressed their lord Marduk,
49. 'Now, lord, seeing you have established our freedom
50. What favour can we do for you?
51. Let us make a shrine of great renown:
52. Your chamber will be our resting place wherein we may repose.
53. Let us erect a shrine to house a pedestal
54. Wherein we may repose when we finish (the work).'
55. When Marduk heard this,
56. He beamed as brightly as the light of day,
57. 'Build Babylon, the task you have sought.
58. Let bricks for it be moulded, and raise the shrine!'
59. The Anunnaki wielded the pick.
60. For one year they made the needed bricks.
61. When the second year arrived,
62. They raised the peak of Esagil, a replica of the Apsû.
63. They built the lofty temple tower of the Apsû

(*Enûma Elish*, tablet 6 lines 47ff[16])

By this account Babylon was built by great gods for the supreme god (Black and Green 1992; Coleman and Davidson 2015).[17] Humans had no hand in its design or construction. At the centre of the city the gods built a shrine – the Esagila – and a ziggurat, a kind of pyramid, to serve as their abode. Babylon was, as the etymology of its name indicates in Akkadian (*bab* = gate, *ili* = of god), and as the Babylonian narrative asserts, the portal of the gods. It was the place where the gods could come down to earth from their heavenly dwelling via the ziggurat they had built.

Ziggurats were typically tiered pyramids with stairways leading to the apex and with sanctuaries on their summits, suitably furnished with luxurious items for the gods to use. These lofty sanctuaries midway between heaven and earth were liminal zones where gods and humans could meet. The *Enûma Elish* goes on to say that when the ziggurat was finished the gods came down

---

16 www.worldhistory.org/article/225/enuma-elish---the-babylonian-epic-of-creation---fu (accessed 25 May 2023).

17 The Anunnaki were Sumerian gods who were the offspring of An, god of the sky, and the earth goddess. Ki (hence the name – AN and KI). Enlil, the god of air was the first-born and was the chief god of the Sumerian pantheon. Until Enlil was born, heaven and earth were inseparable. Note also – E- TEMEN – AN – KI means temple- foundation – heaven – earth.

to it for a big banquet, and they dedicated Babylon to Marduk as his home (see Arnold and Beyer 2002; Heidel 1946).

Architecture as blasphemy

From the Judean perspective ziggurat architecture, and the theology behind it, was blasphemous. The Judeans considered Mt. Zion to be the centre of the earth and the dwelling place of the high god, Yahweh. In their view, Jerusalem was the sacred navel of the world, not Babylon. Babylon was an arrogant upstart. The exiles, like the Babylonians, believed that humans could meet God in high places midway between heaven and earth.

It was the idea of an artificial mountain that offended the exiles. Mt. Zion and Mt. Sinai were natural phenomena created when the earth was formed by Yahweh (Genesis 1). Ziggurats, they believed (despite the narratives), were built by humans and were a testament only to their hubris. Rather than going to places (Mt. Sinai and Mt. Zion) made by God and under his terms, the exiles argued that ziggurats were human constructions designed to entice the gods from heaven on human terms. The Genesis story of the Tower of Babylon inverts the tale from the *Enûma Elish*. Babylon is the abode of humans who aspire to god-like status, and their ziggurats are symbolic of this arrogance.

At the time of the Babylonian Exile there was a ziggurat in Babylon named Etemenanki, which means 'The Tower of the Foundation of Heaven and Earth'. Its origins are obscure. It may have been built originally by the legendary king and lawgiver Hammurabi (who lived and reigned around 1792–1750 BCE or earlier). It had fallen into a state of disrepair, perhaps in part because of the damage caused by the sack of Babylon in 689 BCE by the Assyrian king Sennacherib. Nebuchadnezzar II rebuilt it during the Exile period. A stele, that is, a stone monument carved in relief (MS 2063 Schøyen collection),[18] purportedly from the time, provides an image of the ziggurat and its temple. Next to it is a super-sized image of Nebuchadnezzar, taller than the ziggurat, holding a scroll of the architectural plans for the rebuilding. In part it reads:

> Etemenanki, Ziggurat of Babylon. I made it, the wonder of the people of the world, I raised its top to heaven, made doors for the gates, and I covered it with bitumen and bricks.

Further information about Etemenanki comes from a cuneiform tablet from the third century BCE (probably a copy of an older one), discovered in

---

18 A sketch is reproduced at www.schoyencollection.com/history-collection-introduction/babylonian-history-collection/tower-babel-stele-ms-2063 (accessed 11 November 2023).

Uruk in southern Mesopotamia in 1876 and now housed in the Louvre (AO 6055). It says that Etemenanki was constructed in seven tiers, like a square wedding cake. The exact dimensions are difficult to determine on the basis of the intentionally cryptic Babylonian mathematical system. Here is a sample:

> Measurements of the base of the Etemenanki: here are the length and width to be considered: 3 × 60 is the length, 3 × 60 is the width, measured in standard cubits. Its dimensions are therefore: 3 × 3=9; 9 × 2=18. If you do not know the value of 18, here it is: 3 measures of seed, surface area measured with the small cubit. Base of the Etemenanki: the height is equal to the length and width. Let the initiate show this to the initiate. Let the non-initiate not see it.

The discoverer of the tablet was George Smith, an English Assyriologist, who is most famous for having discovered and translated the original tablets of the Epic of Gilgamesh. He translated the measurements of Entemenanki as follows:

> 1st step 300 × 300 ft, 110 ft high
> 2nd step 260 × 260 ft, 60 ft high
> 3rd step 200 × 200 ft, 20 ft high
> 4th step 170 × 170 ft, 20 ft high
> 5th step 140 × 140 ft, 20 ft high
> 6th step [omitted] conjectured as 20 ft high
> 7th step conjectured as 70 ft × 80 ft, 50 ft high

The tablet states that the ziggurat was as high as the length of its base, so it would have been about 300 feet (91.5 meters) high, an enormously imposing structure given that the rest of the city would have been mostly low dwellings. The actual base of Etemenanki was accidentally discovered by local villagers in the late nineteenth century, when they were attempting to clear land to plant a palm garden. While they did not know what they had found, European engineers working in the area realized what it was. In 1899 German archaeologist and architect Robert Koldewey began excavations, which continued for eighteen years. He measured the base tier as slightly over 91 meters square (around 300 ft^2) – quite close to George Smith's estimate (Koldewey 1914).

Using findings from excavations of other ziggurats, plus the written evidence from clay tablets, archaeologists conjecture that Etemenanki was decorated with glazed bricks which would have been incised with vertical grooves (Harris 2002:50–1; Koldewey 1914). The tablet further indicates that on the highest level of the ziggurat was a temple divided into rooms for various high gods: one for Marduk himself and his wife; others for Nabû (the scribe); Ea (god of water and Marduk's father – also known as Enki); Nusku (god of light); Anu (god of heaven); and Enlil, the Sumerian god who ruled the Mesopotamian pantheon before Marduk superseded him. In an inner courtyard, larger than all the other rooms, was a special bed.

Writing about 100 years after the Exile the Greek historian Herodotus of Halicarnassus (484 BC – c.425 BC) provides this description of Etenmenanki, which helps explain the purpose of the central bedroom:

> In the middle of the precinct there was a tower of solid masonry, a furlong in length and breadth, upon which was raised a second tower, and on that a third, and so on up to eight. The ascent to the top is on the outside, by a path which winds round all the towers. When one is about halfway up, one finds a resting place and seats, where persons are wont to sit some time on their way to the summit. On the topmost tower there is a spacious temple, and inside the temple stands a couch of unusual size, richly adorned, with a golden table by its side. There is no statue of any kind set up in the place, nor is the chamber occupied of nights by anyone but a single native woman, who, as the Chaldaeans, the priests of this god, affirm, is chosen for himself by the deity out of all the women of the land. They also declare – but I for my part do not credit it – that the god comes down in person into this chamber, and sleeps upon the couch.
>
> (Herodotus' *Histories*: book 1:,para 181)

This description contains several errors, such as the dimensions of the ziggurat. For example, a Greek furlong is about 606 feet, more than double the actual length of the base of the tower. Herodotus was probably not an eyewitness but was relying on other sources. Note, though, that he is not completely uncritical about his sources' reports. While he has heard that the god comes down from heaven to sleep on the couch in the temple at the summit with a Babylonian woman of his choosing, he lets his readers know that he is sceptical. What we can take from Herodotus is that this multilayered tower had steps on the outside for the ascent to the top, with places to rest along the way. The only aspect of the interior of the temple that he describes is the central bedchamber for the god.

Whatever it was that the chosen woman experienced in her night in the temple, the Babylonian view of theophany, seeing God face to face, was different from the Judean concept. For the ancient Israelites, meeting God was a potentially fatal event reserved only for the holiest of men (no women allowed). The reason for their meeting was some kind of major revelation such as the giving of the law or the establishment of a sacred place. For the Babylonians the meeting seems to have been sexual, highly reminiscent of the acts of Genesis 6:1–4 (see Chapter 4), the event that precipitated the flood. From the Judean standpoint the Babylonians were playing with fire (or water! – and lots of it).

The remains of Etemenanki, which during the Greek imperial reign (c. fourth century BCE) had once again fallen into a state of disrepair, were torn down to be rebuilt under the orders of Alexander the Great (356–323 BCE). Alexander ordered a huge number of bricks to be made to complete the job, but died before the project could be started. So the ziggurat remained a ruin. Nowadays the base of the ziggurat is exposed, although overgrown somewhat, and satellite images reveal the size and complexity of the temple plaza where it stood. It must have been an awe-inspiring sight.

Etemenanki and the exiles

Because Etemenanki was under reconstruction when the exiles were brought to Babylon it was likely to have been a prominent focus for them. They also undoubtedly heard all the sacred narratives associated with Marduk and the ziggurat. Many scholars argue that much of Genesis is a direct rejection of, or counter-narrative to, the Babylonian creation story. Some take the position that the Judeans deliberately reworked the Babylonian tales to create Genesis (e.g. Arnold and Weisberg 2002). In the Babylonian story, Marduk is groomed as a young god to face the terrifying goddess of watery chaos, Tiamat, who rises up to avenge the death of her husband. After Marduk has slain her, in one of the great battle scenes of ancient narrative, he splits her body in two and fashions the sky and earth from the two halves. Then he sets the sun, moon and stars in the sky, and ordains their passages, which serve to mark years, months and weeks of seven days. Next, he kills one of Tiamat's allies and mixes the blood of the dead god with earth to fashion humans, whose task is to labour to serve the gods. Finally, the gods build Babylon as Marduk's earthly seat, and then celebrate with a huge feast in the temple. Reading the original from the *Enûma Elish*, the echoes of themes from Genesis 1 are unmistakable, making it appear that the Judeans adopted and adapted parts of the Babylonian creation narrative or some related tale.

It is highly likely that the exiles felt the need to counter the Babylonian narrative, which paralleled in so many key ways their own stories of a high god creating order out of watery chaos. Their answer was the story of the Tower of Babylon, which turns the theme of the original Babylonian narrative upside down. According to the exiles, the Babylonian gods did not create Babylon at all, it was a human artefact. More importantly, they did not create order from chaos, but the opposite. In their attempts to be god-like the Babylonians created chaos. Babylon was the seat of chaos and disorder. In the Judean view, cities in general, especially large polyglot imperial capitals, are inherently disordered. Their populations should be scattered across the earth, returned to their original cultural homelands.

The description of the building of the tower in Genesis 11:3 is terse yet perfectly accurate when it comes to the construction of Etemenanki. The description of baked mud bricks and bitumen is exactly paralleled in Nebuchadnezzar's pictorial stele, and in other Mesopotamian texts that emphasize baked bricks as the primordial building material of the gods. Perhaps the Exilic authors were eyewitnesses to Nebuchadnezzar's reconstruction efforts. It is scarcely likely that the building programme could be ignored entirely, even though many exiles lived in enclaves outside the city.

The fact that humans were rebuilding this ziggurat would also make it obvious to the exiles that the story of the tower being built by the gods was pure fantasy. It was self-evidently a human construction with human needs in mind. The Judeans may not have realized that at the time of the rebuilding efforts they were witnessing, the tower was more than 1,000 years old, and that the Babylonians themselves had little idea of its origin. Or they may not have cared. As far as the exiles were concerned it was a human artefact, no matter its age. In the final analysis, the story of the Tower of Babylon was most likely a direct attack on Nebuchadnezzar and his building efforts.

Cities, language and chaos

The central theme of the narrative is that when humans have one language there is virtually no limit to their ambitions. They can congregate in cities and build massive structures. A parallel exists with a short tale within the text of the ancient Sumerian epic (preserved in copies from *c.* twenty-first century BCE), 'Enmerkar and the lord of Aratta':

> On that day when there is no snake, when there is no scorpion, when there is no hyena, when there is no lion, when there is neither dog nor wolf, when there is thus neither fear nor trembling, man has no rival! At such a time, may the lands of Cubur and Hamazi, the many-tongued, and Sumer, the great mountain of the me of magnificence, and Akkad, the land possessing all that is befitting, and the Martu land, resting in security – the whole universe, the well-guarded people – may they all address Enlil together in a single language! For at that time, for the ambitious lords, for the ambitious princes, for the ambitious kings ... Enki, the lord of abundance and of steadfast decisions, the wise and knowing lord of the Land, the expert of the gods, chosen for wisdom, the lord of Eridug, shall change the speech in their

mouths, as many as he had placed there, and so the speech of mankind is truly one.

('Enmerkar and the lord of Aratta', ll. 134–55)[19]

This tale is the exact opposite of the Tower of Babylon story. In this Sumerian narrative, humankind begins with multiple languages and the god Enki (also called Ea, Marduk's father) does not like it. The ambitious lords of the world cannot praise him adequately when they speak different languages, so he commands that they all speak one tongue. This notion would be highly desirable in a hegemonic empire. If you want your subject peoples to do your bidding, they need to speak the same language as you and your overseers.

Language and social control

The periodic effort of some United States legislators to make English the official language of the land is an example of an attempt to use language to dominate minority cultures (including indigenous ones) and foreign immigrants (Lynch 2006). Immigrants can sometimes appear threatening to the mainstream just because they look and act in distinctive manner. If they are off in their own enclaves speaking in unknown tongues, they can appear doubly so. From the immigrant perspective, as well as from that of indigenous peoples, a demand to speak English as the national language in the United States is also, quite rightly, seen as a direct threat to local culture. Pueblo Indians, when performing ancient rituals in kivas in central New Mexico, chant and sing in native Tewa. These songs are not allowed to be translated into English (Ortiz 1969). If the people stop speaking Tewa, this will impact the ability to hold the ritual and indeed the sustainability of the entire culture.

The Catholic mass, by contrast, was for hundreds of years spoken only in Latin worldwide. This signalled the power and universality of the papacy and church hierarchy. In 1900 a Catholic communicant could attend mass in Berlin or Nairobi, and it would be exactly the same. Getting everyone under your control to speak the same language is a powerful mode of subjugation.

Judeans had a vested interest in maintaining their own language and customs, and in not being overpowered by the language of their captors. Apart from the danger of being culturally overwhelmed by the dominant language, a late dialect of Akkadian sometimes simply called Babylonian, the immediate risk was that Judean men and women would start associating with Babylonian people and other subject groups. If the Judeans continued to speak only their local dialects of Hebrew, intermarriage was less likely.

---

19 The Electronic Text Corpus of Sumerian Literature: etcsl.orinst.ox.ac.uk/section1/tr1823.htm (accessed 26 May 2023).

In the story of the Tower of Babylon, Yahweh is in full agreement with Enki; when humans speak only one language there is no limit to what they can accomplish, because they are physically and culturally united. But Yahweh's people are not in the same position as the Babylonians, and so his agenda is quite different from Enki's. The exiles needed to counter the Mesopotamian narratives of domination with a story of their own, to reverse the dynamics of power.

Yahweh's response to the human arrogance of building Etemenanki is analogous to sending the waters of the flood. Humans want to unite heaven and earth, which God has deemed should remain separate since the days of creation. By so doing humans threaten to undo creation by uniting opposites. The result will be a return to chaos, so Yahweh punishes humankind by initiating the confusion they are flirting with – he dis-orders their language. The modern city of Babylon is the result: a place where all different languages are heard and where distinct cultures live in close proximity. This state of affairs is not a symbol of Babylonian power, but of God's terrible judgment.

The story suggests that the name Babel is not derived from Akkadian roots that mean 'the gate of god' but instead means 'confusion' (based on obscure folk etymology – Mckenzie 1995:73). English speakers might say that the place should be called Babble or Babble-On rather than Babel. It is the place where a multitude of languages is spoken, reflecting God's displeasure. Only one solution exists. The peoples who speak these different languages must disperse and go back to where they belong. Nothing good can come from them dwelling in confusion.

The text ends with the peoples speaking different languages scattering over the face of the earth. This dispersion is an absolute condemnation of Babylon and of cities in general. As noted in the next chapter, the Judeans had nothing good to say about cities. People should not be living so close together. The wide-open spaces of the pastoralists living in tents are the ideal. When people live on top of one another, bad things start to happen. Babylon is the symbol of all that is wrong with cities. For the rest of Biblical history (down to the time of Jesus and beyond), the name Babylon is synonymous with corruption.

Further reading

The most recent source of relevant primary materials from Mesopotamia concerning flood narratives is Bill T. Arnold and Bryan E. Beyer's *Readings from the Ancient Near East* (2002). This supersedes Alexander Heidel's *The Gilgamesh Epic and Old Testament Parallels* (1946).

The influence of ancient Babylonian narratives on Genesis has been a contentious issue for Biblical scholars for more than a century. For a good overview of the main issues see Yaacov Shavit and Mordechai Eran's *The Hebrew Bible Reborn* (2007), and Bill Arnold and David Weisberg's 'A centennial review of Friedrich Delitzsch's "Babel und Bibel" lectures' (2002).

Many works on the archaeology of ancient Babylon and of Etemenanki are old, mostly in German, and hard to come by. One article of great interest, if you can find it, is Andrew George (2000), 'E-sangil and E-temen-anki: the archetypal cult-centre'.

For a satellite image of Etemenanki as it now exists, simply search Google Maps, where you can find the remains of the whole ritual complex.

Ancient measurement and mathematical systems preoccupy scholars with a passion. Start with Asger Aaboe's *Episodes from the Early History of Mathematics* (1964) or Georges Ifrah, *A Universal History of Numbers* (1998). For a more complex analysis you can have a go at the works of Jöran Friberg such as, 'The third millennium roots of Babylonian mathematics' (1978) or *Unexpected Links Between Egyptian and Babylonian Mathematics* (2005). You need to be up on algebra and geometry to get much from these sources.

12

The farmer and the cowman can't be friends

It can be puzzling to contemplate why the sophisticated and urbane priests who meticulously kept the historical records of Israel and Judah, and who redacted Genesis, were so enamoured of tent-dwelling cattle and camel herders, and so dismissive of farmers and cities. The previous chapter provides some insights into the ancient Judean views about the evils of cities. But there is much more to the story than that. The redactors of Genesis did not like farmers either, and farming is intimately tied to urbanization and all its evils. The archaeological record shows that intensive farming and the development of cities are interdependent. It is possible that the redactors of Genesis saw farming as the evil prelude to the ills of urban life. The story of Adam and Eve, at the beginning of Genesis, reveals how God's negative attitude towards farming began. The redactors highlighted this story to make the point.

It is possible to interpret the period that Adam and Eve spent in the garden in Eden as symbolic of foraging, the ancient past of all humanity. Adam and Eve did not plant the garden, they did not know how. Yahweh planted it. Adam and Eve simply gathered the fruits of the garden, taking what they needed from the abundance that was there without much work other than a bit of necessary upkeep. In this tranquil and secure world, they were not hunters. No creature in the garden ate meat.

From an anthropological perspective, the story of Adam and Eve is a fable about an idyllic place of non-violence in which all is well if one obeys the rules. Adam and Eve fell from grace with Yahweh when they ate the forbidden fruit in the centre of the garden, and they were rejected from Eden. This part of the story represents the shift from foraging to food production, and it is clearly a transition from good to bad. In terms of human prehistory, the first few chapters of Genesis represent a highly compressed view of the transition from foraging to settled food production. Many anthropologists, myself included, agree with Genesis that the domestication of plants and animals was a fall from grace.

For centuries Western scholars assumed that humans first domesticated plants and animals around 12,000 years ago, and that controlling plant growth and herds lightened their burden of work and increased food security. The assumption was that life in 'the state of nature' was precarious, physically exhausting and dangerous, or as Thomas Hobbes famously put it, 'solitary, poor, nasty, brutish, and short'. A half century of research in archaeology and cultural anthropology has shown that this viewpoint is completely wrong.

The original affluent society

In the 1960s cultural anthropologist Richard Lee offered an entirely different view of the world of foragers, that is, people who provide for their needs through gathering, hunting and fishing. He produced meticulous studies of the diet and work habits of the Ju/'hoansi people (formerly referred to as the !Kung San or Bushmen) of the Kalahari desert in a region crossing the border of Namibia and Botswana (Lee 1979:95). His findings astounded anthropologists. Despite the fact that these people were living in an arid desert, they were prospering. They worked for their food only a few hours every day and generally had enough to eat (based on FDA Recommended Daily Allowances). They were healthy and they had long lifespans. They appeared to be happy and free of interpersonal violence. Lee's findings have since been replicated for other 'undisturbed' forager groups, especially those living in temperate climates (Thomas 2006; Yellen 1986). Unfortunately, it is hard to continue to study the lifeways of foragers because most of their cultures have been integrated, one way or another, into modern cash economies, usually at the bottom of the economic pyramid, and their traditional ways destroyed (DeVore and Lee 1968).

There may be several explanations for why foragers work little but are healthy. First, they harvest what nature offers in the way of food, liquid to drink, and materials for shelter. They do not have to plant, water and fertilize; they do not have to feed livestock and care for sick animals; and they do not need to defend gardens or herds against marauders. They take what they need from nature's bounty. Second, they have an exceptionally simple but efficient technology, Third, they have a limited set of material needs or wants. They do not have to work to earn cash to buy and maintain televisions, computers, mobile phones, dishwashers, cars and air conditioners. Nor, until recently, did they have to support the costly infrastructure of modern states through paying taxes.

Marshall Sahlins, following Lee, called foragers the 'original affluent society' because their needs, as culturally defined, were more than met with minimal effort (Sahlins 1972). Today, we might also call them the 'original green society' because their lifestyle is sustainable and has little or no negative impact on the environment. But, if they were so 'affluent', why did so many peoples abandon the satisfying lifestyle of foraging to pursue the path of plant and animal domestication, that is, farming and herding? The answer to this question probably differs from place to place around the world. In some contexts, people may have taken up farming because of population pressures or climate changes or environmental degradation. No single cause, however, explains the transition in all parts of the globe, and archaeologists do not even agree on the causes for any one area. Multiple factors may have been at work everywhere.

In Mesopotamia, once the initial domestication of plants and animals had occurred around 12,000 years ago in the Levant region, certain cultural changes quickly emerged (Bellwood 2004). The first chapters of Genesis describe those changes, starting with the curse that Yahweh lays on Adam's head as he expels him from Eden (Genesis 3:17–19):

17. And to the man he said...
cursed is the ground because of you;
in toil you shall eat of it all the days of your life;

18. thorns and thistles it shall bring forth for you;
and you shall eat the plants of the field.

19. By the sweat of your face
you shall eat bread...

This poetic curse encapsulates a description of the fate of those who turn to farming. Instead of reaping the harvest of nature, farmers must 'toil' to raise plants. Life becomes work, and it is very hard work. The concept of a weed ('thorns and thistles') surfaces. There are no weeds for the forager. For plants to be deemed weeds you have to have a notion of 'good' plants and 'bad' plants, that is, the plants you want to grow in a certain spot (your cultigens), and the plants you do not want growing there (the weeds). This concept resembles the notion of 'unclean' mentioned in Chapters 3 and 4.

The last sentence in the curse against Adam is the clincher: bread is the cornerstone of the whole cursed edifice. You cannot make bread out of wild grains because they do not contain enough gluten, which is the sticky protein mix that holds flours together to form dough. Bread can be made only from cultivated cereals such as rye, barley and wheat. The emmer wheat that was domesticated in Mesopotamia for bread making is a particular genetic mutation that does not reproduce well in the wild (Zohary 1982; Zohary and Hopf 2000). It must be farmed to be successful and thus people have to stay in one place and tend the fields. Along with sedentary crop cultivation comes the possibility of building houses that are more permanent than the makeshift shelters of foragers – and thus begins a trend toward clustered residences and village life. Such sedentism brings further changes. Settled people can build kilns to make pottery, and also use similar devices to bake yeast breads. They can brew beer from barley. They can do a host of things with their domestic grains they could not do with their wild-grain cousins. In order to gain these advantages, however, they must work harder than the forager: much harder. That is the essence of Yahweh's curse.

Plant domestication provided abundant sources of starchy food that were close at hand. But sedentary farmers faced new risks. If you rely on one or a few crops only, a drought or a disease can wipe them out entirely. Or, people may envy what you have produced and want to grab your land, animals or crops. Get a little ahead and someone will want to take what you have so painfully earned in 'the sweat of your face'. As sedentism increased and population size grew, cities emerged along with powerful governments, social inequality and the concept of private property. Defence against enemies becomes more important. Before long, you have urbanism. That's where Cain, Adam and Eve's first-born, comes into the picture.

Farmer Cain and shepherd Abel

After their expulsion from the garden, Adam and Eve had two sons: Cain and Abel (see also pp. 120ff.). Cain followed in his father's footsteps as a farmer, while Abel became a pastoralist, a shepherd. This division of labour is rightly described using the symbolism of kinship, because the two brothers, as siblings, are both mutually dependent and competitors. Adam, the first human who is not a forager, gives birth to farming (Cain) and pastoralism (Abel) as sibling rivals. These two interrelated economic activities have, since their origins around 12,000 years ago, been in constant and sometimes bitter competition, though they are also mutually dependent. That situation persists into the present.

The domestication of sheep and goats was one of the great miracles of Mesopotamian domestication. Sheep and goats are sure-footed in rocky highlands, they can forage for food in the most inhospitable places, survive in considerable temperature ranges, give birth just about anywhere, and even a child can look after a large flock. Sheep and goats turn things that humans cannot eat (grass and the leaves of woody plants) and that grow on lands that humans cannot cultivate, into products that are immensely useful: milk, and hence the full range of dairy products like cheese and curds; as well as meat, hides, wool, bone and horn. In short, sheep and goats make the inedible edible: they make wild places flow with milk and meat, and with minimal human effort.

Another advantage of goat- and sheep-herding is that it requires little technology. According to the archaeological record for the Levant in the Bronze Age (the period in and around the time purportedly covered by the age of the patriarchs in Genesis, that is, in and around the third millennium BCE), the fortunes of farmers rose and fell. But the pastoralists kept right on going because they needed so little in the way of resources to survive (Dever 2017, 2001; Finkelstein 1996).

Farmers typically take up the best lands: the river bottoms and the fertile plains. They need these lands to survive by growing crops. Unless they are willing to put enormous labour into terracing and irrigation, they cannot do much with the uplands or wilderness. Pastoralists, on the other hand, can thrive in these marginal zones if they have to. Sheep and goats, especially, do well in hilly desert land. However, pastoralists can do better if they have more fertile land and more secure water resources for their flocks. Thus, farmers and herders in early Mesopotamia were, like Cain and Abel, in competition for land.

The fact that Cain, the farmer, was the elder brother and Abel, the shepherd, was the younger reflects the realities of early domestication in general, and in Mesopotamia in particular. Cereals and pulses such as barley, rye, wheat and lentils were first domesticated in Mesopotamia around 12,000 years ago. The domestication of goats and then sheep followed soon thereafter, although the exact dates are much disputed by scholars (Abdurehman 2019; Alberto *et al.* 2018.; Stiner *et al.* 2022) Hunting continued for a time as a mode of providing meat. In Genesis, Esau is the last vestige of the hunting way of life. His father Isaac prefers the wild taste of game, but it is Jacob the herder who is eventually the successful heir to the lineage. Pastoralism will eventually replace hunting.

According to existing archaeological data for Mesopotamia (Mazar 1990), it appears likely that the combination of farming and hunting quickly became untenable, leaving only a limited set of choices for the provision of meat. One possibility was for the farmers to keep domesticated animals, and in some isolated cases this occurred. But the commonest scenario was for the farmers to remain sedentary cereal producers, and for separate classes or ethnic groups to emerge as pastoralists, filling the niche once occupied by the hunter. What followed was a struggle for land resources and, importantly, two quite distinct cultures evolved from the two modes of livelihood (Henry 1989; Price and Gebauer 1995). But who gets which pieces of land and how do the two groups deal with conflicts? In the Levant, the farmers cultivated the best arable lands and the pastoralists worked with the more marginal ones. The two groups needed to find ways to deal with each other on a regular basis, preferably amicably, because each was producing things the other wanted. The farmers needed meat and dairy products, and the pastoralists needed agricultural goods such as grains and flour. In the midst of this trading and competition, which group would arise as the one with the most power?

In many ways, the pastoralists had the power advantage. They lived in places that were difficult to find and easier to defend than the open lowlands. They were mobile. They had perfected the technology of death. They slaughtered animals and had weapons that could also kill people efficiently. They were to be feared by immobile, settled populations who were sitting targets. Genesis is on the side of the pastoralists.

Herding is purity and farming is pollution

All the patriarchs, until Joseph ends up in Egypt, are pastoralists. The Genesis image of the pastoralist as the strong, caring provider – who is nevertheless fearless and deadly – continues through the later books of the Bible down to the tales of the early monarchy. Moses, Joseph's successor in Egypt, begins his life as a rich urbanite, but before he can become Yahweh's chosen leader of the enslaved Israelites he must flee the city and take up herding in the wilderness. Only then is he fit to receive a call from God (Exodus 2:11–22). The narrative of David, the shepherd boy, pitted against Goliath, the archetype of the big, dumb farmer/city dweller, is classic. David's pastoralist background equips him to defeat the Philistine giant and to inherit the monarchy (I Samuel 17).

Why are pastoralists so great and farmers so execrable to the writers of Genesis? The story of the brothers Cain and Abel provides an answer. Part of the tale runs as follows:

> 1. Now the man knew his wife Eve, and she conceived and bore Cain, saying, 'I have produced a man with the help of the Lord.'
>
> 2. Next she bore his brother Abel. Now Abel was a keeper of sheep, and Cain a tiller of the ground.
>
> 3. In the course of time Cain brought to the Lord an offering of the fruit of the ground,
>
> 4. and Abel for his part brought of the firstlings of his flock, their fat portions. And the Lord had regard for Abel and his offering,

5. but for Cain and his offering he had no regard.

(Genesis 4:1–8)

This story has been subjected to endless scholarly analysis (Byron 2011). One common interpretation is that Abel did a better job of sacrificing than Cain, his offering was more pleasing to God. The general impression is that Abel took the choicest animals and dedicated their fattest portions to God, whereas Cain just threw any old offering together because he was not so dedicated to the sacrifice itself. This approach does not pass muster on several grounds.

Beginning with the sacrifice itself as a simple act of thanksgiving on the part of the two brothers, we must remember that such acts were entirely spontaneous. Neither of the men was under any legal or moral obligation to offer anything at all to God. The law concerning sacrifices, and the covenants associated with them, came much later (according to Bible chronology). Their offerings were just nice things to do: acts of thankfulness for God's bounty. If Cain arrived on your doorstep with freshly baked bread as a gift would you sneer at it because it did not meet your expectations?

The passage does not indicate the quality of Cain's offering, although it does make it clear that Abel's was excellent. There is nothing to say that Cain did not examine the first fruits of the harvest and from them picked the very best grains, to make his offering comparable to Abel's. The text is silent on this issue. One could just as easily argue that the redactors at this point were biased against the products of farming and in favour of the products of pastoralism. The bias goes beyond the products alone. In my view, the redactors were biased towards both the products of pastoralism and the way of life of the pastoralist; and most decidedly biased against the products of farmers and their way of life. The foods each produced symbolized the lives they led.

Let us look more closely at the products of the two lifestyles. Hebrew has a term *nephesh*, the root of which – נפש (n-ph-sh) – has the basic meaning of 'breath' (the Hebrew verb *naphash*, means literally 'to breathe'). By extension, the root has a more general sense of 'life', or even 'soul'. Things that have a *nephesh* are living, breathing, soulful, feeling things. According to Genesis 1, things with a *nephesh* were created on the fifth and sixth days of creation. Plants, by contrast, appeared on the third day, and do not have *nephesh*. One might go further and suggest that in the ancient Hebraic conception, plants were not truly living in the same way as animals and humans. Without breath they did not have life: they were things that sprang naturally from the soil. The act of creation makes this point (Genesis 1:11–12):

11. Then God said, 'Let the earth put forth vegetation: plants yielding seed, and fruit trees of every kind on earth that bear fruit with the seed in it.' And it was so.

12. The earth brought forth vegetation: plants yielding seed of every kind, and trees of every kind bearing fruit with the seed in it.

God did not create the plants in the same way that he created animals and humans. He endowed the soil with generative power and let it bring forth the vegetation on its own (a process of 'autochthony', meaning 'from the earth itself'). The soil is richly fertile, so that it generates things that are good to eat; but it cannot bring forth life/*nephesh*. Only God can make things with *nephesh*, and he has higher regard for them than for the things that spring from the soil.

You may protest that in the creation account in Genesis 2, God makes Adam out of the soil. This is quite true, but closer examination of the passage reveals the difference between this creation and that of plants (Genesis 2:7):

7. then the Lord God formed man from the dust of the ground, and breathed into his nostrils the breath of life; and the man became a living being.

The man does not grow out of the earth; God shaped the earth and, much more importantly, breathed his own breath into the inanimate clay form he had made in order to give it life. The phrase here translated as a 'living being' is literally 'a being with *nephesh*'. The *nephesh* comes from God: animals and humans have it; plants do not.

Plants are not bad to eat, and they are vital to human diets. But when it comes to sacrificing and appealing to God directly, the sacrifice of plants will not have the same power as sacrifices of animals. In the ancient Hebraic world-view, killing an animal is a potent act, while reaping wheat or plucking a pear lacks the same emotive force. When animals die they cry, they bleed, they lose breath. Wheat and barley give up to the reaper's blade without a whimper (at least not one that the farmer can hear). Animals lose their *nephesh*; plants do not. The herder who has the ability to sacrifice animals has Yahweh's favour.

Oklahoma!: the farmer and the cowman

Think of the difference between the cowboy and the farmer in modern North America. There are precious few movies about the life of the Western farmer, but cowboy movies are innumerable. In the classic musical *Oklahoma!* (one of the songs from which, 'The Farmer and the Cowman Must Be Friends', inspired the title of this chapter), the farmers are all neat, clean and harmless (boring) and the ranchers are dark, foreboding and dangerous (as well as sexually attractive). Don't mess with the ranchers. The themes of *Oklahoma!* and Genesis are starkly antithetical. *Oklahoma!* wants the farmers and cowboys to be friends, for their daughters to intermarry, and in the process for the cowboys to settle down and be tamed. Genesis wants the pastoralists to stay as far away from the farmers as possible, to avoid intermarriage, and to remain mobile and free.

Although Genesis contains some ambiguity about where the pastoralists belong, the general impression is that they should live in tents and dwell in the wilderness. The references to Abraham, Isaac and Jacob as tent dwellers are unmistakable and often repeated. In relation to the patriarchs, the word 'tent' – Hebrew, אהל (*ohel*) – appears twenty-one times in Genesis. Even when Lot and Abraham part company, and Lot goes to live with the city people in the plains, he lives (initially) in a tent (Genesis 13:12):

> 12. Abram settled in the land of Canaan, while Lot settled among the cities of the Plain and moved his tent as far as Sodom.

As he becomes more citified (corrupt) he shifts from a tent to a house.

In the Deuteronomic history, Yahweh himself prefers living in a tent to a permanent house (2 Samuel 7:4–7):

> 4. But that same night the word of the Lord came to Nathan:
>
> 5. Go and tell my servant David: Thus says the Lord: Are you the one to build me a house to live in?
>
> 6. I have not lived in a house since the day I brought up the people of Israel from Egypt to this day, but I have been moving about in a tent and a tabernacle.
>
> 7. Wherever I have moved about among all the people of Israel, did I ever speak a word with any of the tribal leaders of Israel, whom I commanded to shepherd my people Israel, saying, 'Why have you not built me a house of cedar?'

Living in a tent in the wilderness and herding sheep is the archetype for the people of Israel and the preference of Yahweh himself. That is why he had regard for Abel's sacrifice. He likes shepherds and all they represent. He likes the wilderness where they keep their sheep; he likes what the wilderness does for them. The wild places where sheep and goats and their keepers live are places of simplicity and honesty and purity.

As further evidence that the wilderness is the place that God prefers, consider some of the great moments of revelation in the Hebrew Bible. There is, for example, the moment when God appears to Moses at the site of the burning bush (Exodus 2). At the time Moses is keeping his father-in-law's sheep in the wilderness. Or there is Elijah's great moment of conflict when he flees the wrath of Jezebel (1 Kings 19:4–5):

> 4. But he himself went a day's journey into the wilderness, and came and sat down under a solitary broom tree. He asked that he might die: 'It is enough; now, O Lord, take away my life, for I am no better than my ancestors.'

From this place of renewal and restoration Elijah journeys to Horeb, where he meets God. Such instances could be repeated many times. The Israelites, when they left their captivity in Egypt, spent forty years in such places: purifying themselves and readying themselves for the Promised Land. The Judean exiles would do well to follow in their footsteps.

Beware the bright lights of the city

Abel the pastoralist is immediately Yahweh's favourite. Cain the farmer has little value in Yahweh's eyes. He is a murderer and thus an outcast. He is also the founder of cities (Genesis 4:17):

> 17. Cain knew his wife, and she conceived and bore Enoch; and he built a city, and named it Enoch after his son Enoch.

It is not useful to ask whether Cain built the city all by himself with his own hands, and who populated it besides his wife and son (given that in Genesis the only other people at the time were Adam and Eve). The story is not meant to be understood within a modern logical framework. Rather, it presents a metaphor – farming and farmers are inherently corrupt, and their sedentary lifestyle leads to all kinds of evils, including cities. From the perspective of the exiles, Babylon is the worst of all.

In Genesis, most cities are associated with Canaanites and little good is said of them. They are places for the pastoralists to stay away from, or treat warily. Moral tales of the critical need to avoid the Canaanites begin with the story of Abraham and Lot's journey to Bethel in central Canaan after a sojourn in Egypt. Once in Canaan they agree to go their separate ways because they need their own grazing lands:

The farmer and the cowman can't be friends

> 5. Now Lot, who went with Abram, also had flocks and herds and tents,
>
> 6. so that the land could not support both of them living together; for their possessions were so great that they could not live together,
>
> 7. and there was strife between the herders of Abram's livestock and the herders of Lot's livestock. At that time the Canaanites and the Perizzites lived in the land.
>
> 8. Then Abram said to Lot, 'Let there be no strife between you and me, and between your herders and my herders; for we are kindred.
>
> 9. Is not the whole land before you? Separate yourself from me. If you take the left hand, then I will go to the right; or if you take the right hand, then I will go to the left.'
>
> 10. Lot looked about him, and saw that the plain of the Jordan was well watered everywhere like the garden of the Lord, like the land of Egypt, in the direction of Zoar; this was before the Lord had destroyed Sodom and Gomorrah.
>
> 11. So Lot chose for himself all the plain of the Jordan, and Lot journeyed eastwards; thus they separated from each other.
>
> 12. Abram settled in the land of Canaan, while Lot settled among the cities of the Plain and moved his tent as far as Sodom.
>
> 13. Now the people of Sodom were wicked, great sinners against the Lord.
>
> (Genesis 13:5–13)

Abraham and his nephew make very different decisions. As the story unfolds, the consequences of this become manifest. Although Lot is a classic pastoralist, he is greedily attracted to the well-watered plains surrounding the cities. It looks like the easy life. There is a catch, however. The city brings with it a lifestyle that ultimately leads to destruction: cities create surplus wealth, which creates occupational specialization, class divisions, hierarchies of power and, along with these changes, social injustice, exploitation of the poor, abuses of absolute power and decadent consumption. As the story progresses Lot gets sucked further and further into the city life. Abraham, by contrast, repudiates the cities of the plains and moves to what was later to become Judah, in the hill country of Mamre (Genesis 13:18). The text indicates that Lot has made a bad choice while affirming Abraham's apparent generosity in letting him have the 'best' and keeping the 'worst' for himself. It turns out not so much an act of kindness as Abraham's wise method of insulating himself against the ills of the city. Let the Judeans in exile looking greedily at Babylon take note!

As Lot becomes more deeply entrenched in city life, he meets his potential downfall on two separate occasions. The first incident is brief; the full narrative is found in Genesis 14. The cities of the plain, including Sodom, entered into a vassal agreement with a set of powerful kings who united in an attempt to build a vast empire by threat of force; but after a number of years the cities rebel. The kings send large expeditionary forces to crush the cities and compel their obedience. Sodom is conquered and plundered. Lot is carted off as a prisoner and his goods confiscated. This cautionary tale says essentially that the life of the city may look good until something like this inevitably happens. So, stay away from the decadence and flesh pots of Babylon.

Abraham hears of Lot's plight and raises an army comprised of raiding bands of pastoralists who fall on the mighty armies of the kings at night and slaughter them wholesale. He then restores all of Lot's possessions to him. On his way home Abraham meets the king of Sodom, who offers to reward him:

> 21. Then the king of Sodom said to Abram, 'Give me the people, but take the goods for yourself.'
>
> 22. But Abram said to the king of Sodom, 'I have sworn to the Lord, God Most High, maker of heaven and earth,
>
> 23. that I would not take a thread or a sandal-thong or anything that is yours, so that you might not say, 'I have made Abram rich.'
>
> (Genesis 14:21–3)

The wealth of cities is corruptly attained and, in turn, further corrupts. No doubt the possessions of the king of Sodom had been stolen on raids to other cities. Abraham wants none of it. He is content to return to his flocks and his tents in the highlands. Exiles take note again.

The second incident is the famed destruction of Sodom and Gomorrah, the full story of which appears in Genesis 18 and 19. The tale parallels the details of the Flood narrative, with some important differences. The fact that these cities are wicked is signalled repeatedly in previous chapters of Genesis, but the exact nature of the wickedness is not spelled out until the time of destruction.

The tale begins with three 'men' (Yahweh and two angels of destruction) passing by Abraham's tent in Mamre. Abraham's response is typical of the

The farmer and the cowman can't be friends

pastoralist, only more generous. He invites them to sit in the cool of a shade tree, bathe their feet, and eat with him. He orders Sarah to make bread of the finest flour, and sends out a servant to slaughter a choice fat calf and prepare it for the table. These magnificent foods he serves to his guests along with milk and curds (similar to yogurt).

> 6. And Abraham hastened into the tent to Sarah, and said, 'Make ready quickly three measures of choice flour, knead it, and make cakes.'
>
> 7. Abraham ran to the herd, and took a calf, tender and good, and gave it to the servant, who hastened to prepare it.
>
> 8. Then he took curds and milk and the calf that he had prepared, and set it before them; and he stood by them under the tree while they ate.
>
> (Genesis 18:6–8)

This is a royal feast, the kind of feast that a generous pastoralist who has done well can produce for honoured guests.

In return for his superb hospitality Abraham receives two prophecies. First, he is told that Sarah will have a son within a year. Sarah is amused. She is ninety years old, and openly says that she is well past menopause. So, from a simple biological point of view she cannot help but be incredulous, as she is in this touching verse:

> 12. So Sarah laughed to herself, saying, 'After I have grown old, and my husband is old, shall I have pleasure?'
>
> (Genesis 18:12)

The verse raises sexual and reproductive themes again. Even an old woman and her companion of a lifetime can have pleasure with one another's bodies, and if it is Yahweh's will, she will give birth. That is what being a strong, generous, and righteous pastoralist can do for you.

Second, Yahweh tells Abraham he is disgusted with Sodom and Gomorrah and is bent on destroying the cities. The two angels of destruction walk away towards Sodom to carry out their fateful mission, leaving Abraham face to face with Yahweh. A bartering exchange between Abraham and Yahweh follows. Abraham is concerned that the righteous will perish along with the wicked in Sodom and Gomorrah. He pleads with Yahweh to spare Sodom if fifty righteous people can be found in it. Yahweh agrees. Then, by degrees, Abraham seeks reprieve for the city, even if fewer and fewer righteous can be found in it. Eventually he has Yahweh down to ten. But not even ten righteous people were found, condemning the city as a cesspool of immorality (Genesis 18:16–19:3).

The two destroying angels reach Sodom by nightfall and find Lot sitting at the city gate. This is a sign, among others, that Lot has by now become fully integrated into city life. The city gate was the place where the rich and powerful sat to transact public business. Lot no longer dwells in a tent as a pastoralist should, but in a house. What follows is a repeat of Abraham's hospitality, but under very different circumstances. He urges the 'men' to come to his house to wash their feet and rest. After an initial refusal, which would be common in Near Eastern etiquette then and now, they acquiesce to Lot's entreaties. The English text usually says that Lot prepares a 'feast with unleavened bread'. The type of bread indicates that it was prepared in haste. The word 'feast' is more interesting, though. It translates the Hebrew word *mishteh* which comes from a root whose primary meaning is to drink, and which, therefore, can mean a drinking bout or a banquet with wine.

The presence of wine at the meal is a subtle sign that Lot's feast is more suited to city dwellers than Abraham's. If you read the segments of Abraham's and Lot's hospitality in parallel, you see that many of their acts, and the Hebrew phrasing, are identical. Where they differ, therefore, there must be of some significance – as in the fact that Abraham greets the angels at the door of his tent, while Lot does so at the city gate. Abraham offers the strangers a meal of meat and dairy products; Lot gives them a meal with wine. Lot's meal says it all: Lot is citified.

(Same) sex and the city

The next scene, and the one which gives Sodom's name to the sexual act, has caused an immense amount of controversy among interpreters of the Bible. The men of the town surround Lot's house and demand that he sends out his two male guests so that they can gang rape them. Lot, playing the good host, will not allow this to happen and offers his virgin daughters in their stead. Commentators (Loader 1990) are normally shocked by this outrageous offer, and try to explain it away in some fashion; for example, that this is Lot's last-ditch effort to protect his guests at all costs and that daughters were not highly valued and so could be sacrificed. I think the commentators are missing a key point. In offering his daughters, Lot is providing the option of heterosexual sex, which they refuse. They have specifically come for homosexual acts. If Lot were simply being a courageous and self-sacrificing host he could have offered himself up as the rape victim. But then, the narrator could not then have shown that the Sodomites were not interested in heterosexuality.

This story is a close parallel to the story of the angel marriages and the Nephilim which immediately precedes the Flood narrative (Genesis 6:4). The homosexuality of the men of Sodom is a key component in the condemnation and destruction of the city. Modern commentators who want to soften this judgment have put forth many arguments that seek to show that the crimes of the men of Sodom were less sexual and of a more general nature (Harland 1943; Jordan 1999:89–95). They want the crimes to be more about wanton acts of violence, the breaching of laws of hospitality, and the disrespect of traveling strangers. All these aspects are there. But if the redactor just wanted the Sodomites to be seen as wicked in a general way, he could have had them come to Lot's house with the intent to rob the men or kill them or do some other nasty thing to them (Fields 1997; Loader 1990).

As discussed in earlier chapters of this book, the exiles in Babylon who compiled the text of Genesis could not tolerate any sexual acts that were non-reproductive. So, they condemned cultures that practised homosexuality. Canaanite cities are universally condemned in Genesis for their immoral ways but Sodom and Gomorrah are specifically condemned for their homosexuality.

My interpretation of this passage is based on an understanding of it strictly in the context of the Babylonian exile, not in the context of the twenty-first century. Genesis is not addressed to the modern world; it is addressed to the exiles. Turning it into a timeless moral tale that sets up a permanent sexual ethic for all peoples in all places, as many Christian conservatives would, loses the force of its original intent: if an oppressed minority in exile were to practise homosexual acts, that would go against the commandment to 'be fruitful and multiply'. Cross-cultural studies of sexual practices worldwide show that societies under severe population pressure are much more likely to accept birth control, abortion and homosexuality than societies that are not (McEwen 2019; Reczek *et al.* 2017; Werner 1979). Ancient Canaanite cities teeming with people were more likely to be liberal about homosexuality than less populated regions. Pastoralists living in wide expanses and whose prime wealth lay in the fertility and reproduction of their animals might be less inclined in that direction. The patriarchal narratives portray pastoralists as strongly committed to heterosexual reproduction, and painfully aware of the consequences of childlessness.

Although commentators on these two chapters of Genesis see the close parallels between the narratives of the hospitality of Abraham and of Lot, down to the actual wording in many places, many are reluctant to follow the threads to the conclusions that the redactors want us to see (e.g. Hamilton 1995). Abraham is a faithful pastoralist living in a tent. He is old but his wife can imagine the pleasures of sex with him. In consequence for his hospitality he is promised a son who will be the start of a long line of descendants whose number will be uncountable. He is also promised the land of Canaan as his inheritance.

Lot has given up the pastoral life and become a man of the city. His hospitality is followed by attempted acts of homosexuality, which lead to the utter destruction of the city and all who live there. Lot, his wife, and his daughters are the sole survivors, because the angels allow them to flee. They are told not to look back, presumably because this act would signal that they had regrets about leaving. Lot's wife disobeys and is turned into a pillar of salt. The land that the Canaanites have lost will become Abraham's, and Lot is left to produce sons by having sex with his daughters.

Henceforth Sodom, like Babylon, becomes a synonym for urban decadence. The prophets Amos, Zephaniah, Isaiah, Jeremiah and Ezekiel all compare corrupt cities to Sodom. Isaiah even makes the express link with Babylon in his prophecy on the destruction of the city and the restoration of Israel:

> 9. And Babylon, the glory of kingdoms,
> the splendour and pride of the Chaldeans,
> will be like Sodom and Gomorrah
> when God overthrew them.
>
> (Isaiah 13:19)

Even Jerusalem does not escape God's wrath as a corrupt city. According to Deuteronomic history (I Kings 8:27), God never wanted a city and a temple for a home. He never wanted kings ruling Israel. Kings are the products of the excesses of city life. He wanted his people to follow the pastoralist ethic and for the Ark of the Covenant to reside in a tent.

Exile and restoration

Genesis and the prophets indicate that city-dwellers tend towards the fat, lazy and corrupt. The northern kingdom of Israel became dominated by the ethic of farming and cities, so it fell to destruction. Jerusalem started on the same path and the consequences were the same. In his poetic Book of Lamentations, Jeremiah condemns the city ways that Jerusalem had fallen into in latter days before the exile, and compares the punishment to that of Sodom:

> 5. Those who feasted on delicacies
> perish in the streets;
> those who were brought up in purple
> cling to ash heaps.
>
> 6. For the chastisement of my people has been greater
> than the punishment of Sodom,

> which was overthrown in a moment,
> though no hand was laid on it.
>
> (Lamentations 4:5–6)

The time of the wilderness wandering during the Exodus was one of the purification of the Israelites following their captivity in Egypt. During that period, they were nomadic pastoralists. They had escaped from bondage, but they could not enter the Promised Land until they were fully purged of all the images of wealth and luxury of the Egypt of the pharaohs that they hankered after, even when they had been delivered from slavery. No one was destined to enter Israel who had laid eyes on Egypt (Deuteronomy 31:51–2). The desert time was a liminal time of cleansing and re-ordering. The pastoralist ethic could be restored to them in that time. Then they would be fit to inherit a new land.

The exiles in Babylon saw themselves in the same role as the desert wanderers. They needed to get away from Babylon and restore themselves in exile. They had to content themselves with the fact that time must pass before they were purged and restored. A generation must pass before they can return. If there was ever to be a New Jerusalem it had to be created by people with a pastoralist mentality, not by those grown fat and sleek in the fleshpots of the city. They must be lean and hungry. They must be accustomed to deprivation, and able to survive in the wilderness. They must be purified by the rigors of the desert.

Further reading

The classic anthology on foragers is Irven DeVore and Richard Lee's *Man the Hunter* (1968); they also wrote *Kalahari Hunter-Gatherers* (1976). For an in-depth analysis of hunter-gatherers in history and in the modern world, see Tim Ingold *et al.* (1988), *Hunters and Gatherers*. Counter-narratives to the 'man the hunter' model are found in Frances Dahlberg (ed.) *Woman the Gatherer* (1981). Elizabeth Marshall Thomas lived with the Kalahari Bushmen in the Nyae Nyae region in Angola, starting in the 1950s, and she writes about the devastating changes they have experienced since then in her book, *The Old Way* (2006).

The scholarly literature on domestication of plants and animals is vast. Peter Bellwood's, *First Farmers* (2004), describes the transition to farming in Mesopotamia and beyond. For Israel, see Donald Henry, *From Foraging to Agriculture* (1989). Some excellent articles on Mesopotamia are included in the anthology by T. Douglas Price and Anne Birgitte Gebauer, *Last Hunters-First Farmers* (1995). An excellent brief book about the Neolithic in the Middle East is Colin Tudge's, *Neanderthals, Bandits and Farmers* (1999). There is little consensus in this area about the causes of the transition to farming, so please read critically.

The origins of animal domestication and pastoralism in the Near East have been the subject of considerable archaeological interest. Two works provide a good overview: Ofer Bar-Yosef and Anatoly Khazanov, *Pastoralism in the Levant* (1992), and Israel Finkelstein, *Living on the Fringe* (1995).

The study of the rise and character of the city and city states in the Near East is as complex archaeologically as these other investigations. Of particular interest are Volkmar Fritz, *The City in Ancient Israel* (1996), Marc Van de Mieroop, *The Ancient Mesopotamian City* (1999) and Norman Yoffee, *Myths of the Archaic State* (2005).

For an overview of references to homosexuality in the Bible from a gay perspective, read Daniel A. Helminiak, *What the Bible Really Says about Homosexuality* (2000). The Christian conservative position is represented by Robert A. J. Gagnon *The Bible and Homosexual Practice* (2001).

13

It isn't over even when it's over

❦

The book of Ezra begins with this amazing pronouncement (Ezra 1:1–4):

1. In the first year of King Cyrus of Persia, in order that the word of the Lord by the mouth of Jeremiah might be accomplished, the Lord stirred up the spirit of King Cyrus of Persia so that he sent a herald throughout all his kingdom, and also in a written edict declared:

2. 'Thus says King Cyrus of Persia: The Lord, the God of heaven, has given me all the kingdoms of the earth, and he has charged me to build him a house at Jerusalem in Judah.

3. Any of those among you who are of his people – may their God be with them! – are now permitted to go up to Jerusalem in Judah, and rebuild the house of the Lord, the God of Israel – he is the God who is in Jerusalem;

4. and let all survivors, in whatever place they reside, be assisted by the people of their place with silver and gold, with goods and with animals, besides freewill-offerings for the house of God in Jerusalem.

The Babylonian Exile was officially over! Cyrus of Persia conquered Babylon in 539 BCE and in the first year of his reign in Babylon he issued this edict. A great many historical and archaeological problems surround the exact nature of the exiles' return to Jerusalem and the timing of events, including how many people went in how many waves over what period of time. However, for our purposes, these details are irrelevant. What matters is that there was an end to the Exile, and in consequence the city of Jerusalem and the temple were eventually rebuilt.

Judah under Persian rule

The Persian view of imperial control differed from that of the Assyrians and Babylonians before them. Cyrus believed that peace would be maintained better if subject ethnic groups, such as the Judeans, were sent back to their original homelands, where, provided the vassal states did what they were told, they could practise their own customs in peace. They were still subject to strict political and economic control by the Persian ruler, and rebellion was not to be tolerated. Meanwhile, the Persian empire made a huge profit from their tribute, more than could made with them living in exile in Babylon.

It took decades for significant numbers of the exiles to return to Judah, though there are inadequate sources for precise dates and numbers . Once back in Judah, rebuilding efforts included reconstructing the temple and the city walls along with new housing. This process was difficult, because there were conflicting opinions as to what should be done and how. The twin books of Ezra and Nehemiah (to be read, as ever, with a large pinch of salt) present the full story of these rebuilding efforts and the disputes that were involved.

The rough chronology of the return of the exiles and the rebuilding of Jerusalem, in what is called the Persian period, can be summarized thus (even though much of this history is under dispute). Around 538 BCE Cyrus decreed that Sheshbazzar, called a 'prince of Judah', should take possession of the temple vessels that Nebuchadnezzar had carted to Babylon, and he should return with a group of exiles to restore the temple in Jerusalem (Ezra 1:1–4). Sheshbazzar quickly disappears from the scene to be replaced by Zerubbabel, grandson of Jehoiakin, who became governor of Judah and oversaw the initial restoration process. One of the first reconstruction projects of the returned exiles was the building of an altar in Jerusalem, so that the sacrificial and ritual cycle could be renewed. Under the spiritual guidance of the prophets Haggai and Zechariah, the Second Temple was dedicated in 515 BCE, along with a celebration including a massive sacrifice of animals, followed by a huge Passover feast. This feast echoed closely, and quite deliberately, the Passover feast Josiah hosted when he had earlier restored the temple under the guidance of the Deuteronomists.

The symbolic value of this Passover is evident. The exiles had returned from their bondage, just as the ancient Israelites had returned from their captivity in Egypt. The temple was restored to its former glory and purpose by the exiles, just as it had been in the days of Josiah. The people had been purged of all their 'foreign' ways. The concepts of 'cleanness' and 'holiness' and 'purity' and 'separation' that are so important to the Jews of all eras as symbolic of their ethnic identity are repeated in the description of the event (Ezra 6:19–21):

> 19. On the fourteenth day of the first month the returned exiles kept the Passover.
>
> 20. For both the priests and the Levites had purified themselves; all of them were clean. So they killed the Passover lamb for all the returned exiles, for their fellow-priests, and for themselves.
>
> 21. It was eaten by the people of Israel who had returned from exile, and also by all who had joined them and separated themselves from the pollutions of the nations of the land to worship the Lord, the God of Israel.

Because they are back in their home land, and because they are following laws of purity, the Jews are now 'separated' (the text uses the same triliteral root, בדל (b–d–l), as for the acts of creation in Genesis 1) from the other nations such as Egypt, Persia and the Canaanites. The Creation, the Exodus, the Deuteronomic reforms and the Exile are all tied together in one ritual package. While all now seems right in the homeland, a serpent lurks in what otherwise looks like a new paradise for the former exiles.

The perils of the return

One might think that, with the restoration of the exiles and the re-establishment of a Jewish state, the social lessons of Genesis would cease to have much relevance. In fact, the opposite is the case. In the long run, the return of the exiles was almost disastrous for the ethnic purity and integrity of the Jews in Judah. In Babylon, the exiled Judeans faced the obvious problem: they either kept to themselves, fiercely, or they would be assimilated wholesale – swallowed up in the great urban multicultural hotchpotch, and never heard of again. In Judah it was a different story. This was home. Here they could be safe from the problems of assimilation, or so they thought. But nothing could be farther from the truth. Josiah could have told them that. He would never have had to purge the temple and the city of so many foreign religions and customs (2 Chronicles 34) if the simple act of living in Judah had meant that the Judean people would remain pure and separate.

By the middle of the fifth century BCE, the scribes Nehemiah and Ezra were facing a near disastrous situation. Both Ezra and Nehemiah had lived with the exiles in Babylon, and each had led new waves of Jews back to Judah. The degradations that they found on their return shocked them. Ezra 9:1–4 gives a sample:

> 1. After these things had been done, the officials approached me and said, 'The people of Israel, the priests, and the Levites have not separated

themselves from the peoples of the lands with their abominations, from the Canaanites, the Hittites, the Perizzites, the Jebusites, the Ammonites, the Moabites, the Egyptians, and the Amorites.

2. For they have taken some of their daughters as wives for themselves and for their sons. Thus the holy seed has mixed itself with the peoples of the lands, and in this faithlessness the officials and leaders have led the way'.

3. When I heard this, I tore my garment and my mantle, and pulled hair from my head and beard, and sat appalled.

4. Then all who trembled at the words of the God of Israel, because of the faithlessness of the returned exiles, gathered around me while I sat appalled until the evening sacrifice.

A similar sentiment is found in Nehemiah 9:23–5:

23. In those days also I saw Jews who had married women of Ashdod, Ammon, and Moab;

24. and half of their children spoke the language of Ashdod, and they could not speak the language of Judah, but spoke the language of various peoples.

25. And I contended with them and cursed them and beat some of them and pulled out their hair; and I made them take an oath in the name of God, saying, 'You shall not give your daughters to their sons, or take their daughters for your sons or for yourselves.

The language of Ezra in particular echoes the sentiments of Genesis: 'the Levites have not *separated* themselves from the peoples of the lands' and 'the holy seed has *mixed* itself with the peoples of the lands' (Ezra 9:1–2, emphasis added). Once again there is nothing for it but to purge the nation of foreign elements. Ezra decrees that any man who has married a foreign woman must confess his sin publicly and must divorce her immediately – and abandon the children of the marriage as well. And thus it goes. Without the lessons of Genesis constantly in the forefront, the Jews were just as likely to end up losing their culture on their own doorstep as when they were exiled in Babylon.

Eventually, the Persian empire was overtaken by Alexander the Great (during the 330s BCE). In turn, the Greek empires of his successors, the Ptolemies and Seleucids, were supplanted by the Romans. The province of Judea came under Roman control in 64 BCE after a brief period of independence in between Seleucid and Roman rule. Judah was no more than a tiny, but troublesome, state in the ever-expanding imperial colossus of the ancient Graeco-Roman world. Some of the flavour of the political realities of life under the Romans is captured in the early gospels – Mark, Matthew and Luke – and especially in Luke's sequel to his gospel, The Acts of the Apostles. Other sources on the ever-changing fortunes of the Jewish state during this period include canonical and extra-canonical works such as the Books of Maccabees and the historical writings of the Jewish author Josephus.

In 70 CE the final catastrophe struck. Jewish zealots rebelled against the domination of Rome in 66 CE. Consequently, the full might of the Roman imperial army came crashing down on Jerusalem. Roman forces laid siege to the city and it eventually fell, with unimaginable bloodshed. The emperor commanded that the temple and much of the city be torn apart, stone by stone, so that only a few monuments remained standing to show that a mighty capital had once existed there. Such a policy of destruction would serve as a stern warning to others who might be thinking of following suit.

Following the destruction of the temple and the city in 70 CE until the mid-twentieth century, the Jews were in a constant state of exile from a homeland: a centuries-long reprise of the Babylonian captivity, but this time with the complications of diaspora added. It was supremely fortuitous for the Jews of diaspora that the first exile in Babylon carved out for them a survival strategy in the form of the principles established in Genesis. This strategy could be re-used in the ongoing effort to avoid assimilation into dominant cultures across the globe. To be sure, the Jews of Europe and Asia did not always have a choice to practise a social policy of isolationism. It was sometimes brutally forced upon them. But even under the bitterest of circumstances they had a cultural survival manual to hand.

Before the temple and Jerusalem were sacked, Christianity had emerged as a sect of Judaism within Judea. It was also spreading as a new religion in opposition to paganism in large sections of Asia Minor and Europe, largely due to the evangelizing efforts of the apostle Paul. He had been raised as a strict Jewish Pharisee, and therefore was conversant with Genesis and the law, and writes in favour of a 'Genesis option' style isolationism (see p. 16) for the Christian church as a mode of survival in the face of pressure to assimilate into local cultures across the ancient world. The 'Genesis option' speaks to Christians as well as Jews when they face the same cultural problems. In II Corinthians 6, for example, Paul says:

> 14. Do not be mismatched with unbelievers. For what partnership is there between righteousness and lawlessness? Or what fellowship is there between light and darkness?

15. What agreement does Christ have with Beliar? Or what does a believer share with an unbeliever?

16. What agreement has the temple of God with idols? For we are the temple of the living God; as God said,
> 'I will live in them and walk among them,
> and I will be their God,
> and they shall be my people.

17. Therefore come out from them,
> and be separate from them, says the Lord…

While Paul advocates separation and segregation, he does not promote other components of the Genesis option. He seems convinced that the end of the world is near and, therefore, marriage and reproduction are irrelevant or even counterproductive. He follows some of the basic principles from Genesis because he was raised within that tradition. It resonates with him when planning a survival strategy for Christians facing a hostile world.

The Genesis option beyond the Babylonian exile

Historically, like Paul's early Christians, few cultures have been willing to adopt the Genesis option wholesale. But several examples exist of separationist groups who have gone part of the way in this schema. The Shakers, for example, radically separated themselves from mainstream America in the eighteenth and nineteenth centuries. Their complete rejection of marriage and sexual relations, however, meant that the group would eventually die out. Recruitment from the outside world did not keep pace with the decline of the population through death and departure (Andrews 2011).

Some Pueblo cultures of the American Southwest have managed to maintain considerable separation from the mainstream. The Tewa, who occupy several pueblos in the Rio Grande valley north of Santa Fe, New Mexico, went from being open and engaged with much of mainstream North America in the early twentieth century to being much more isolationist after the Second World War. Now, their kiva rituals are secret and exclusive. They refuse to teach the Tewa language to outsiders, even to people who marry in. Photography and other forms of documentation of the pueblos, the people and their rituals by outsiders (including anthropologists) is either completely forbidden or tolerated in narrowly defined ways and at considerable expense (Ortiz 1969).

In many ways, however, the Tewa are forcibly connected to the outside world. Since the initial colonization of the region by Spanish conquerors, a

Roman Catholic presence has been strong in all of the pueblos. In addition, several public rituals and dances performed by the Tewa originated in Spain (Forrest 1984:ch. 1–3). The traditional economic base of the pueblos of farming and hunting collapsed in the twentieth century, leaving the inhabitants no options but to accept government assistance or to work for outsiders. Modern technology is readily evident in all the pueblos: televisions, video-game systems, dishwashers, pickup trucks and automobiles, electric stoves, computers and mobile phones. At first, such innovations were resisted or limited because of the scarcity of disposable income. With the advent of wage-paying jobs outside the pueblos, the technological hallmarks of Western culture have followed. As such they are much more like Memmi's group, 'the colonized who resist the colonial situation' (see Chapter 1)than fitting the Genesis option of complete separation and isolation.

The Old Order Amish are a contemporary culture that closely follows the principles of radical isolationism and disengagement from the dominant culture laid down in Genesis. Among the Amish as a whole are many different styles of Amish culture, some of which engage with mainstream American culture to some degree or another, including use of electricity, telephones and automobiles. The Old Order Amish, the strictest and most traditional of the US communities of Anabaptists, are quite severe in their efforts to limit the use of 'modern' technology.

American and Canadian Amish populations trace their roots to German-Swiss Anabaptists of the sixteenth century, who emigrated from their native homes in the seventeenth and eighteenth centuries because of religious persecution. When they arrived in North America they gravitated to rural areas, where they would be able to farm. Their communities are self-governing and largely self-sufficient. Their primary language is a dialect of German. They adhere to a strict religious code, which includes shunning of community members who have illicit contact with the outside world. Conservative Old Order Amish communities still use draft animals (horses or mules) for farming needs and for transportation. The Amish horse-drawn buggy is an archetypical symbol of the lifestyle. Electricity in homes is banned, and so the array of Western technology that relies on it is absent as well (Kraybill, Johnson-Weiner and Nolt 2013).

But Amish communities are not totally self-sufficient, so some contact with the outside world is inevitable. They do not manufacture cloth, for example. They make their own clothes, but they need to purchase the material. Therefore, they need cash, which means that they have to sell some of their farm produce. If they want to sell milk, they have to follow the Food and Drug Administration codes that demand that they pasteurize and refrigerate it. In consequence, they have to make limited exceptions to the ban on electricity.

They also have to pay certain taxes, and they are forced to accept a number of federal and state laws, though they spend considerable effort resisting them.

The Old Order Amish have rigid codes of endogamy. The section of II Corinthians 6 cited above is prominent in their code of conduct. They place a high value on having many children. Strong family bonds are extremely important and divorce, although allowed, is frowned upon and generally found only in cases of domestic violence, abuse or adultery. Generally speaking, therefore, the Old Order Amish follow the Genesis option of separation highly successfully. Old Order Amish communities in North America are flourishing and growing steadily. What is more, Amish culture is not shaped by an ideology of opposition to mainstream culture or by any other engagement with the mainstream. Amish culture takes its shape from its own historical and religious circumstances, not because it is rebelling against the mainstream. What 'the English' do is irrelevant. In many ways they are more successful at applying the lessons of Genesis than even the most orthodox of Jewish groups in the contemporary world. This success is largely attributable to their rural agrarian economic base, which provides them with a considerable degree of autonomy because they can be self-sufficient in so many key ways.

There are some significant negative consequences to maintaining a radically separatist group within a large and powerful dominant culture. One is that isolated groups, especially those with a different language and distinct dress or appearance, may be targets of suspicion, paranoia and even irrational hatred. The Amish are constant victims of random acts of violence in some parts of North America. In most cases they do not respond because of their general stance of pacifism, and because to involve authorities of any kind brings the outside world into their lives. When some crime within the Amish community comes to light in the mainstream media, especially one involving sexual abuse, a torrent of hostility is directed towards the Amish as a whole, as if their privacy and isolation were mere covers for a corrupt lifestyle. Again, the Amish choose not to respond, so these unfounded attacks remain unchallenged in the media. To challenge is to engage, and to do so would void the Genesis option.

For the Amish the negative aspects of cultural isolation are outweighed by the perceived positive benefits. Their policies of isolation give them some power with respect to local, state and federal law. They do not draw social security, so they have successfully petitioned to be allowed not to pay into the scheme. They are exempt from military service as pacifists. They are allowed to remove their children from school after eighth grade even though this is well below the official school-leaving age. The key to their success may well be that their desires in these legal arenas are fuelled by religious beliefs, and the courts are often sympathetic to such arguments.

The policy of 'be fruitful and multiply' has led to steady increases in their numbers and rapid expansion of their communities. They have low infant-mortality rates, lower than average rates of disease and mortality, and a prohibition against birth control leads to an average of seven live births per married couple. The total Old Order Amish population doubles around every twenty-two years, and they are one of the fastest-growing populations in the world.[20] When Old Order Amish communities reach a certain population limit, they fission and form new communities elsewhere. These are currently springing up at a rate of about one every eight days in the USA. That is a staggering increase when you compare it with the US Presbyterian Church, which, as of 2018, loses a church about every ten days.[21] The Old Order Amish demonstrate convincingly that the social policies outlined in Genesis can work very well for people other than the Judeans in exile in Babylon.

The Genesis option for Jews today

The historical development of Judaism and Jewish culture in Babylon and beyond give a basis for understanding Jewish culture today. Although the decree of Cyrus initiated the return of the exiles to Jerusalem, a considerable number of Jews stayed in Babylon. They did not assimilate to Babylonian culture but continued to use the principles of Genesis to remain separate and segregated. From the point of view of the ultimate survival of Judaism, their existence proved critical. When the temple was destroyed by the Romans in 70 CE the Babylonian community became the centre of Judaism. For approximately 1,000 years the Jewish scholars of Babylon were enormously influential in establishing the foundations of non-temple worshipping Judaism that are still in force today. Babylonian rabbis developed much of the ritual practice of the synagogue and many of the classic prayers. They also gathered together commentaries on the Torah into what is now called the Babylonian Talmud, still an indispensable source for many Jewish sects. Much of contemporary Judaism is built on a foundation laid by the descendants of Babylonian exiles who continued to follow the central tenets of the Genesis option (see, for example, Rejwan 1985).

---

20 See groups.etown.edu/amishstudies/files/2017/08/Population_Change_1992-2017.pdf (accessed 15 August 2023); also www.worldometers.info/world-population/#growthrate (accessed 8 November 2023).

21 www.christianpost.com/news/pcusa-lost-over-140-churches-nearly-5-percent-of-active-members-in-2018.html (accessed 15 August 2023).

Throughout the Jewish diaspora, whether by force or choice, Jews followed the Genesis option and managed to survive as an identifiable cultural group. But how does the Genesis option function for modern Jews? Is it still, in fact, an option? The answers to these questions are exceedingly complex because the nature of Judaism and Jewish culture in the modern world is complex, and this is not my area of expertise. I summarize some key points here.

On the surface it seems as if some ultra-orthodox groups in North America and Europe are still taking the Genesis option. For example, the main tenets of the Genesis option are evident in the communities of Chabad-Lubavitch, Hasidic Jews also known as Lubavitchers, who live in New York and the north-east of the United States. They have distinctive styles of clothing and worship practice, and generally speak a language other than English, usually Yiddish, as their first language. They place high value on endogamy and large families. They work hard at remaining physically and culturally isolated from the US mainstream in their home communities. But they are not as separatist as might be required for complete success.

Because their communities are not agricultural, they are not as economically self-sustaining as the Old Order Amish. Many of the members are required by the dynamics of the marketplace to interact with outsiders, even if the interaction is deliberately limited to economic transactions. The last rebbe, or leader, of Chabad-Lubavitch, Menachem Mendel Schneerson (1902–94), actively embraced much modern technology, such as television, so as not to deter new members. Although Schneerson followed the doctrines of Hasidism in avoiding secular politics, because engagement might lead to other forms of assimilation, he allowed visits by a variety of politicians, who used such occasions as photo opportunities (suggesting some kind of endorsement by Schneerson). He did, however, practise a radical form of physical isolationism for himself within the Crown Heights area of Brooklyn, refusing to leave to go to a hospital even when he had a heart attack.

Despite a community ethic of radical separatism, it is impossible for Lubavitchers in and around Brooklyn to sustain constant isolation from surrounding cultures, even though they appear to do a good job of maintaining the hallmarks of their own identity in appearance and customs, and try as much as possible to avoid contact with non-Hasidic people in the vicinity. The 1991 Crown Heights Riots,[22] although an extreme example of undesirable

---

22   The riots began on 19 August 1991, after two children of Guyanese immigrants were accidentally struck by a car running a red light while following the motorcade of Rebbe Menachem Mendel Schneerson, the leader of Chabad. One child died and the second was severely injured. Looting of Jewish stores and attacks on Jews in the streets followed.

social interaction between orthodox Jews and other ethnic communities in Brooklyn, demonstrate that it is both physically and socially impossible for the Lubavitcher community to preserve its isolation from the outside world. The physical separateness of the wilderness pastoralist is an unattainable ideal because the Lubavitchers live in an urban commercial environment. Yet it is still an important ideal, even if a metaphorical one, in the modern world.

If in the modern world the Genesis option cannot work perfectly even for the most orthodox of Jewish communities, then one might suppose that it is even less viable for other Jewish sects living and working in the mainstream of the Western world. Yet among the most secular of Jews there is still a sense that the Genesis option has its importance, even if in diluted form. The high value placed on endogamy is an example. Among North American secular Jews, that is, people who self-identify as ethnically Jewish but who have no religious affiliations, there is sometimes talk of a crisis of Jewish culture because of the prevalence of intermarriage of secular Jews with non-Jews.[23] Even though these people are neither learning Hebrew nor reading the Torah, they maintain certain traditions that have high value as cultural markers. Certain foods are important, hence secular Jews are sometimes disparagingly called 'kugel Jews' by the more orthodox.[24] Many secular Jews also celebrate the High Holy days, especially Passover, with limited or no religious observance, but still with a sense that the days are important Jewish holidays, and hence important to keep in some fashion for the preservation of Jewish identity. Many secular Jews, therefore, perceive exogamy as a serious threat to the continued existence of Jewish ethnicity.

Another component of the Genesis option, the dangers inherent in assimilation into mainstream culture, is a contentious issue for European and American Jews. The Reform movement within Judaism began in the nineteenth century with many religious and political aims, one of them being a desire on the part of many Jews to become more active participants in the cultures in which they lived in Europe. Reformers, especially in Germany, placed an emphasis on conforming to the norms of European culture in dress and habits, and the abandonment of many, but not all, of the codes of Jewish law, such as the strict adherence to *kashrut* (Jewish dietary laws, also called kosher food laws), which they considered to be an assortment of ancient superstitions and taboos with no relevance to the modern world.

---

23 See, for example: www.vox.com/2019/7/10/20687946/israel-minister-second-holocaust-intermarriage (accessed 16 August 2023).
24 Kugel being a noodle dish that is popular among Ashkenazi Jews on the Sabbath and festival days.

Despite a desire to accept the norms of mainstream culture, European Jewish reformers, and their American emulators, saw limits to assimilation. In a straightforward sense they actively rejected the fundamentals of the Genesis option. They saw isolation and separatism as counterproductive. They positively accepted the intellectual heritage of the Enlightenment (and much of Protestant theology in modified form), because to do so brought them in line with contemporary culture. They wanted to look and act like 'normal' Europeans and North Americans. Nonetheless, there was a general sense that it was possible to go too far. Underneath all the changes was a golden nugget of Jewish culture that was valuable and needed to be preserved.

Novels, plays, and movies continually lament the ills of assimilation and the loss of Jewish identity because of it. There are classic stage musicals and plays turned Hollywood movies, such as, *Cabaret, Crossing Delancey* and *Fiddler on the Roof* (which likewise addresses the problem of exogamy). Or there are fictionalized autobiographical accounts of Jewish immigrants such as Barry Levinson's trilogy *Diner, Avalon,* and *Tin Men*. *Avalon* focuses directly on the radical changes in a Jewish immigrant family in Baltimore over three generations as they gradually assimilate into American culture, and laments the loss of Jewish heritage through a series of sentimental flashbacks. The conflict of the old and new ways, and the ever-present dangers of assimilation in even orthodox communities, are constant themes in the literary output of Jewish authors such as Chaim Potok and Isaac Bashevis Singer, providing fodder for playwrights and screenplays.

While there may be nostalgia for the traditions of the past among modern secular Jews, two of the pillars of the Genesis option are almost or completely absent. Secular Jews tend to be monolingual, speaking the dominant language of the culture where they live, perhaps occasionally sprinkled with a Yiddish slang word or expression (kvetch, schnorrer, schlepp, schmuck). Likewise, the admonition to be 'fruitful and multiply' is valueless among secular Jews. Contraception within the Jewish community as a whole is a measure of orthodoxy. The more orthodox a community, the more likely it is to see large families as a blessing and birth control as problematic, and vice versa.

Ultimately, the Genesis option for Jews and oppressed peoples is that it provides a powerful solution to an eternal problem. It hinges on the ability of a culture to completely disengage from discourse with the dominant culture about its identity. To engage is to lose, not least because you end up letting the discourse from the dominant culture define who you are. The Genesis option requires that oppressed cultures define themselves on their own terms, refusing to be seduced into interaction with anyone else about that identity.

In *Anti-Semite and Jew* Jean-Paul Sartre, who was not Jewish, claimed 'It is the anti-Semite who creates the Jew' (1948:143) In a similar vein Hannah

Arendt, the Jewish German political theorist whose works were of great important in the aftermath of the Second World War, wrote 'If one is attacked as a Jew, one must defend oneself as a Jew. Not as a German, not as a world-citizen, not as an upholder of the Rights of Man, or whatever.' (Bernstein 1996:21). Both Sartre and Arendt, writing in the wake of the Holocaust and in the midst of Stalinist racism in the Soviet Union, asserted that to allow others to define Jewish identity is disastrous. Both Nazis and Stalinists used racial and lineage criteria for their definitions. The person labelled a Jew by these criteria had no say in the matter.

The Genesis option starts from the other side of the equation. It says, 'We will define what it means to be Jewish and we will not be questioned or drawn into debate concerning our conclusions.' This is what the state of Israel did when it first asked the legal question *'Mihu Yehudi'* ('Who is a Jew?'). The question had deep implications for the state in terms of immigration, settlement and citizenship. The answers to the question are complex and divisive, but the important point is that Jews themselves were asking the question, and providing the answers without being involved with stereotypes and labels from the outside (Litvin 2012).

While the Genesis option has many important components, as well as subtleties, it rests in the end on the notion that a culture which defines itself in its own terms is much stronger than one that is defined by others, or engages with others in such definition. That is the ultimate point of the continued adulation of wilderness pastoralists in Genesis and throughout the Hebrew Bible. Pastoralists, alone in the wilderness with their herds, are free to define themselves in any way that they choose. The Genesis option contains the implied sentiment that the world as a whole outside one's own culture needs to be treated as a wilderness, and each oppressed culture needs to see itself as pastoralists, eking out a living from that land. Take what you need from it, but do not let it be your master. Prosper in isolation from other cultures whose values will serve to do nothing except corrupt you.

One of the great wilderness narratives of the Hebrew Bible is the story of Moses at the burning bush (Exodus 3). Moses is keeping his father-in-law's sheep in the wilderness when he has an encounter with God, who sets him the task of freeing the Israelites from bondage in Egypt. At a critical moment in the narrative Moses asks God to tell him his name (capitals in the original):

> 13. But Moses said to God, 'If I come to the Israelites and say to them, "The God of your ancestors has sent me to you," and they ask me, 'What is his name?', what shall I say to them?'

14. God said to Moses, 'I am who I am.' He said further, 'Thus you shall say to the Israelites, 'I am has sent me to you.'

'I AM WHO I AM' is the perfect name for the God of the people who are to live according to the Genesis option. Their God defines himself for himself rather than being defined by others, and derives his power from himself and not from others. If they do likewise they too will become powerful and will break the chains of their bondage to another culture.

Further reading

To understand the history and theology of the post-exilic period, you can consult Peter Ackroyd's *Exile and Restoration* (1968). It is seriously dated, but it remains a good guide to the literature of the period. Check out also the relevant sections of Paula McNutt's *Reconstructing the Society of Ancient Israel* (1999). You might also want to look at a commentary on the books of Ezra and Nehemiah. One that is readable and strong on historical context is F. Charles Fensham's *The Books of Ezra and Nehemiah* (1982). For a popular work on the history of Jerusalem from its foundations through the Exile and destruction in 70 CE and beyond, consult Karen Armstrong's *Jerusalem* (1996).

The previously noted two-volume work *Archeology of the Land of the Bible* (Ephraim 2001) is the best overview of the current state of archaeology in the Levant. It meshes the biblical historical record with the archaeological facts. See also William G. Dever's *What Did the Biblical Writers Know and When Did They Know It?* (2001). Israel Finkelstein, William Dever, and Amihai Mazar (and the whole Mazar family), have produced countless articles and numerous books on the history of the Levant region, some dealing with the post-Exilic situation.

Flavius Josephus was a Jew, but he was also the puppet of imperial Rome. His historical vision of Jewish history, while biased, is of paramount importance in adding to the Biblical narrative. Any edition of *The Wars of the Jews* (Josephus 2020) will be rewarding reading. The scene he paints of the destruction of Jerusalem is extraordinary.

Good books on contemporary Pueblo culture are rare because of their isolationist stance. The classic on the Tewa is Alfonso Ortiz, *The Tewa World* (1969). Ortiz has a privileged view because he was raised in a Tewa pueblo. See also Jill Sweet's *Dances of the Tewa Pueblo Indians* (2004). She explores the many changes that the Tewa are undergoing and how they are coping with survival in the face of massive pressures to assimilate to the Anglo world. Also take a look at Ramón A. Gutiérrez's *When Jesus Came, the Corn Mothers Went Away* (1991). To learn how Spanish culture and colonization have influenced the dance and ritual of the Tewa you could look at my own work, *Morris and Matachin* (Forrest 1984).

A definitive study of Old Order Amish culture is Donald B. Kraybill's, *The Riddle of Amish Culture* (1989). Check out also Donald B. Kraybill, Karen M. Johnson-Weiner, and Steven M. Nolt's, *The Amish* (2013). Changes in an Amish community in Lancaster County, Pennsylvania, are documented in Donald B. Kraybill and Steven M. Nolt's *Amish Enterprise* (1995). I also recommend Joe Wittmer's *The Gentle People* (2006). Wittmer was raised in an Amish community but left as a teenager. He now acts as an insider/outsider guide to traditional Amish life.

For a history of the Jews in Babylonia, see Nissim Rejwan's, *The Jews of Iraq* (1985). For the more contemporary scene I suggest Reeva Simon, Michael Laskier and Sara Reguer's *The Jews of the Middle East and North Africa in Modern Times* (2003) and Norman Stillman's *The Jews of Arab Lands in Modern Times* (1991).

For information on Lubavitchers in the modern world there are numerous choices. You could start with Avrum M. Ehrlich's *Leadership in the Habad Movement* (2000) and Jan L. Feldman's *Lubavitchers As Citizens* (2003).

For analyses of Jewish identity through history and in modern times, consult Mel Konner's *Unsettled* (2003), Lynn Davidman's, *Tradition in a Rootless World* (1991), Jack Kugelmass's *Between Two Worlds* (1988), Sascha Goluboff's *Jewish Russians* (2003) and Matti Bunzl's *Anti-Semitism and Islamophobia* (2007). For the question, 'Who is a Jew?' consult Morris Kertzer's *What is a Jew?* (1996) and Lauren Siedman's *What Makes Someone a Jew?* (2007).

REFERENCES

Aaboe, A. 1964. *Episodes from the Early History of Mathematics*. Washington, DC: New Mathematical Library.

Abdurehman, A. 2019. 'Origin, domestication, current status, trend, conservation and management of sheep genetic resource in Africa with specific reference to Ethiopia', *Advances in Life Science and Technology* 71:8–14.

Ackroyd, P. 1968. *Exile and Restoration: A Study of Hebrew Thought of the Sixth Century B.C.* London: SCM Press.

——— 1970. *Israel under Babylon and Persia*. Oxford: Oxford University Press.

Ager, S.L. 2005. 'Familiarity breeds: incest and the Ptolemaic dynasty', *The Journal of Hellenic Studies* 125:1–34.

Alberto, F.J., Boyer, F., Orozco-terWengel, P., Streeter, I., Servin, B., de Villemereuil, P., Benjelloun, B., Librado, P., Biscarini, F., Colli, L., Barbato, M., Zamani, W., Alberti, A., Engelen, S., Stella, A., Joost, S., Ajmone-Marsan, P., Negrini, R., Orlando, L., Rezaei, H.R., Naderi, S., Clarke, L., Flicek, P., Wincker, P., Coissac, E., Kijas, J., Tosser-Klopp, G., Chikhi, A., Bruford, M.W., Taberlet, P. and Pompanon, F. 2018. 'Convergent genomic signatures of domestication in sheep and goats', *Nature Communications* 9:813.

Albertz, R. 2000. 'The riddle of the Deuteronomists'. In T. Römer (ed.), *The Future of the Deuteronomistic History*, pp. 119–27. Leuven University Press.

Alexander, P.S. 1992. 'Early Jewish geography'. In D.N. Freedman (ed.), *Anchor Bible Dictionary* 2, pp. 977–88. Garden City, NJ: Anchor.

Alford, R.D. 1988. *Naming and Identity: A Cross-cultural Study of Personal Naming Practices*. New Haven: HRAF.

Alstola, T. 2020. *Judeans in Babylonia: A Study of Deportees in the Sixth and Fifth Centuries BCE*. Leiden: Brill.

Andreasen, N.-E. 1972. *The Old Testament Sabbath: A Tradition-Historical Investigation*. Atlanta, GA: Society of Biblical Literature.

Andrews, E.D. 2011. *The People Called Shakers*. Mineola, NY: Dover.

Arensberg, C. 1937 [1968]. *The Irish Countryman: An Anthropological Study*. London: Macmillan.

Armstrong, K. 1996. *Jerusalem: One City, Three Faiths*. New York: Knopf.

Arnold, B.T. 2014. *Introduction to the Old Testament*. Cambridge: Cambridge University Press.

Arnold, B.T. and Beyer, B.E. 2002. *Readings from the Ancient Near East: Primary Sources for Old Testament Study*. Grand Rapids, MI: Baker Academic.

Arnold, B.T. and Weisberg, D. 2002. 'A centennial review of Friedrich Delitzsch's 'Babel und Bibel' Lectures', *Journal of Biblical Literature* 121(3):441–57.

Ausloos, Hs. 2015. *The Deuteronomist's History. The Role of the Deuteronomist in Historical-Critical Research into Genesis–Numbers* (Old Testament Studies 67). Leiden: Brill.
Baden, J.S. 2009. *J, E, and the Redaction of the Pentateuch*. Tübingen: Mohr Siebeck.
——— 2012. *The Composition of the Pentateuch: Renewing the Documentary Hypothesis* (Anchor Yale Reference Library). New Haven: Yale University Press.
Bar-Yosef, O. and Khazanov, A. (eds) 1992. *Pastoralism in the Levant: Archaeological Materials in Anthropological Perspective*. Madison, WI: Prehistory Press.
Barstad, H.M. 1996. *The Myth of the Empty Land: A Study in the History and Archaeology of Judah during the 'Exilic' Period*. Oslo: Scandinavian University Press.
Bellwood, P. 2004. *First Farmers: The Origins of Agricultural Societies*. Oxford: Blackwell.
Bernstein, R.J. 1996. *Hannah Arendt and the Jewish Question*. Cambridge, Mass: M.I.T Press.
Best, R.M. *Noah's Ark and the Ziusudra Epic: Sumerian Origins of the Flood Myth*. University Park, PA: Eisenbrauns.
Black, J. and Green, A. 1992. *Gods, Demons and Symbols of Ancient Mesopotamia: An Illustrated Dictionary*. London: The British Museum Press.
Blenkinsopp, J. 2002. *Isaiah 40–55: A New Translation with Introduction and Commentary*. New York: Doubleday
Borgerhoff Mulder, M. 1995. 'Bridewealth and its correlates: quantifying changes over time', *Current Anthropology* 36(4):573–603.
Brenner, A. 1985. *The Israelite Woman: Social Role and Literary Type in the Biblical Narrative*. Sheffield: JSOT Press.
Breidenbach, G. and Harris, H. 1971. *The Nuer* (film). Cambridge, MA: Harvard University.
Bridge, E.J. 2012. 'Female slave vs female slave: אמה and שפחה in the Hebrew Bible', *Journal of Hebrew Scriptures* 2, DOI: 10.5508/jhs.2012.v12.a2.
Brondz, I. 2018. 'Why do Judaism and Islam prohibit eating pork and consuming blood as a food?', *Norwegian Drug Control and Drug Discovery Institute (NDCDDI)* 4(2), DOI:10.4236/vp.2018.42003.
Bunzl, M. 2007. *Anti-Semitism and Islamophobia: Hatreds Old and New in Europe*. Chicago: Chicago University Press.
Byron, J. 2011. *Cain and Abel in Text and Tradition: Jewish and Christian Interpretations of the First Sibling Rivalry*. Leiden: Brill Publishers.
Carr, D. 2011. *The Formation of the Hebrew Bible: A New Reconstruction*. Oxford: Oxford University Press.

——— 2014. 'Changes in Pentateuchal criticism'. In M. Saeboe, J.L. Ska and P. Machinist (eds), *Hebrew Bible/Old Testament. III: From Modernism to Post-Modernism. Part II: The Twentieth Century – From Modernism to Post-Modernism*, pp. 431–66. Bristol, CT: Vandenhoeck & Ruprecht.

Chagnon, N. 1968. *Yanomamö: The Fierce People*. New York: Holt.

Charlesworth, J.H. (ed.) 1985. *The Old Testament Pseudepigrapha, Vol. 2: Expansions of the Old Testament and Legends, Wisdom and Philosophical Literature, Prayers, Psalms, and Odes, Fragments of Lost Judeo-Hellenistic Works*. New York: Doubleday.

Chattopadhyay, K.P. 1922. 'Levirate and kinship in India', *Man* 22:36–41.

Chen, Y.S. 2013. *The Primeval Flood Catastrophe: Origins and Early Development in Mesopotamian Tradition*. Oxford: Oxford University Press.

Christin, A.-M. 2002. *A History of Writing: From Hieroglyph to Multimedia*. Paris: Flammarion.

Clifford, R. 1994. *Creation Accounts in the Ancient Near East and in the Bible*. Washington, DC: Catholic Biblical Association.

Cohen, A. and Kangas, S.E. 2010. *Assyrian Reliefs from the Palace of Ashurnasirpal II: A Cultural Biography*. Boston, MA: Brandeis University Press.

Cohen, H.H. 1974. *The Drunkenness of Noah*. Tuscaloosa: University of Alabama Press.

Cohn, N. 1996. *Noah's Flood: The Genesis Story in Western Thought*. New Haven: Yale University Press.

Coleman, J.A. and Davidson, G. 2015. *The Dictionary of Mythology: An A–Z of Themes, Legends, and Heroes*. London: Arcturus Publishing Limited.

Collins, A.Y. (ed.) 1985. *Feminist Perspectives on Biblical Scholarship* (Society of Biblical Literature Centennial Publication 10). Chico, CA: Scholars Press.

Collins, J.J. 2002. 'Current issues in the study of Daniel'. In J.J. Collins, P.W. Flint and C. VanEpps (eds), *The Book of Daniel: Composition and Reception*. Leiden: Brill.

Crawford, J. 2000. *At War With Diversity: U.S. Language Policy in an Age of Anxiety*. Bristol, UK: Multilingual Matters.

Crossan, J.D. 1991. *The Historical Jesus: The Life of a Mediterranean Jewish Peasant*. San Francisco, CA: Harper.

——— 1994. *Jesus: A Revolutionary Biography*. San Francisco, CA: Harper.

Crowley, T. 2000. *The Politics of Language in Ireland 1366–1922: A Sourcebook*. London, Routledge.

Crystal, D. 2000. *Language Death*. Cambridge: Cambridge University Press.

Dahlberg. F. (ed.) 1981. *Woman the Gatherer*. New Haven: Yale University Press.

Dalley, S. 2000. *Myths from Mesopotamia: Creation, the Flood, Gilgamesh, and Others* (rev. edn.). Oxford: Oxford University Press.

Dalton, J. and Leung, T.C. 2014. 'Why is polygyny more prevalent in western Africa? An African slave trade perspective', *Economic Development and Cultural Change* 62(4):601–4.

Davidman, L. 1991. *Tradition in a Rootless World: Women Turn to Orthodox Judaism*. Berkeley: University of California Press.

Davies, G.I. 1998. 'Introduction to the Pentateuch'. In J. Barton (ed.), *Oxford Bible Commentary*, pp. 1–47. Oxford University Press.

Davies, P.R. 1992. *In Search of 'Ancient Israel'*. Sheffield: JSOT Press.

Derrida, J. 1990 [1953–4]. *The Problem of Genesis in Husserl's Philosophy* (tr. M. Hobson). Chicago: University of Chicago.

Dever, W.G. 2001. *What Did the Biblical Writers Know and When Did They Know It?: What Archaeology Can Tell Us About the Reality of Ancient Israel*. Grand Rapids, MI: William Eerdmans Publishing.

——— 2017. *Beyond the Texts: An Archeological Portrait of Ancient Israel and Judah*. Atlanta: SBL Press.

DeVore, I. and Lee, R. (eds). 1968. *Man the Hunter*. Chicago: Aldine Press.

——— 1976. *Kalahari Hunter-Gatherers: Studies of the !Kung San & Their Neighbors*. Cambridge, MA: Harvard University Press.

Domingue, V.R. and Metzner, E. 2017. 'Special section on nativism, nationalism, and xenophobia: what anthropologists do and have done', *American Anthropologist* 119:518–19.

Dosse, F. 1998. *History of Structuralism* (2 vols.). Minneapolis: University of Minnesota Press.

Douglas, M. 1966. *Purity and Danger: An Analysis of Concepts of Pollution and Taboo*. New York: Frederick A. Praeger.

Dozeman, T.B. 2010. *Methods for Exodus*. Cambridge: Cambridge University Press.

Dundes, A. 1999. *Holy Writ as Oral Lit: The Bible as Folklore*. Lanham, MD: Rowman and Littlefield.

Ehrlich, A.M. 2000. *Leadership in the Habad Movement: A Critical Evaluation of Habad Leadership, History, and Succession*. New York, NY: Jason Aronson.

Eliade, M. 1954. *The Myth of the Eternal Return*. New York: Bollingen.

Ellickson, R.C. and Thorland, C.D.1995. 'Ancient land law: Mesopotamia, Egypt, Israel', *Chicago-Kent Law Review* 71(1):12.

Ellicott, C. (ed.) 2019 [1897]. *An Old Testament Commentary for English Readers*. Omaha, NB: Patristic Publishing.

Ensminger, J. and Knight, J. 1997. 'Changing social norms: common property, bridewealth, and clan exogamy', *Current Anthropology* 38(1):1–24.

Evans-Pritchard, E.E. 1940. *The Nuer: A Description of the Modes of Livelihood and Political Institutions of a Nilotic People*. Oxford: Oxford University Press.

——— 1951. *Kinship and Marriage among the Nuer*. Oxford: Oxford University Press.

Fanon, F. 1967. *Black Skin, White Masks* (tr. C.L. Markmann). New York: Grove Press.

——— 2004 [1967]. *The Wretched of the Earth* (tr. R. Philcox). New York: Grove Press.
Farb, P. 1975. *Word Play: What Happens When People Talk*. New York: Random House.
Feldman, J.L. 2003. *Lubavitchers As Citizens: A Paradox of Liberal Democracy*. Ithaca, NY: Cornell University Press.
Fedorak, S.A. 2013. *Global Issues: A Cross-Cultural Perspective*. Toronto: University of Toronto.
——— 2017. *Anthropology Matters* (3rd edn.). Toronto: University of Toronto.
Fensham, F.C. 1982. *The Books of Ezra and Nehemiah*. Grand Rapids, MI: William Eerdmans Publishing.
Ferry, D. 1993. *Gilgamesh: A New Rendering in English Verse*. New York: Farrar, Straus and Giroux.
Fields, W.W. 1997. *Sodom and Gomorrah: History and Motif in Biblical Narrative*. London: A&C Black.
Finkelstein, I. 1995. *Living on the Fringe*. Sheffield: Sheffield Academic Press.
——— 1996. 'The archaeology of the united monarchy: an alternative view', *Levant* 28:177–87.
——— 2013. *The Forgotten Kingdom: The Archaeology and History of Northern Israel*. Atlanta, GA: Society of Biblical Literature.
Finkelstein, I. and Mazar, A. 2007. *The Quest for the Historical Israel: Debating Archeology and the History of Early Israel*. Atlanta, GA: Society of Biblical Literature.
Finkelstein, I. and Silberman, N.A. 2001. *The Bible Unearthed: Archaeology's New Vision of Ancient Israel and the Origin of Its Sacred Texts*. New York: Simon and Schuster.
Finkelstein, I. and Silberman, N.A. 2007. *David and Solomon: In Search of the Bible's Sacred Kings and the Roots of the Western Tradition*. New York: Simon and Schuster.
Fischer, S. 2001. *The History of Writing*. London: Reaktion.
Fishman, J. (ed.) 2000. *Can Threatened Languages Be Saved: Reversing Language Shift, Revisited: A 21st Century Perspective*. Clevedon: Multilingual Matters.
Fontaine, P.F.M. 1986. *The Light and the Dark: A Cultural History of Dualism*. Amsterdam: J.C. Gieben.
Forrest, J. 1984. *Morris and Matachin: A Study in Comparative Choreography* (Centre for English Cultural Tradition and Language Publications 4). Sheffield: University of Sheffield.
——— 1999. *The History of Morris Dancing, 1458–1750*. Toronto: University of Toronto.

Forrest, J. and Forrest-Blincoe, B. 2018. 'Kim Chi, K-Pop, and taekwondo: the nationalization of South Korean martial arts', *Ido Movement for Culture: Journal of Martial Arts Anthropology* 18(2):1–14.

Fortes, M. and Evans-Pritchard, E.E. (eds) 1940. *African Political Systems*. Oxford: Oxford University Press.

Fox, R. 1980. *The Red Lamp of Incest*. New York: Dutton.

French, J.R.P. and Raven, B. 1959, 'The bases of social power'. In D. Cartwright (ed.), *Studies in Social Power*, pp. 150–67. Ann Arbor, MI: Institute for Social Research.

Fretheim, T.E. 1991. *Exodus*. Westminster: John Knox Press.

Freud, S. 1950 [1913]. *Totem and Taboo*. New York: Routledge and Kegan Paul.

Friberg, J. 1978. *The Third Millennium Roots of Babylonian Mathematics. I. A Method for the Decipherment, Through Mathematical and Metrological Analysis, of Proto-Sumerian and Proto-Elamite Semipictographic Inscriptions*. Göteborg: Department of Mathematics, University of Göteborg.

——— 2005. *Unexpected Links Between Egyptian and Babylonian Mathematics*. Singapore: World Scientific Publishing.

Friedman, R.E. 1987. *Who Wrote the Bible?* San Francisco: Harper.

Fritz, V. 1996. *The City in Ancient Israel*. Sheffield: Sheffield Academic Press.

Frymer-Kensky, T. 2002. *Reading the Women of the Bible: A New Interpretation of Their Stories*. New York: Schoken Books.

Fuchs, E. 2000. *Sexual Politics in the Biblical Narrative: Reading the Hebrew Bible as a Woman*. Sheffield: Sheffield Academic Press.

Gagnon, R.A.J. 2001. *The Bible and Homosexual Practice: Texts and Hermeneutics*. Nashville: Abingdon Press.

Garsiel, M. 1991. *Biblical Names: A Literary Study of Midrashic Name Derivations and Puns*. Ramat Gan: Bar-Ilan University Press.

Geertz, C. 1973. *The Interpretation of Cultures*. New York: Basic Books.

Gell, A. 1992. *The Anthropology of Time: Cultural Constructions of Temporal Maps and Images*. Oxford: Berg.

George, A. 2000. 'E-sangil and E-temen-anki: the archetypal cult-centre', *Babylon: Focus mesopotamischer Geschichte, Wiege früher Gelehrsamkeit, Mythos in der Moderne* 2:67–86.

——— 2003. *The Babylonian Gilgamesh Epic: Introduction, Critical Edition and Cuneiform Texts* (2 vols.). Oxford: Oxford University Press.

Ginsburg, F. and Rapp, R. (eds) 1995. *Conceiving the New World Order: The Global Politics of Reproduction*. Berkeley: University of California Press.

Goldenberg, D.M. 2003. *The Curse of Ham: Race and Slavery in Early Judaism, Christianity, and Islam*. Princeton, NJ: Princeton University Press.

Gollaher, D. 2000. *Circumcision: A History of the World's Most Controversial Surgery*. New York: Basic Books.

Goluboff, S. 2003. *Jewish Russians: Upheavals in a Moscow Synagogue*. Philadelphia: University of Pennsylvania Press.

Gonen, R. 2002. *The Quest for the Ten Lost Tribes of Israel*. Northvale, NJ: Jason Aronson.

González, N. 1999. 'What will we do when culture does not exist anymore?', *Anthropology & Education Quarterly* 30(4):431–5.

Goody, J. 1990. *The Oriental, The Ancient and The Primitive: Systems of Marriage and the Family in the Pre-Industrial Societies of Eurasia*. Cambridge: Cambridge University Press.

Goody, J. and Tambiah, S.J. 1974. *Bridewealth and Dowry*. Cambridge: Cambridge University Press.

Grabbe, L.L. (ed.) 1998. *Leading Captivity Captive: The Exile as History and Ideology*. Sheffield: JSOT Press.

——— 2007. *Ancient Israel: What Do We Know and How Do We Know It?* New York: T&T Clark.

Graeber, D. 2011 *Debt: The First 5,000 Years*. Hoboken, NJ: Melville House.

Greenhalgh, S. (ed.) 1995. *Situating Fertility: Anthropology and Demographic Inquiry*. Cambridge: Cambridge University Press.

Grossman, K., Paulette, T. and Price, M. 2017. 'Pigs and the pastoral bias: the other animal economy in northern Mesopotamia (3000–2000 BCE)', *Journal of Anthropological Archaeology* 48:46–62.

Guillaume, P. 2018. 'Debunking the latest scenario on the rise of the pork taboo', *Études et Travaux* 31:144-66.

Guinnane, T. 1997. *The Vanishing Irish: Households, Migration and the Rural Economy in Ireland, 1850–1914*. Princeton, N.J.: Princeton University Press.

Gutiérrez, R.A. 1991. *When Jesus Came, the Corn Mothers Went Away: Marriage, Sexuality, and Power in New Mexico, 1500–1846*. Stanford: Stanford University Press.

Ham, K. 2006. *The New Answers Book: Over 25 Questions on Creation/Evolution and the Bible, Book 1*. Green Forest, AK:. Master Books.

Hamilton, V.P. 1995. *The Book of Genesis: Chapters 18–50*. Grand Rapids, MI: Eerdmans.

Hanson, K.C. (tr. and ed.) 2011. *Hermann Gunkel, Israel and Babylon: The Babylonian Influence on Israelite Religion*. Cambridge: James Clarke & Co.

Harkin, M.E. (ed.) 2004. *Reassessing Revitalization Movements: Perspectives from North America and the Pacific Islands*. Lincoln: University of Nebraska Press.

Harland, J.P. 1943. 'Sodom and Gomorrah: the destruction of the cities of the plain', *The Biblical Archaeologist* 6(3):41–54.

Harris, M. 1975. *Cows, Pigs, Wars and Witches: The Riddles of Culture*. London: Hutchinson & Co.

References

Harris, S.L. 2002. *Understanding the Bible.* New York: McGraw-Hill.
Harrison, P. 2006. 'Poststructuralist theories'. In S. Aitken and G. Valentine (eds.), *Approaches to Human Geography*, pp. 122–35. London: SAGE Publications.
Heidel, A. 1942. *The Babylonian Genesis* (2nd edn.). Chicago: University of Chicago Press.
――― 1946. *The Gilgamesh Epic and Old Testament Parallels.* Chicago: University of Chicago Press.
Helminiak, D.A. 2000. *What the Bible Really Says about Homosexuality.* Tajique, NM: Alamo Square Press.
Hendel, R. 2012. *The Book of 'Genesis': A Biography* (Lives of Great Religious Books). Princeton, NJ: Princeton University Press.
Henry, D. 1989. *From Foraging to Agriculture: The Levant and the End of the Ice Age.* Philadelphia: University of Pennsylvania Press.
Hinton, A.L. (ed.) 2002. *Annihilating Difference: The Anthropology of Genocide.* Berkeley: University of California Press.
Holy, L. 1996. *Anthropological Perspectives on Kinship.* Sterling VA: Pluto Press.
Huebner, S.R. 2007. '"Brother-sister" marriage in Roman Egypt: a curiosity of humankind or a widespread family strategy?', *The Journal of Roman Studies* 97:21–49.
Ifrah, G. 1998. *A Universal History of Numbers: From Prehistory to the Invention of the Computer.* London: Harvill Press.
Ingold, T., Riches, D. and Woodburn, J. 1988. *Hunters and Gatherers* (2 vols.). Oxford: Berg.
James, W. and Mills, D. (eds) 2004. *The Qualities of Time: Anthropological Approaches.* Oxford: Berg.
Jeansonne, S. 1990. *The Women of Genesis: From Sarah to Potiphar's Wife.* Minneapolis: Fortress Press.
Johnson, M.D. 1969. *The Purpose of the Biblical Genealogies, with Special Reference to the Setting of the Genealogies of Jesus.* Cambridge: Cambridge University Press.
Jordan, M. 1999. *The Invention of Sodomy in Christian Theology.* Chicago IL: University of Chicago Press.
Josephus, F. 2020. *Wars of the Jews: Or, History of the Destruction of Jerusalem.* (tr. W. Whiston). Overland Park, KS: Digireads.
Kertzer, M. 1996. *What is a Jew?* New York: Touchstone.
Kirkpatrick, P. 1988. *The Old Testament and Folklore Study.* Sheffield: JSOT Press.
Koldewey, R. 1914. *The Excavations at Babylon* (tr. A.S. Johns). London: Macmillan.
Konner, M. 2003. *Unsettled: An Anthropology of the Jews.* New York: Penguin.
Kraybill, D.B. 1989. *The Riddle of Amish Culture.* Baltimore: Johns Hopkins University Press.

Kraybill, D.B. and Nolt, S.M. 1995. *Amish Enterprise: From Plows to Profits*. Baltimore: Johns Hopkins University Press.

Kraybill, D.B., Johnson-Weiner, K.M. and Nolt, S.M. 2013. *The Amish*. Baltimore: Johns Hopkins University Press.

Kroeber, A. 1935. 'History and science in anthropology', *American Anthropologist* 35:539–69.

Kugelmass, J. (ed.) 1988. *Between Two Worlds: Ethnographic Essays on American Jewry*. New York: Cornell University Press.

Lachs, R.1980. *Women and Judaism*. Garden City, NY: Doubleday & Co.

Lambert, W.G. 2013. *Babylonian Creation Myths*. Winona Lake, IN: Eisenbrauns.

Lange, A. and Meyers, E.M. (eds) 2011. *Light Against Darkness: Dualism in Ancient Mediterranean Religion and the Contemporary World*. Göttingen: Vandenhoeck & Ruprecht.

Leach, E. 1969. *Genesis as Myth and Other Essays*. London: Jonathan Cape.

——— 1970. *Claude Lévi-Strauss*. Chicago: University of Chicago Press.

——— 1976. *Culture and Communication: The Logic by which Symbols are Connected*. Cambridge: Cambridge University Press.

Leavitt, G. 1990. 'Sociobiological explanations of incest avoidance: a critical claim of evidential claims', *American Anthropologist* 92:971–93.

——— 2013. 'Tylor vs. Westermarck: explaining the incest taboo', *Sociology Mind* 3(1):45–51.

Lee, R.B. 1979. *The !Kung San: Men, Women and Work in a Foraging Society*. Cambridge: Cambridge University Press.

Leonard, S.A. and McClure, M. 2004. *Myth and Knowing*. McGraw-Hill.

Leeming, D.A. and Leeming, M.A. 2009. *A Dictionary of Creation Myths* (Oxford Reference Online edn.). Oxford: Oxford University Press.

Levenson, J.D. 2004. 'Genesis: introduction and annotations'. In A. Berlin and M.Z. Brettler (eds.), *The Jewish Study Bible*. Oxford: Oxford University Press.

Lévi-Strauss, C. 1963. *Structural Anthropology*. New York: Basic Books.

Levine, B.A. 2003. *Leviticus*. Philadelphia, PA: JPS Torah Commentary.

Linton, R. 1943. 'Nativistic movements', *American Anthropologist* 45:230–40.

Litvin, B. 2012. *Jewish Identity: Who Is A Jew?* Brooklyn, NY: KTAV Publications.

Loader, J.A. 1990. *A Tale of Two Cities: Sodom and Gomorrah in the Old Testament, Early Jewish and Early Christian Traditions*. Leuven, Belgium: Peeters Publishers.

Lynch, W. 2006. 'A nation established by immigrants sanctions employers for requiring English to be spoken at work: English-only work rules and national origin discrimination', *Temple Political and Civil Rights Law Review* 65:65–7.

Malina, B. 1981. *The New Testament World: Insights from Cultural Anthropology*. Atlanta: John Knox.

Mazar, A. 1990 [1973]. *Archaeology of the Land of the Bible: 10,000–586 B.C.E.* Garden City, NJ: Anchor Bible Reference Library.

McEwen, H. 2019. 'Suspect sexualities: contextualizing rumours of homosexuality within colonial histories of population control', *Critical African Studies* 11(3):266–84.

McNutt, P. 1999. *Reconstructing the Society of Ancient Israel.* Louisville: John Knox Press.

Memmi, A. 1962. *Portrait of a Jew* (tr. E. Abbott). New York: Orion Press.

——— 1965. *The Colonizer and the Colonized* (tr. H. Greenfeld). New York: Orion Press.

——— 2006. *Decolonization and the Decolonized* (tr. R. Bonnono). Minneapolis: University of Minnesota Press.

Middlemas, J. 2005. *The Troubles of Templeless Judah.* Oxford: Oxford University Press.

Mckenzie, J.L. 1995. *The Dictionary of the Bible.* New York: Simon and Schuster.

Murdoch, B. 1994. 'Sethites and Cainites: the narrative problem of Adam's progeny in the early middle high German Genesis poems'. In V. Honemann (ed.), *German Narrative Literature of the Twelfth and Thirteenth Centuries: Studies Presented to Roy Wisbey on his Sixty-Fifth Birthday*, pp. 701–17. Berlin: Max Niemeyer Verlag.

Murphy, Y. and Murphy, R. 2004 [1974]. *Women of the Forest.* New York: Columbia University Press.

Nelles, W. (ed.) 2003. *Comparative Education, Terrorism and Human Security: From Critical Pedagogy to Peacebuilding?* London: Palgrave.

Nicholson, E.W. 2003. *The Pentateuch in the Twentieth Century.* Oxford: Oxford University Press.

Niditch, S. 1987. *Underdogs and Tricksters: A Prelude to Biblical Folklore.* San Francisco: Harper.

——— 1993. *Folklore and the Hebrew Bible.* Minneapolis: Augsburg Fortress.

——— 1996. *Oral World and Written Word: Ancient Israelite Literature.* Louisville: John Knox Press.

Noegel, S.B. (ed.) 2000. *Puns and Pundits: Word Play in the Hebrew Bible and Ancient Near Eastern Literature.* Bethesda, MA: CDL Press.

O'Brien, J. (ed.) 1953. *The Vanishing Irish: The Enigma of the Modern World.* New York: McGraw-Hill.

Ong, A. 1999. *Flexible Citizenship: The Cultural Logics of Transnationality.* Durham, NC.: Duke University Press.

Ortiz, A. 1969. *The Tewa World: Space, Time, Being, and Becoming in a Pueblo Society.* Chicago: University of Chicago Press.

Pagels, E. 1989. *Adam, Eve and the Serpent.* New York: Vintage Books.

Parfitt, T. 2002. *The Lost Tribes of Israel: The History of a Myth*. London: Weidenfeld & Nicolson.

Partridge, E. 1983. *Origins: A Short Etymological Dictionary of Modern English*. New York: Greenwich House.

Peters-Golden, H. 2012. *Culture Sketches: Case Studies in Anthropology* (6th edn.). New York: McGraw-Hill.

Pleins, D.J. 2004. 'When myths go wrong: deconstructing the drunkenness of Noah', *Culture and Religion* 5(2):219–27.

Portes, A. and Zhou, M. 1993. 'The new second generation: segmented assimilation and its variants', *Annals* 530(1):74–96.

Potter, S.H. 1977. *Family Life in a Northern Thai Villlage: A Study in the Structural Significance of Women*. Berkeley: University of California Press.

Prager, D. 2020. *Genesis: God, Creation, and Destruction*. Washington, DC: Regnery Faith.

Price, T. D. and Gebauer, A.B. (eds) 1995. *Last Hunters-First Farmers: New Perspectives on the Prehistoric Transition to Agriculture*. Santa Fe: School of American Research.

Pritchard, J.B. (ed.) 1969. *Ancient Near Eastern Texts Relating to the Old Testament* (3rd edn.). Princeton: Princeton University Press.

Reczek,C., Spiker, R., Liu, H. and Crosnoe, R. 2017. 'The promise and perils of population research on same-sex families', *Demography* 54(6):2385–97.

Rejwan, N. 1985. *The Jews of Iraq: 3000 years of History and Culture*. London: Weidenfeld and Nicolson.

Reyhner, J. (ed.) 1999. *Revitalizing Indigenous Languages*. Flagstaff, AZ: Northern Arizona University, Center for Excellence in Education.

Richards, E.G. 1999. *Mapping Time: The Calendar and its History*. Oxford: Oxford University Press.

Robben, A.C.G.M. and Sluka, J.A. 2012. *Ethnographic Fieldwork: An Anthropological Reader* (2nd edn.). Oxford: Wiley-Blackwell.

Ruether, R.R. (ed.) 1974. *Religion and Sexism: Images of Woman in the Jewish and Christian Traditions*. New York: Simon and Schuster.

Ryan, W. and Pitman, W. 1998. *Noah's Flood: The New Scientific Discoveries about the Event that Changed History*. New York; Touchstone.

Saeboe, M., Ska, J.L. and Machinist, P. (eds) 2014. *Hebrew Bible/Old Testament*. Göttingen: Vandenhoeck & Ruprecht.

Sahlins, M. 1972. *Stone Age Economics*. Chicago: Aldine-Atherton .

Sailhamer, J.H. 2008. *Genesis (The Expositor's Bible Commentary)*. Grand Rapids, MI: Zondervan.

——— 2011. *Genesis Unbound: A Provocative New Look at the Creation Account*. North Sydney, NSW: Dawson Media.

Salzmann, Z. 2004. *Language, Culture, and Society: An Introduction to Linguistic Anthropology* (3rd edn.). Boulder, CO: Westview Press.

Sapir-Hen, L., Bar-Oz, G., Gadot, Y. and Finkelstein, I. 2013. 'Pig husbandry in Iron Age Israel and Judah: new insights regarding the origin of the 'taboo', *Zeitschrift des Deutschen Palästina-Vereins* 129(1):1–20.

Sarna, N.M. 2001. *The JPS Torah Commentary: Genesis*. Philadelphia: Jewish Publication Society.

Sartre, J.-P. 1948. *Anti-Semite and Jew*. New York: Shocken Books.

Sawyer, B. and Sawyer, P. 1993. *Medieval Scandinavia: From Conversion to Reformation, Circa 800–1500*. Minneapolis: University of Minnesota Press.

Schearing, L.S. and McKenzie, S.L. (eds) 1995. *Those Elusive Deuteronomists: The Phenomenon of Pan-Deuteronomism*. London: T&T Clark.

Schechner, R. 1971. 'Incest and culture: a reflection on Claude Lévi-Strauss', *Psychoanalytic Review* 58(4):563–72.

Scheper-Hughes, N. 2001. *Saints, Scholars, and Schizophrenics: Mental Illness in Rural Ireland, Twentieth Anniversary Edition*. Berkeley: University of California Press.

Shanks, H., Dever, W., Halpern, B. and McCarter, K. 2012 *The Rise of Ancient Israel* (2nd edn.). Washington, DC: Biblical Archeology Society.

Shavit, Y. and Eran, M. 2007. *The Hebrew Bible Reborn: From Holy Scripture to the Book of Books: A History of Biblical Culture and the Battles over the Bible in Modern Judaism* (tr. C. Naor). Berlin: Walter de Gruyter.

Shectman, S. 2022. 'Women's status and feminist readings of Genesis'. In B.T. Arnold (ed.), *The Cambridge Companion to Genesis*, pp. 188–208. Cambridge: Cambridge University Press.

Shepher, J. 1983. *Incest: A Biosocial View*. New York: Academic Press.

Shipley, J.T. 1984. *The Origins of English Words: A Discursive Dictionary of Indo-European Roots*. Baltimore: Johns Hopkins University Press.

Siarl, F. 2013. 'Brief history of the Cornish language, its revival and its current situation', *E-Keltoi* 2(2):199–227.

Siedman, L. 2007. *What Makes Someone a Jew?* Woodstock, Vermont: Jewish Lights Publishing.

Silberman, A. and Finkelstein, I. 2002. *The Bible Unearthed: Archaeology's New Vision of Ancient Israel and the Origin of Its Sacred Texts*. New York: Simon and Schuster.

Simon, R., Laskier, M. and Reguer. S. (eds) 2003. *The Jews of the Middle East and North Africa in Modern Times*. New York: Columbia University Press.

Ska, J.-L. 2006. *Introduction to Reading the Pentateuch*. Winona Lake, IN: Eisenbrauns.

Smith, D.L. 1989. *The Religion of the Landless: The Social Context of the Babylonian Exile*. Bloomington, IN: Meyer-Stone Books.

Southwood, K.E. and Halvorson-Taylor, M. 2017. *Women and Exilic Identity in the Hebrew Bible*. London: Bloomsbury.

Steinberg, N. 1993. *Kinship and Marriage in Genesis: A Household Economics Perspective*. Minneapolis, MN: Fortress.

Stern, E. 2001. *The Archeology of the Land of the Bible Volume II: The Assyrian, Babylonian, and Persian Periods*. New York: Doubleday.

Stillman, N. 1991. *The Jews of Arab Lands in Modern Times*. Philadelphia: Jewish Publication Society.

Stiner, M.C,, Munro, N.D., Buitenhuis, H., Duru, G., Özbaşaran, M. 2022. 'An endemic pathway to sheep and goat domestication at Aşıklı Höyük (Central Anatolia, Turkey)', *Proceedings of the National Academy of Sciences* 119(4):e2110930119.

Stone, L. 2006. *Kinship and Gender: An Introduction* (3rd edn.). Boulder: Westview Press.

Stromberg, J. 2011. *An Introduction to the Study of Isaiah*. London: T&T Clark.

Sweeney, M.A. 2001. *King Josiah of Judah: The Lost Messiah of Israel*. Oxford: Oxford University Press.

Sweet, J. 2004. *Dances of the Tewa Pueblo Indians: Expressions of a New Life* (2nd edn.). Santa Fe: School of American Research Press.

Talon, P. 2005. *The Standard Babylonian Creation Myth Enūma Eliš* (SAACT 4). Helsinki: State Archives of Assyria Cuneiform Texts .

Thomas, E.M. 2006. *The Old Way: A Story of the First People*. New York: Farrar, Straus and Giroux.

Tobolka, R. 2003. 'Gellner and Geertz in Morocco: a segmentary debate', *Social Evolution & History* 2(2): https://www.sociostudies.org/journal/articles/140489 (accessed 18 September 2023).

Tov, E. 1992. *Textual Criticism of the Hebrew Bible*. Minneapolis, MN: Fortress Press.

Tsumara, D.T. 1989. *The Earth and the Waters in Genesis 1 and 2: A Linguistic Investigation*. Sheffield: Sheffield Academic Press.

——— 2005. *Creation and Destruction: A Reappraisal of the Chaoskampf Theory in the Old Testament*. Winona Lake, IN: Eisenbrauns.

Tremayne. S. (ed.) 2001. *Managing Reproductive Life: Cross-Cultural Themes in Fertility and Sexuality*. Oxford: Berghahn Books.

Tudge, C. 1999. *Neanderthals, Bandits and Farmers: How Agriculture Really Began*. New Haven: Yale University Press.

Turner, V. 1967. *The Forest of Symbols: Aspects of Ndembu Ritual*. Ithaca: Cornell University Press.

——— 1969. *The Ritual Process: Structure and Anti-Structure*. Chicago: Chicago University Press.

Tylor, E.B. 1871. *Primitive Culture*. New York: J.P. Putnam's Son.

van den Berghe, P.L. 2010. 'Human inbreeding avoidance: culture in nature', *Behavioral and Brain Sciences* 6:91–102.
van de Mieroop, M. 1999. *The Ancient Mesopotamian City*. Oxford: Oxford University Press.
van Gennep, A. 1909. *Les rites de passage*. Paris: Émile Nourry.
von Rad, G. 1961. *Genesis*. London: Westminster.
van Seters, J. 1992. *Prologue to History: The Yahwist as Historian in Genesis*. Westminster: John Knox Press.
vom Bruck, G. and Bodenhorn, B. (eds) 2006. *The Anthropology of Names and Naming*. Cambridge: Cambridge University Press.
Wall, R., Hareven, T.K. and Ehmer, J. (eds). 2001. *Family History Revisited: Comparative Perspectives*. Newark, DE: University of Delaware Press.
Wallace, A.F.C. 1956. 'Revitalization movements', *American Anthropologist* 58:264–81.
Waters, M.C. Tran, V.C., Kasinitz, P. and Mollenkopf, J.H. 2010. 'Segmented assimilation revisited: types of acculturation and socioeconomic mobility in young adulthood', *Ethnic Racial Studies* 33(7):1168–93.
Wellhausen, J. 1878. *Geschichte Israels* (vol. 1). Berlin: Druck und Verlag von Georg Reimer.
――― 1883. *Prolegomena zur Geschichte Israels* (vol. 1, 2nd edn.). Berlin: Druck und Verlag von Georg Reimer.
――― 1894. *Israelitische und jüdische Geschichte* (vol. 2). Berlin: Druck und Verlag von Georg Reimer.
Werner, D. 1979. 'A cross-cultural perspective on theory and research on male homosexuality', *Journal of Homosexuality* 4(4):345–62, DOI: 10.1300/J082v04n04_03.
West, A. 1981. 'Genesis and patriarchy', *New Blackfriars* 62(727):17–32.
Whitcomb, J.C. and Morris, H. 1961. *The Genesis Flood: The Biblical Record and Its Scientific Implications*. Philadelphia: Presbyterian & Reformed Publishing.
White, D.R. 1988. 'Rethinking polygyny: co-wives, codes, and cultural systems', *Current Anthropology* 29:529–72.
Wilkinson, R.J. 2015. *Tetragrammaton: Western Christians and the Hebrew Name of God*. Leiden: Brill.
Wittmer, J. 2006. *The Gentle People: An Inside View of Amish Life* (3rd edn.). Washington, IN: Black Buggy Restaurant & General Store.
Wolf, A.P. and Durham, W.H. 2004. *Inbreeding, Incest, and the Incest Taboo: The State of Knowledge at the Turn of the Century*. Stanford, CA: Stanford University Press.
Yellen, J. 1986. 'Optimization and risk in human foraging strategies', *Journal of Human Evolution* 15(8):733–50.
Yoffee, N. 2005. *Myths of the Archaic State: Evolution of the Earliest Cities, States, and Civilizations*. Cambridge: Cambridge University Press.

Zavella, P. 2011. *I'm Neither Here Nor There*. Durham, NC: Duke University Press.
Zerubavel, E. 1985. *The Seven Day Circle: The History and Meaning of the Week*. New York, NY: Free Press.
Zohary, D. and Hopf, M. 2000. *Domestication of plants in the Old World*. Oxford: Oxford University Press.
Zohary, M. 1982. *Plants of the Bible*. Cambridge: Cambridge University Press.

Index

Abel   53, 75, 120, 176–9, 181–2
Abishag   106, 140, 160
Abraham   6, 53, 82, 88–92, 94–5, 97, 100, 103–7, 112, 116, 120, 124, 126, 131, 133, 136–7, 142, 146, 149–51, 154–7, 159, 181–8; *see also* Abram
Abram   88, 100–6, 122, 133, 181, 183–4; *see also* Abraham
Absalom   106, 140, 160
Adah   119–20
Adam   1, 42, 44, 47, 52–3, 65, 74–6, 80, 116, 119, 121–2, 128, 146, 152–4, 173, 175, 176, 180, 182
Adonijah   140, 160
adultery   111, 198
agency   19, 97, 111, 150–3, 155, 157
agriculturalists   61
Akkadian   164, 170–1
Alexander the Great   168, 194
Amish   *see* Old Order Amish
Ammon and Ammonites   90, 92–3, 127, 194
Amnon   89, 160
Amorites   123–5, 143, 196
Amos   10, 188
angel   52, 142, 151, 155, 157, 184–6, 188
archaeologists and archaeology   4, 7–9, 17, 23, 25, 32, 39, 71, 166, 172–5, 177, 190–1, 204
ark/Ark   1, 7, 34, 70, 73, 79–80, 82, 188
Asenath   92, 98–9
Asher   92, 126
assimilation   12–16, 27, 30, 36–9, 60, 77–8, 81, 101, 193, 195, 199–202, 204
Assyria and Assyrians   8–11, 25–7, 30, 34, 72, 165, 192
Atra-hasis   72, 74
autochthony   180

Ba'al   27
Babel   59, 162–3, 171–2
Babylon and Babylonians   11–20 *passim*, 25, 30–40, 45, 54, 59–60, 67, 69, 71–2, 77, 80–1, 86, 88–9, 105, 107, 122, 128, 138, 144–7, 154, 159, 163–72, 182, 184, 187–9, 191–6, 199, 205
Babylonian captivity   *see* Exile
barley   175–7, 180
Beersheba   155

Benjamin   8, 92, 97–8, 126, 139, 150
Bethel   29, 49, 150, 182
Bethlehem   150
Bible-Babel   59
Bilhah   92, 96–7, 126, 140
bilineal   132
binary oppositions   63–5
bitumen   162, 165, 169
book of the law   28–9
bread   138, 149, 155, 175–6, 179, 185–6
bricks   162–6, 168–9
brideservice   95, 97–8
bride wealth   91, 93, 95, 97–8, 100, 102–3, 109, 113
Brooklyn   200–1

Cain   53, 75, 78, 114–15, 119–22, 176–9, 182
calves   105, 185
camels   91, 131, 156, 158, 173
Canaan and Canaanites   7, 17–18, 27, 89–91, 93–5, 98–9, 101, 108, 111, 118, 123–5, 133–7, 141–2, 150–1, 155, 157–8, 161, 181–3, 187–8, 193–4
cattle   21, 38, 56–7, 67, 91, 102, 131, 152, 173
Cave of Machpelah   150
Chaim Potok   202
chaos   1, 41, 58, 78, 119, 163, 168–9. 171
circumcision   37, 98, 100, 104, 106–7, 113, 116
clean (*also* unclean)   38, 47, 66–7, 80, 134, 175, 181, 189, 192–3
colonialization   12–14, 22, 25, 196–7, 204
cousins   82–3, 85–8, 91, 93, 95, 115–16, 126, 176
covenant   29, 34, 104–7, 122, 157, 179, 188
creation   20, 37, 41, 50, 55, 57–65, 68–71, 73–4, 77–80, 153, 163–4, 168, 171, 179–80, 193; *see also* procreation
cunning   116, 137
Cyrus   191–2, 199

Dan   92, 96–8, 126
Daniel   32
darkness   1, 55–6, 58, 62–5, 68, 78–9, 106, 181, 195
David   viii, 10, 23, 27–8, 30, 32, 39, 42, 89, 93–4, 111, 128, 130, 132, 140, 144, 160, 178, 181

Deutero-Isaiah ix, 5, 35
Deuteronomy and Deuteronomists 5, 10, 20, 26–9, 33–5, 46, 73, 90, 93, 112, 130, 132, 139–40, 160, 181, 188–9, 192–3
diet 174, 180
dietary laws 37–9, 201
Dinah 98–9
divorce 102–4, 194, 198
documentary hypothesis 5–6, 9, 21–2
domestication 39, 68, 79, 131, 174–7, 189–90
Douglas, M. viii, 39, 66
drunkenness 7, 70, 90, 134–5, 145

Egypt and Egyptians 9, 17, 23, 25–7, 30–2, 34, 52, 85, 90, 95, 98–9, 101, 123–5, 135, 137, 141, 143, 154–5, 159, 172
embodiment 16, 52–3, 64
endogamy 83, 86–8, 93–4, 98, 119, 198, 200–1
Enki 167, 169–71
Enoch 115, 120–1, 182
Enûma Elish 163–5, 168
Ephraim 92, 98, 126, 141–4, 204
Er 108–10, 115
Esau 43–4, 51, 92–5, 137–9, 144, 148–51, 155–7, 177
Etemenanki 165–6, 168–9, 171–2
ethnocide 11, 22
Eve 1, 44, 52–3, 75, 152–4, 173, 176, 178, 182
exile, exiles and the Judean Exile vi–vii, ix, 5, 11–13, 15–16, 18–21, 26, 31–41, 45, 49, 51–4, 59–61, 70–3, 75, 77, 81–2, 86, 88–9, 95, 97, 102, 105, 107, 119, 122, 128, 131, 133, 136–8, 143–4, 146–51, 154, 159–61, 163, 165, 167–9, 171, 182, 184, 187–8, 191–6, 199, 204
exodus and Exodus viii, 16, 26, 30, 34, 36, 46, 66–7, 142–3, 154–5, 178, 182, 189, 193, 203
exogamy 83, 86–8, 99, 201–2
Ezekiel ix, 5, 45–6, 49, 51–2, 76, 188
Ezra 37, 191–4, 204

fertility 25, 74, 97, 99–102, 104, 112, 149–50, 154, 177, 180, 187
floods and the Flood 7, 59–60, 68, 70–5, 77–80, 82, 119, 122, 134, 162, 168, 171, 184, 186
foragers and foraging 21, 173–6, 189
Freud 83–4, 99

Gad 92, 126
Garden of Eden 1, 44, 173, 175
gender 6, 21, 93, 99, 106, 146, 149, 151
Genesis option 15–16, 21, 73, 147, 195–204
genitor 97, 109
genitrix 97–8
genocide 11, 22
Gilgamesh 71–2, 74, 80, 166, 171
goats 38, 51, 67, 91, 104, 131, 139, 149, 176–7, 182

Hagar 90, 92, 95, 101–3, 137, 150, 154–5
Haggai 192
Ham and Hamites 121–5, 134–5, 137
Haran 88–9, 92, 95, 101, 122, 124, 133
Harris, M. viii, 39–40, 67
Hebrew vi, viii–ix, 1–3, 8–9, 20–2, 25, 30, 36, 41–4. 46–50, 52–4, 59, 64, 76, 96–7, 105–6, 114, 121, 138–40, 153, 159–61, 163, 170, 172, 179, 181–2, 186, 201, 203
Hebron 150
heterosexuality 186–7
Hittites 93–4, 150, 194
Holocaust 203
holy 20, 22, 27, 36, 45–6, 194, 201
homosexuality 186–8, 190
Hosea 10
Hoshea 25
houses and households 2, 28–9, 31, 33, 45, 49, 51, 83–5, 90, 101–2, 106–7, 109–12, 117, 132, 139, 147–8, 151, 155, 157–60, 164, 166, 176, 181, 186–7, 191

immigrants 77–8, 81, 170, 200, 202–3
incest 21, 83–8, 90, 99, 103, 140
incremental repetition 57, 61
Isaac 6, 51, 82, 90–5, 102–4, 112, 116, 131–2, 137, 142, 146, 148–51, 155–8, 177, 181
Ishmael and Ishmaelites 32, 90, 92, 95, 97, 102–3, 131, 137, 151, 155
Israel and Israelites viii, 7–11, 17–18, 23, 25–7, 30–1, 34, 39–40, 44–5, 51, 66, 71, 82, 89–90, 93, 97–9, 112, 114, 116–18, 120, 124–6, 130, 132–5, 137, 140–4, 146, 150, 154–5, 157–8, 160–1, 167, 173, 178, 181–2, 188–94, 201, 203–4
Issachar 92, 126

Index

Jabal 119–20
Jacob 6, 8, 17, 19, 42–4, 47, 49, 51, 82, 92–8, 100–1, 103, 115–18, 126, 131–2, 137–44, 146, 148–51, 155–9, 177, 181
Japheth 121–2, 134
Jehoiachin 31
Jehovah 46, 48
Jeremiah 32–3, 46, 105, 188, 191
Jerusalem 9–11, 15, 20, 23, 25, 27–37, 49, 60, 105, 118–19, 126, 138, 140, 165, 188–9, 191–2, 195, 199, 204
Jesus vii, 128, 171, 204
Jezebel 160, 182
Joseph 6, 42, 82, 92, 97–9, 117–18, 126, 131–2, 139, 141–4, 148, 150–1, 154–5, 158–60, 178
Josephus 195, 204
Joshua 10, 22, 26, 30, 126
Josiah 26–31, 33–5, 42, 122, 192–3
Jubal 119–20
Judah viii, 7–11, 18, 20, 23, 25–7, 29–34, 36, 39–41, 43, 60, 67, 71, 89–90, 92, 105, 108–11, 114–15, 118, 122, 126, 128, 130–2, 138, 140, 144–5, 147, 151, 160, 173, 183, 191–5
Judaism 15, 35, 150, 160, 195, 199–201
Judeans vi, 5, 8, 10–12, 15–20, 23, 26–8, 30–4, 36–9, 41–2, 45–7, 58–62, 64, 67, 70–1, 76–7, 82, 86, 88–9, 94, 100, 107, 112, 115, 119, 126, 128–9, 132, 134–5, 138, 143, 147, 149, 151, 154, 159–61, 163, 165, 167–71, 173, 182, 184, 192–3, 199
Judges 10, 26

Kenites 120, 131
Keturah 112
Kings 9–10, 26, 29–31, 76, 93, 132, 140, 182, 188

Laban 92, 95, 116, 138, 151, 157–9
lambs 35–6, 38, 52, 193
Leah 42–3, 92, 95–8, 103, 115–16, 126, 139, 149–50, 157–8
Lee, R. 174, 189
Levant 7, 23, 25, 71, 124, 154, 175, 177, 190, 204
Levi and Levites 8, 43, 92, 118, 126, 141, 193–4
levirate 109–10, 112–13, 115
Leviticus viii, 5, 16, 68, 84, 89, 107, 135–6, 140, 150
Lilith 152–3
liminal states 64–6, 68–9, 124, 164, 189

Lost Tribes 8–9, 26, 40
Lot 88–90, 92, 126, 149, 151, 181–4, 186–8
Lubavitchers 200–1, 205

Maccabees 195
Mamre 149, 183–4
Manasseh 92, 98, 117–18, 126, 141–4
Marduk 163–5, 167–8, 170
marriage v–vi, ix, 5, 14, 16, 20–1, 76–8, 82–3, 85–9, 91–4, 98–9, 103–4, 107, 109, 112–13, 119, 128, 137, 145, 153, 156–7, 170, 181, 186, 194, 196, 201
Masoretes 47–8
mater 97–8
matrilines and matrilineality 99, 132, 157
Megiddo 30
Memmi, A. 12–15, 22, 197
messiahs 10, 27, 36
Michelangelo 55, 145
milk 176–7, 185, 197
miscegenation 78
Moab and Moabites 31, 90, 92–3, 126, 194
Moses 30, 42, 46, 66, 117–18, 135, 178, 182, 203–4
Mount Zion 11
Mundurucú 148

Nahor 88, 91–2, 101, 116, 122, 133
Naphtali 92, 96–8, 126
nativists 13–15, 27, 60
Nebuchadnezzar 31–2, 165, 169, 192
Nehemiah 37, 192–4, 204
nephesh 179–80
Nephilim 75–8, 186
Noah 1, 7, 70, 73–4, 78–80, 82, 121–4, 134, 145
Nuer 22, 128, 131
Numbers 76, 117–18, 172

Old Order Amish 78, 197–200, 205
Onan 108–10, 144

Paddan-aram 95, 156, 157–8
Passover 30, 34–5, 38, 154, 192–3, 201
pastoralists 61, 67, 91, 102, 120, 131–2, 171, 176–9, 181–90, 201, 203
pater 97, 109
patriarchs and patriarchy 6, 82–3, 86, 88, 94, 98–100, 131–2, 144, 146–7, 151, 154, 160, 177–8, 181, 187

patrilines and patrilineality 97, 102–3, 108–12, 114–22, 124, 128, 130–3, 137, 140, 145–6, 151, 153, 155, 157–8
patrilocality 102–3, 153, 158
Paul 195–6
Perez and Perezites 144
Persia 39, 191–4
pigs 39, 67, 151
polygyny 93, 113, 119, 121, 150
post-Exile 15, 37, 204
Potiphar 148, 159–60
primogeniture 115, 130–2, 139, 145–6
procreation see also creation
Proto-Isaiah 10

Rachel 42, 92, 95–8, 101–3, 115–16, 126, 139, 148–51, 157–60
Rebekah 91–4, 148–51, 155–8, 160–1
redactors ix, 4–5, 19, 45, 71, 77, 114, 132, 143, 147, 156, 173, 179, 187
Reuben 41, 43, 92, 97, 116–17, 126, 139–41
revitalization 22, 26–7, 30, 39
Romans 49, 194–5, 197, 199

Sabbath 37, 46, 63, 69, 201
sacrifice 11, 15, 27, 34–6, 41–2, 52–3, 70, 72, 116, 179, 180–1, 186, 192, 194
Samuel 9–10, 26, 89, 132, 140, 144, 178, 181
Sarah 88, 90, 92, 95–7, 103, 112, 137, 149–50, 154–7, 159–61, 185; see also Sarai
Sarai 88, 100–4; see also Sarah
Schneerson, M.M. 200
science 19, 55, 80
Second Temple 192; see also temple
segmentary lineages 114, 119–24, 126, 128–9, 146
separation 11, 16, 21, 23, 32, 36–8, 46, 55–6, 58–60, 63–6, 68, 77–80, 89, 104–7, 116–19, 123, 137, 171, 177, 182–3, 192–4, 196–9, 201; see also separatism
separatism 14, 200, 202; see also separation
Shakers 196
sheep 35, 38, 67, 91, 110, 131, 139, 176–8, 181–2, 203
Shelah 108, 110–11, 122
Shem 82, 121–4, 134
shepherds 21, 25, 71, 142, 145, 149–50, 157, 176–8, 181
Shinar 162–3
Shur 155
Simeon 8, 42–3, 92, 118, 126, 141
Sinai 65–6, 165

Singer, I.B. 202
Sodom 89, 135, 149, 151, 181, 183–8
Solomon viii, 10–11, 23, 27–8, 30–1, 39, 42, 93–4, 132, 140, 160

Talmud 119, 199
Tamar 89, 108–11, 144, 147, 151
temple viii, 2, 9–11, 15, 20, 23, 25, 27, 29, 31–2, 34–7, 41, 50, 60, 100, 128, 150, 164–5, 167–8, 188, 191–3, 195–6, 199; see also Second Temple
tents 119, 134–5, 158, 171, 173, 181, 183–8
Terah 88–93, 95, 99, 103, 111, 116, 122, 131, 133, 137
Tewa 170, 196–7, 204–5
Tiamat 163, 168
Torah 2, 41, 46, 51, 54, 199, 201
Tubal-cain 119–20

ultimogeniture 130–3, 136, 138, 141, 143–6
unclean see clean
Ur 88–9, 104, 133, 166
Utnapishtim 72

water 1, 40, 55–6, 58, 60–3, 65–6, 68–73, 79, 81, 101, 140, 150, 155, 163, 167–8, 171, 174, 177, 183
week, the 37–8, 59–61, 69, 73–4, 168
wheat 149, 175, 177, 180
wilderness 34, 60, 67, 71, 155, 177–8, 181–2, 189, 201, 203
Women of the Forest 148

Yahweh 10, 20, 34–6, 45–6, 48–9, 76–7, 91, 105–6, 116, 148–9, 152, 155, 157–8, 162, 165, 171, 173, 175–6, 178, 180–2, 184–5
Yehudah 8
Yiddish 200, 202

Zebulun 92, 126
Zechariah 192
Zedekiah 32
Zerah 144
Zerubbabel 42, 192
ziggurats 164–9
Zillah 119–20